Library of
Davidson College

CASTE IN A PEASANT SOCIETY

Caste in a Peasant Society

A CASE STUDY IN THE DYNAMICS OF CASTE

BY MELVIN M. TUMIN

GREENWOOD PRESS, PUBLISHERS
WESTPORT, CONNECTICUT

Library of Congress Cataloging in Publication Data

Tumin, Melvin Marvin, 1919-
   Caste in a peasant society.

   Reprint of the ed. published by Princeton University Press.
   Bibliography: p.
   Includes index.
   1. Caste--Guatemala. 2. San Luis Jilotepeque, Guatemala. 3. Peasantry--Guatemala. I. Title.
[HN150.S3T8 1975]   301.44'97281   75-29328
ISBN 0-8371-8390-1

Copyright, 1952 by Princeton University Press

Originally published in 1952 by Princeton University Press, Princeton, N.J.

Reprinted with the permission of Melvin Tumin

Reprinted in 1975 by Greenwood Press,
a division of Williamhouse-Regency Inc.

Library of Congress Catalog Card Number 75-29328

ISBN 0-8371-8390-1

Printed in the United States of America

TO MY MOTHER
AND TO THE MEMORY OF
MY FATHER

PREFACE

About ninety miles east of Guatemala City, Central America, is the pueblo of San Luis Jilotepeque. Within this peasant farming society are 2,400 Indians and 1,100 Ladinos, the latter claiming to be of Spanish descent. The two groups live together in a self-sufficient community isolated from surrounding areas and free from regular contact with the outside world. Their culture patterns are different, their roles in the community diverge, a caste system flourishes—and yet the two must live and work together to maintain their common existence. The result is a state of peaceful tension.

Social scientists have been much concerned with caste systems and what they reveal about human society. Why is it that some castes are more durable than others? Why are some more responsive to the stimuli of Western industrialization? Why do subordinate castes accept such a large burden of the responsibilities and labor without receiving ample reward? These are but some of the vital questions to be asked. When raised in the proper way, they probe to the heart of social structure.

While the general outlines of caste systems are similar in some degree wherever they are found, it is also true that there are numerous and important differences among them. An understanding of these differences, as well as the similarities, is essential to a true knowledge of castes. Sound and genuinely comparable materials from a number of different caste systems are therefore needed. Simple comparisons of structure will not suffice; what is required is intensive inquiry into the basic attitudes underlying the structure. What life values and perspectives do the castes share? How do they differ? What images do they have of themselves and of each other? How do the different castes define the social arrangements?

When we have found the answers to these questions for a number of different societies, we will understand more

PREFACE

fully and more systematically the nature of caste, its structure, and its function. This understanding will in turn contribute to our knowledge of what is and what is not possible in human social relationships.

The present study represents an attempt to provide such materials for one particular variation on the theme of caste, to be found in operation in the pueblo of San Luis Jilotepeque. The book is the culmination of a field trip to Guatemala which began in July of 1942 and ended late in April of 1943. About ten years will have elapsed from the date of first entry into the field to the date of final publication. During the stay in the field and in the years which have passed since then I have been aided in a variety of ways by a number of persons and institutions to whom I should like, at this point, to express my appreciation.

My greatest single debt is to Dr. John Gillin, Professor of Anthropology of the Institute for Research in Social Sciences at the University of North Carolina. I had come to Guatemala as an enthusiastic but green field worker, with little experience in the actual techniques of field investigation, considerable apprehension as to where and how one started, and, of course, I was a total stranger to the people and the area. Dr. Gillin had already been in residence in the pueblo of our mutual concern for several weeks. He had laid a basic groundwork of rapport with the people and achieved a working familiarity with the area. He had already selected some first-rate informants. He had begun to sketch in the ethnographic foundations. I was the fortunate heir of all of these accomplishments.

More than that, Dr. Gillin was kind and patient enough to take me under his tutelage from the outset and to spend a good deal of his valuable time in teaching me how to work in the field and in sharing his already acquired insights with me. It is unquestionable that a substantial portion of whatever merit this work may have is to be attributed to the relationship I enjoyed with Dr. Gillin.

Over the years which have passed since our joint resi-

PREFACE

dence in San Luis Jilotepeque, Dr. Gillin and I have exchanged our data freely; we have read and criticized each other's materials closely; we have, in short, shared in some of the very best features of scientific collaboration. All of this has been of marked benefit to me, especially since Dr. Gillin has been back to the area several times since our first visit, and has studied the pueblo, in collaboration with others, from a variety of perspectives. He has been generous and kind enough to make these later materials available to me without stint or reservation.

During my stay in the field, and in the subsequent ordering and presentation of materials for publication, I have had the continuing helpful criticism of Drs. Robert Redfield and Sol Tax of the Department of Anthropology of the University of Chicago. They performed the invaluable service of reading my field notes as I shipped them out from Guatemala during my stay, and criticizing those notes in detail. They directed my attention numerous times to gaps in my investigations, to improbabilities in my estimates, and to collateral similarities with other Latin American materials. The fact that they had both had considerable experience in Guatemalan materials themselves made their critiques all the more valuable. They were truly sponsors of my field trip in the best sense of the word, and I should like here to acknowledge how deeply grateful I am to them not only for their professional assistance but for their personal interest and support as well during some of the most trying days of my stay in Guatemala.

In San Luis itself, a number of persons were of invaluable assistance to me, both personally and professionally. It is impossible to specify the kind and degree of aid they rendered, but their names must here be included among those who made this volume possible. They are Don and Doña Oscar Guerra; Don Victor Sandoval; Don Jose Yaque; and, finally, my good friend and splendid informant, now deceased, Don Luis Najera.

My original interest in anthropology springs from the stimulus, encouragement, and training I received from

PREFACE

several colleagues and teachers. These include Dr. Wendell Bennett, Yale University; Mr. Herbert Passin; Mr. Frederic Camper; Mr. Saul Bellow; and Dr. Melville J. Herskovits, Northwestern University. It was primarily under the rigorous and skillful teaching of Dr. Herskovits that I first acquired such basic skills in the discipline as I subsequently have found useful.

Throughout the years since my field trip, a number of colleagues have been kind enough to read and offer suggestions on various articles written on the field materials gathered. These include Dr. Kurt Wolff of Ohio State University; Dr. Paul Hatt of Northwestern University; Dr. Norman Humphrey of Wayne University; Dr. Don J. Hager of Princeton University; Dr. Harry Bredemeier of New Jersey College for Women; and Dr. Wilbert Moore of Princeton University. The latter has done me the great service of reading through the manuscript in its entirety and offering cogent and helpful suggestions.

In 1946 I made the acquaintance of Dr. William J. Goode, now of Columbia University. He has at all times been a source of invaluable intellectual and personal stimulation and comradeship. The benefit I have derived from my continuing relationship with him runs too deeply and too generally throughout my own work for me to be able to specify it. Let the record stand here, therefore, of a sense of appreciation for the meaning of my friendship with Dr. Goode, whose extent he will full well recognize.

The field trip on which this report is based was made possible by a pre-doctoral field fellowship of the Social Science Research Council to whom grateful acknowledgment is here tendered.

I wish also to acknowledge here the assistance of the Carnegie Institution of Washington, and especially the staff attached to their Guatemalan office, who helped smooth the path in ways too numerous to mention.

The University Research Committee of Princeton University has been more than generous in the financial assistance they have provided me, making it possible for me to

PREFACE

spend considerable time in reevaluating my materials and reordering their presentation for publication. Their final important generosity consists in their providing a partial subsidy for the publication of this volume. Their continuing encouragement has helped materially in bringing this task to completion.

Finally, my deepest gratitude must here be tendered to my wife, Sylvia Yarost Tumin. She has not only suffered the ordinary trials and tribulations which attach to a household while a manuscript is being completed; she has rendered, as well, the kind of technical, intellectual, and personal aid and support throughout, without which it is indeed true this manuscript would not have seen the light of publication.

The present volume is only one of several works already published on the pueblo of San Luis Jilotepeque. The full body of published materials includes, among other things, a microfilm reproduction of all of my basic field notes; specialized articles on results of Rorschach testing in the pueblo; and a full-length volume by John Gillin entitled *The Culture of Security in San Carlos* (Publication No. 16, Middle American Research Institute, the Tulane University of Louisiana, New Orleans, 1951).

The reader's attention must be particularly called to Gillin's volume. It represents a special summing up of some of the basic facets of the security systems of San Luis (which Gillin has chosen to call by the pseudonym San Carlos). As such, it wisely involves a presentation of some of the basic ethnographic data. Unfortunately, the volume was received just too late for it to be possible to iron out some discrepancies between it and this volume. However, almost without exception, these discrepancies are minor. The most serious difference involves a question of the total number of people to be found in the area we studied. But this is primarily a function of the known distortions in census-taking in the area, and it is certain that where the

PREFACE

figures represent those collected by us rather than by the agents of the official census, we are in total agreement.

Gillin's volume and the present one bear sufficiently on each other to commend their being considered as one large work in two volumes, rather than two separate works. Because of this close connection of the two volumes, it would have meant an impossibly laborious apparatus of footnotes to refer the reader of this volume to relevant materials in Gillin's. As a result I have chosen the expedience of citing here Gillin's volume as being relevant almost in its entirety and its details to my own. The following table of contents of the Gillin volume should therefore be taken as a kind of generic citation: Chapter 1, The Problem of Security. 2, The Situation. 3, The Land and Its Products. 4, Habitations. 5, Food. 6, Clothing and Ornament. 7, The Need for Money. 8, The Social Structure as a Source of Satisfaction and Frustration. 9, Political and Control Structure. 10, Formal Christianity a la San Carlos. 11, The Fiesta of the Patron Saint. 12, Informal Religion and Psychiatry. 13, The Balance of Threat and Security.

A comparison of this table of contents with my own will quickly reveal the extent to which the two works represent an interconnected body of data and observations.

MELVIN M. TUMIN

Princeton, N.J.

CONTENTS

PREFACE	vii
INTRODUCTION	3

PART I. THE SETTING

CHAPTER 1.	ECONOMIC AND POLITICAL FRAMEWORK	11
CHAPTER 2.	SOCIALIZATION, EDUCATION, AND RECREATION	25
CHAPTER 3.	RELIGION, MEDICINE, AND MAGIC	38
CHAPTER 4.	THE PUEBLO: ITS RELATIONS AND REPUTATION	50

PART II. LADINO-INDIAN SIMILARITIES AND DIFFERENCES

CHAPTER 5.	PHYSICAL FACTORS AND THEIR SOCIAL DEFINITIONS	59
CHAPTER 6.	LANGUAGE, LITERACY, AND EDUCATION	71
CHAPTER 7.	CLOTHING	84
CHAPTER 8.	HOUSING: QUALITY, STYLE, AND LOCATION	99
CHAPTER 9.	ECONOMIC ACTIVITY AND ATTITUDES	109

PART III. TENSIONS AND EQUILIBRIA

CHAPTER 10.	THE GODPARENT COMPLEX	125
CHAPTER 11.	THE DIFFERENTIAL STRUCTURE AND FUNCTIONS OF RELIGION	141
CHAPTER 12.	THE DIFFERENTIAL STRUCTURE AND FUNCTIONS OF KINSHIP	155
CHAPTER 13.	WHERE THE PEOPLE MEET	169
CHAPTER 14.	WHERE THE PEOPLE STAY APART	189
CHAPTER 15.	INTRA-GROUP STRATIFICATION	209
CHAPTER 16.	GROUP IMAGES	234
CHAPTER 17.	LEVELS OF ASPIRATION AND ASSIMILATION	250
BIBLIOGRAPHICAL NOTE		273
APPENDIX:	I. METHODOLOGY	277
	II. THE SCHEDULE	282
	III. LADINO OPINIONS ABOUT INTERMARRIAGE	286
INDEX		293

CASTE IN A PEASANT SOCIETY

INTRODUCTION

It is now generally agreed among sociologists that all known human societies are stratified to some degree or other. This holds even in the cases of the most isolated and nonliterate groups. That the fact of stratification is universal makes the term itself central to sociological analysis.

A number of competing positions have been taken regarding the necessity of stratification for the continuity of any human society. Among these is the familiar Marxian view which holds that stratification is primarily classlike in character and that it disappears as a feature of human organization with the completion of the communist revolution, which marks the disappearance of classes.

A contrary view in current sociological thinking is that some stratification is inherent in and indispensable to any continuing society. The supporting reasoning starts with the idea that all continuing social structures require individuals to fill differently skilled roles. In order to motivate the more talented persons to undergo the training and sacrifices requisite to acquiring high-level skills, it is necessary, the argument runs, that they shall be differentially rewarded. This differentiation of rewards, invidiously and honorifically appraised by the society, thus emerges as a natural fact of any going social order.

One fundamental difference of opinion between this and the Marxian conception rests on the question of whether or not it is possible to induce human beings to do tasks which are judged to be more difficult and more functionally important than the ordinary, without their expecting an extraordinary reward in return.

Various bodies of evidence from the early history of the Soviets and from current events in the new state of Israel suggest that some closer approximation to the condition of "equal rewards for unequal work" is possible than formal sociological analysis is yet prepared to admit. At the same time, evidence from the more recent history of the Soviets,

INTRODUCTION

and some emerging features in Israel, strongly suggest that such a condition may at best be a temporary feature of societies in transition and that it is incapable of being permanently institutionalized.

By virtue of the nature of the sociological materials involved, a crucial experiment to determine the issue with some finality seems out of the question. As a minimum there would be required control and experimental groups of people who would be characterized by no previous experience with work motivations or other values regarding work. Such a condition is scarcely likely to be encountered or to be instigatable. Moreover, one would have to raise questions regarding the quality of the rest of the institutional structure in which such a condition was possible. By and large we must therefore content ourselves with closely reasoned inferences drawn from the known range of variation in historical or contemporaneous societies.

Sociological theory is therefore more likely to profit from a close study of existing and historical systems of stratification in which the consequences for the members of the societies are determinable. The relative efficiency of various arrangements of stratification for stated societal ends thus becomes possible of discovery. Moreover, posed this way, the question avoids the highly unproductive tendency, found in some modern sociological quarters, of making sweeping generalizations about structural imperatives and necessities on the basis of imperfect analyses of a limited portion of the range of human possibilities. That this is important is clear from the fact that while the reputations of some individual sociologists can be made by posing systematically relevant and important questions and hypotheses, the reputation of sociology as a total enterprise will suffer unless it can begin to provide systematically definitive answers which have a surefooted basis in empirical materials.

To this goal of providing answers, the present study proposes to contribute, by presenting in an orderly fashion the details of one case of a stratified social order, with some

INTRODUCTION

special reference to the system of tensions in equilibrium to which it adds up. As a single case it has no necessary greater theoretical implications nor any wider relevance to systematic sociology than any other single case might have. The community in question does represent, however, a kind of variation on the general theme of societal stratification which is likely to be found duplicated to some degree by many societies presently on, or about to move onto, the fringe of the influences of westernization and Europeanization. As such, if closely described and properly analyzed, the materials are likely to throw additional light on the question of what is and what is not possible in such human social arrangements. A knowledge of the consequences for the people of such societies of the normative order under which they live should be of considerable assistance to planners of social policy.

The descriptions and analysis to follow pertain to a Guatemalan community as it was observed in the fall and winter of 1942 and the spring and early summer of 1943. Events subsequent to those dates, especially those which flow from the national revolution of 1944, have somewhat altered the arrangements as they are to be described. These alterations, however, constitute a specially focused study, and do not, in any event, alter the pertinence to general sociological theory of the data as found at the time specified.

The community in question is San Luis Jilotepeque, Guatemala, C.A., located some 90 miles east of Guatemala City. Resident in this community are two groups of people who are relatively distinct in some basic aspects of their culture patterns. There are the Ladinos, numbering approximately 1,100, consisting of peoples who are identified by themselves and others as being of Spanish descent and culture-type, and having no hereditary connections with Indian ancestors. In continuous day-by-day contact with them is a group of some 2,400 Pokoman-speaking (Maya-Quichoid) Indians.

Together these groups form a relatively self-sufficient interacting community whose continuity appears to de-

INTRODUCTION

pend on their joint participation in the business of life. Isolated as the community is from surrounding areas, and free as it virtually is from the impact of visitors and travelers, certain working arrangements with regard to social relations among Indians and Ladinos have evolved which, though in some broad respects common to all of Eastern Guatemala, may also be said to be relatively unique to San Luis in other particular features.

This study will attempt to describe the general round of life, in which participation of both groups is requisite to its continuity. It will then seek to describe in detail the similarities and differences between the two groups, considered as social strata, hierarchically organized with reference to each other. In this connection, there will be considered the symbols of identification of social group membership; the round of activities in which each engages, both separately and together; the differential distribution of rewards which are available in the community; the extent to which the barriers of demarcation between the two strata are rigid and impermeable; and, finally, the study will focus on some incipient and other well-developed sources of strain and tension which are present in the social structure.

Since this work employs "tension and equilibrium" as core concepts, a word is in order with regard to the manner in which these terms are here employed. Any society may be viewed as a system or organization of forces and factors interlocked and integrated, in one way or another, by norms which govern behavior in the various parts of the system and determine the statuses to be filled in that system. The existing arrangement of these interrelated forces at any moment in the history of the society may be taken as the condition of equilibrium. It becomes immediately possible, then, to determine which factors are operating to produce a different arrangement of forces on the one hand, and those, on the other, which tend to reinforce the existing values and practices. The former may reasonably be termed sources of tension or "disequilibrium." In short, the status quo at any moment is taken as

INTRODUCTION

the point of equilibrium, and any force or factor which has as a consequence, either possible or actual, some alteration of that status quo may be viewed as a source of tension in the society.

The concept of social equilibrium has been under attack in the recent literature of sociology, partly on the grounds that the word commonly carries a positive value connotation which, by transfer, becomes identified with the status quo, and hence presumably makes of the sociologist who employs the term a "defender" of that status quo. Needless to say, this is largely a semantic confusion, since the term as here employed and as generally used in sociological literature carries no value connotations. We have come sufficiently far in our understanding of social structure and function to realize that societies are profitably viewed as systems of moving equilibria, which immediately implies the existence at all times in all societies of certain sources of strain. Both strain and equilibrium, then, are equally natural facts of any social structure, and are therefore indispensable terms for the student of society. By role-definition, the sociologist has no preferences in these matters. His primary ambition is to formulate systematically the variety of types of equilibrium systems which are found in the human social habitat.

To achieve this ambition, there is required a considerable amount of information about the subjective definitions of the cultural situation which are prevalent in the system under study. Typical ethnographic procedure, relying heavily as it does upon intensive work with a limited number of informants, is therefore somewhat limited in its usefulness for this end. A wider basis of information and insight is required if one is to talk sensibly and reliably about tension and equilibrium in a human society. Hence, in this study, some of the most crucial data to be presented were derived from a series of questionnaires administered to a sample of approximately 10 per cent of the male heads of both Ladino and Indian households. By comparison with such reports as rely mainly on a few informants, it is

INTRODUCTION

unquestionable that one can reasonably feel more secure about generalizations which are based on information from a wider population sample. While there is no serious contention that the sample is measurably representative, there is, nevertheless, the certainty that the margin of possible error has to a significant degree been reduced by the technique of inquiry used.

At the same time, the use of simple and participant observation, and of a small number of trained and sensitized informants, is recognizably indispensable to sound ethnography. Many of the observations, therefore, about the general round of life and the situations of joint and separate participation, are derived from this type of evidence, rather than from questionnaire materials. The latter primarily refer, on the one hand, to certain material questions of fact which involve enumeration, and, on the other, to certain questions concerning attitudes about which no simple inference from overt behavior could reasonably have been made. Further details of these matters will be found discussed in detail in the Appendix on Methodology.

PART I
THE SETTING

CHAPTER 1

ECONOMIC AND POLITICAL FRAMEWORK

GUATEMALA is divided into twenty-two departments or states. Each of these consists of a number of *municipios*[1] or municipalities. In turn, each of these is constituted by a capital *pueblo* or town, surrounded by a number of *aldeas*, or hamlets. One of the twenty-two states of Guatemala, called Jalapa, has, as one of its seven municipios, San Luis Jilotepeque, whose capital pueblo bears the same name. The present study primarily concerns this pueblo.

San Luis—as we shall hereafter refer to the pueblo—contains about 3,500 people, of whom some 2,400 are identified as Indian and the remaining 1,100 as Ladinos, or peoples of presumptive Caucasoid racial descent and Spanish-culture provenience. The hamlets which surround the pueblo contain approximately 3,900 residents, of whom some 2,600 are Indian and 1,300 Ladino. The largest of these hamlets has 560 residents, the smallest 261. Only one of these, El Camaron, is all-Indian in population; none is all-Ladino.

The municipio itself is approximately 400 square kilometers in dimension, with the pueblo occupying but 2 square kilometers. It is quite clear, therefore, that, relative to the rest of the municipio, the pueblo of San Luis is densely populated, since it contains almost 1/2 of the whole municipio population within 1/20 of the entire available area.

The altitude of the pueblo is approximately 676 meters. It lies some 41 kilometers distant from the department capital of Jalapa, and some 146 kilometers from Guatemala City itself. Its climate is roughly describable as semitropical. The hottest months are April, May, and June

[1] All non-English words will be italicized the first time they appear in the text, at which time their English equivalents will also be given. Whenever such words appear subsequently in the text, they will not be italicized.

11

THE SETTING

while the relatively coldest weather occurs in November, December, and January. The rainy season occurs during the months of May to October inclusive, at which times rain falls, sometimes abundantly, several afternoons a week. There is scarcely any rain whatsoever between the middle of October and the middle of April.

The type of agriculture is describable as lowland, without irrigation. In scattered portions of the municipio, where the terrain becomes decidedly mountainous, there is a limited amount of mountain agriculture, and some irrigable lands are scattered throughout the municipio as well. Both of these, however, are very limited by comparison with the amount of lowland agriculture which prevails.

The resources of the area which are most often brought into use are fish, baking clay, stone for various tools, maguey and other fiber plants; corn, beans, rice, chile, and all kinds of semitropical fruits and vegetables; fowl, livestock, and dairy products; wild herbs and shrubs; wild animals for skin and meat; limestone, used primarily for cooking, disinfection, and softening of cooked products; some coffee, cane sugar, pitchwood for illumination and shrub wood for fire. Almost anything and everything else San Luis people use or buy is brought from outside the municipio by traveling merchants from surrounding municipios, while such things as cloth, canned goods, and various manufactured items are shipped on consignment from manufacturing or importing houses usually located in Guatemala City. A considerable amount of small items for personal or household use is brought in by Indian men on their return from their own sales trips to neighboring municipios, and even as far as the neighboring countries of San Salvador and Honduras.

Agriculture is the primary economic enterprise in San Luis, and figures on the size of plots held are therefore revealing. The range is from landlessness to holdings totaling 20 *caballerias*, or about 14 square kilometers. The distribution of landholding is concentrated overwhelmingly at the lowest end of the scale, so that a man who owns one square kilometer of land is locally considered as wealthy. Considering only those who own land, a rough approximation gives 48 *cuerdas*, or 1/15 of a square kilometer, as the average landholding.

A caballeria, or approximately .7 of a square kilometer, is valued at between $200 and $1,000, depending on the location and quality of the land. Since it is generally agreed that most of the land is only marginally productive, the average value falls far nearer the lower figure. Land that is situated where it can be irrigated and where cane sugar and coffee can be raised is considered the most valuable.

Guatemalan landowners pay a tax of $3 per $1,000 evaluation. The assessment of the value is nominally the task of a local pueblo board, but, it is said, this board simply submits its "suggestions" to department officials, who are reputed to raise the evaluation by half, the raised evaluation in turn then being submitted to national officials who are reported to double that figure and assess taxes on that basis. Since highly individual arrangements are often made, according to reports, it is most difficult to get any accurate figure on current assessed evaluations, and consequently most difficult to give any accurate overall picture of land wealth, except in these general terms already described.

Any sources of income other than those already mentioned are nominal and trivial. The chief focus of economic activity can thus clearly be seen to be the land. Several other considerations combine to make this a central facet of pueblo life. First, there is a high positive evaluation by Indian culture of the dignity of manual labor. Given the fact that the Indians have few if any economically productive skills other than those directly relevant to raising their staple crops of corn and beans, the expectable result is a high positive orientation toward land and work upon it. Matching and opposed to this is the high negative evaluation in Ladino culture which attaches to manual labor upon the land, and an expectable and ever-present positive evaluation of the prestige-value of landownership. These facts in combination have the consequence that the diverse elements in the community are bound to each other as interacting units in a common division of labor. As will later be seen, this fact is productive of a high degree of social stability under certain conditions, and under others is importantly contributive to social tension.

A further characteristic of the agricultural nexus in San Luis is the concentration on corn and beans as both the principal staple crops for local consumption and for market exchange and sale. One consequence entailed by these facts is that the pueblo tends to operate on a level of survival, which, relative to other known standards in the Western hemisphere, appears to be minimal. A further issue of this dependence on corn and beans is the relative unimportance of San Luis as an exporting community, with consequent social isolation, on the one hand, and the "facing inward" of horizons of aspiration, on the other. These in turn contribute to making the community one which is relatively highly conscious of itself, and consequently highly attentive to problems of local social arrangements. Since the results of the structure of organized work in San Luis do not extend significantly beyond the pueblo limits, and since, therefore, there is no extra-pueblo status system toward which local residents can pitch their social horizons with any degree of reality, there is the predictable and openly expressed concern with minute details of local rating.

The predominant occupation for all males both in the pueblo and the municipio as a whole is farming in one form or another. The vast majority of those engaged in agriculture, however, own so little land that their official work classification is *jornalero*, or day-worker, or wage-hand, and, as such, they are subject to the vagrancy law which requires that they demonstrate through registry in a work book that they have worked for other people a

ECONOMIC AND POLITICAL FRAMEWORK

number of days a year, to a maximum of 150, depending on the amount of land they themselves own. For instance, in the municipio, there were 1,535 able-bodied males between the ages of 18 and 60. Of these, some 1,341, or almost 90 per cent, were classified as jornaleros. The remaining 194 were listed as other than jornaleros, and were classified as follows: 63 landowners devoted to agriculture; 37 landowners devoted to commerce; and 94 *obreros*, or workers. In this last group were listed 9 masons, 19 woodworkers, 15 carpenters, 3 tailors, 12 iron workers, 4 barbers, 1 "monthly contractor," 12 stone workers, 6 roofers, 3 slaughterers, 1 shoemaker and 1 marimba player.

In the pueblo itself, there were some 690 males between the ages of 18 and 60. Of these 540, or almost 80 per cent, were classified as jornaleros. The other occupations fall into the same categories as those listed above for the municipio as a whole. The division of labor is more complex, however, than such classifications would tend to suggest. For there are many part-time work specialties which are performed, but which cannot be claimed to be the primary source of income, and therefore may not be officially considered as the occupation of the individuals concerned.

The remaining occupations, both full- and part-time, include: dressmaker, musician, tile and adobe maker, saddlemaker, horse trainer, bee raiser, midwife, curer, bonesetter, masseur, baker, candlemaker, rope and lasso maker, pension and dining-room keeper, dairy-product manufacturer, diviner, storekeeper, writer of documents, pharmacist, practical doctor, schoolteacher, telegraph officer, military and civil official, soapmaker, water-supply tender, policeman, veterinarian, religious leader, lime worker, hatmaker, pottery worker, wizardry, animal castrator, and fish-net manufacturer.

Storekeeping is rather ubiquitous though informal. Stores in San Luis are classified as first or second class. The first-class stores, of which there are eleven, are those which do a gross business of more than $15 a month; the

THE SETTING

second-class stores, of which there are two, are those which gross between $10 and $15 a month. The pueblo and its environs are dotted with little stores which do less than $10 a month gross trade and are therefore neither listed in treasury reports nor do they pay matriculating taxes. By contrast, the first-class stores pay 25 cents a month tax and the second-class, 15 cents a month. In addition, any store where scales are employed pays a tax of 50 cents a year to the pueblo.

The largest general store in town is owned by the three Chinese in the municipio. It is estimated that they do a gross business of between $3,000 and $4,000 a year. The second largest general store is estimated to gross approximately $1,400 to $1,600 a year. No other store in town except the pharmacy even approximates the gross trade of these two.

Aside from the stores, there are the open-air all-day markets held in the main plaza of the pueblo every Thursday and Sunday. To these markets come buyers and sellers from all over the municipio, and occasionally one sees inhabitants of other departments as well. Food stuffs are the main items of commerce. Conversations with the sellers reveal that they are well satisfied to earn ten cents during the day. Most of them are women, for whom market days are almost holidays as well. Market starts about 8 a.m. and ends about 4 p.m. Anywhere from 60 to 300 persons may be there, depending on the goods available and the promise of attendance. Sunday is far and away the larger of the two days, inasmuch as it is also the day when compulsory military drill is held in the plaza, to which from 300 to 1,300 men come in accordance with their military classification.

Prices of goods and services in the pueblo vary from season to season, and from seller to seller, but some rough means can be struck. The following lists approximate generally prevailing prices for some of the most common items of commerce and exchange. For purposes of conversion into labor units, it should be noted that unskilled

ECONOMIC AND POLITICAL FRAMEWORK

Indian labor receives 10 cents a day for approximately 10 hours, or about 1 cent an hour, plus food, worth perhaps 5 cents more, totaling, therefore, 15 cents a day, or 1.5 cents an hour. Skilled Indian labor receives from 15 to 25 cents a day plus 5 cents worth of food for a ten-hour day, equalling between 2 cents and 3 cents an hour. Unskilled Ladino labor receives 15 cents a day and 5 cents worth of food, or approximately 2 cents an hour, and skilled Ladino labor receives 25 cents a day and food, or about 3 cents an hour. The prevailing wage scale, then, ranges between 1.5 cents an hour and 3 cents an hour.

FOODS

Coffee (bean)	4¢ lb.	Potatoes	4-10¢ lb.
Coffee (ground)	8¢ lb.	White onions	4-8¢ lb.
Sugar (unrefined)	2¢ lb.	Green onions	1-3¢ a bunch
Sugar (refined)	4¢ lb.	Tomatoes	1-5 for 1¢
Corn (grain)	15-30¢ lb.	Chile (small bowl)	3-5¢
Beans (shelled)	35-70¢ lb.	Egg cake	25¢ lb.
Drinking alcohol	8¢ ½ pt.	Soda pop	7¢ for 8 oz.
Beef	8-15¢ lb.	Cocoa	8¢ lb.
Pork	4-10¢ lb.	Sour cream	30¢ quart
Oranges	3-8 for 1¢	Cheese	20¢ lb.
Bananas	3 for 1¢	Tortillas	6-15 for 1¢
Avocados	1-4 for 1¢	Eggs	8-15¢ doz.
Garlic	3 for 1¢	Chickens	15-25¢ each

CLOTH AND CLOTHING

Cotton cloth (slightly under a yard)	$ .20- .45 vara	Cotton shawl	$ .75- up
Cotton trousers (ready made)	1.00- 2.50	Cotton stockings (women's)	.20- .40
Cotton shirts (ready made)	.85- 1.50	Cotton socks (men's)	.20- .50
Cotton jacket (ready made)	1.50- 2.00	Handkerchief	.08- .15
Cotton jacket (made to order)	1.50- 3.00	Wool suit (men's)	15.00-25.00
Cotton dress	1.00- 3.00	Necktie	.20- 1.00
Cotton slip	.50- 1.50	Wool shawl	3.00- 8.00
		Straw hat (men's)	.25- .40
		School uniform (children's)	.75- 3.00

TOOLS

Machete	$.50-2.00	Long knife	$.50-1.00
Hoe	.75-3.00		

MEDICINES

Aspirins	1-5¢ each	Quinine injection	$ .50
Liver extract	$2.00	Alimentation injection	.50

17

THE SETTING

ANIMALS

Hogs	$ 2.00-15.00	Mules	$15.00-35.00
Cows	5.00-25.00	Horses	15.00-75.00

SERVICES

Doctor's visit	25¢	Phone call	50¢ for five minutes (flat rate)
Marimba and 4-man crew	40¢ an hr.		
Mule for hire	15-25¢ a day	Postage	4¢ oz.
Baptism	60¢	Official documents	30¢
Wedding	$3.00	Certificate of residence	2¢
Telegrams	3¢ a word		

MISCELLANEOUS

Cigars	½ to 1¢ a piece	Crepe paper	20¢ a roll
Cigarettes	12 for 2¢ to 20 for 15¢	Pitchwood	20-40¢ armful
Combs	10-20¢	Firewood	2-5¢ armful
Earrings	8-25¢ a pair	Gasoline	20-25¢ for 4/5 liter
Rings	25-75¢ each	Roofing and flooring tiles	½¢ each
Lipstick	15-25¢ a stick	Candles	1-10¢ each
Toothpaste (miniature tube)	15¢	Sheet of paper and envelope	1½¢
Wool blankets	$1.00-5.00	Candy sticks and bars	½¢-5¢
Tablecloths	.75-3.00		

When these figures on the cost of living are set next to figures which describe the prevailing incomes, a picture of a relatively low standard emerges. However, the people of San Luis tend toward considerable exaggeration of the incomes of others and toward considerable minimization of their own. Thus, for instance, one person seriously estimated the wealth of two women storekeepers as anywhere up to $4 million in cash and untold holdings in real estate. But more reliable figures are available from sample budgets which were collected. From these it is possible to make the rough estimate that average income, inclusive of the value of food and other goods produced, is approximately $100 a year per family. With an average family of five individuals, this reduces to an average yearly income of $20 per capita. It is impossible to estimate closely how much of this is cash and how much goods, but it is reasonable to assert that the largest portion of the income for the average person is acquired in goods which he produces.

If it were assumed that half of the average income is cash, totaling about $50 a year per family, even this amount

ECONOMIC AND POLITICAL FRAMEWORK

would stand in marked contrast to the extremes of cash income characteristic of a number of people. A fairly reliable calculation of the income of the local pharmacist, for instance, puts it at approximately $50 a month in cash from his store alone, plus a much larger amount from the sale of goods produced on his lands. By contrast with this, a significant number of families in San Luis earn perhaps $10-15 in cash the entire year, and produce goods with a cash value of perhaps $50 altogether. Thus, even at the reduced standard of living which prevails, there are sharp and noticeable differentiations in economic rewards. These enter significantly, as will later be seen, into the determination of political power and social prestige.

GOVERNMENT

In San Luis, as in any community structure, there are both formal and informal systems for the maintenance of social order. The sharp stratification which prevails in San Luis results in four independent but interlocking systems of social control which can be identified. There is, first, the formal structure of government, repeating microcosmically in the pueblo the macrocosmic configuration of officialdom which is found generally characteristic of Guatemala. Second, one finds the informal arrangement of folkways and mores which govern behavior of the Ladino group. Third, there is the matching phenomenon for the Indian group. And fourth, at all times one is kept conscious and aware of that informal system of regulations which governs behavior between the Indians and Ladinos at their frequent points of juncture. The single unitary pattern of these four is the formal system of government controls which is compulsive, restraining, and guiding of behavior commonly for all citizens of the pueblo.

The chief local official is an appointed *intendente*, or mayor, who derives his authority and secures his appointment from the *Jefe Politico*, the chief authority of the department as a whole. The Jefe Politico is a personal appointment of the president, and exercises authority over life and death, subject only to the approval of the president. The intendente, deriving authority both in spirit and letter from the Jefe, is an extremely powerful individual, having rights and prerogatives with regard to dispensation of pueblo and personal matters far beyond what is customary in more democratic types of governmental organization. He is principal magistrate and legislator in the community, at the same time that he is the commanding officer of whatever local police structure he wishes to create or has already created.

In theory, the intendente is guided in his decisions by a board of six *regidores*, or aldermen, who are sometimes elected and sometimes appointed, depending in part on official momentary whims. The regidor is an unpaid position and while some special occasions induce various individuals to vie for it, by and large it is not desired by the majority of citizens. Even less desirable is the position of assistant regidor, also unpaid, who is more subject still to arbitrary whim and assignment to menial work than is the regidor. Lowest down in the ranks is the position of *sirviente*, or servant, of whom there are thirty in attendance at any one time. This, too, is an unpaid position, the sole reward being the exemption for nine weeks of such service from local taxes, amounting to $3 a year.

Whereas the regidores are nominally elected from arbitrarily designated slates of candidates, the sirvientes are peremptorily chosen by the intendente, with the advice of local informal community leaders. The attempts to free oneself from this "voluntary service" to the government are even more frequent and persisting than those which characterize the office of regidor. Petitions for such exemptions are, however, often entertained. If a petitioner can prove that he has already given such service for several years, but that one of his neighbors has not, it is not unusual for the neighbor to be called for service and the original designatee to be released.

The servants and aldermen take rotating turns at serving, each turn lasting a week, so that at any given time there are in attendance one alderman and his assistant and five servants. The working day is from sunup to sundown, but these people may be and often are called at any time of the night to perform a service, sometimes as menial but as taxing as running a message to a neighboring pueblo or hamlet.

Assisting the intendente in his administrative duties are two salaried officers, a secretary and a scribe. These positions are largely clerical, but because they are often Ladino-occupied, these men often exercise informal mandatory powers over the Indian aldermen and servants. The duties of the intendente extend, as have been noted, over all phases of local community organization. With or without the aid of precedent in the civil code, the intendente makes criminal and civil decisions, marries, jails, settles disputes, awards damages, and assesses fines. Effectively, nothing of any public significance can be done in the pueblo without the implicit or explicit permission of the intendente. In turn, however, he rarely feels free except in petty local matters to make decisions which might conceivably be of interest to the Jefe Politico, who has summary power of removal over him. Moreover, as is to be expected, there are considerable informal restraints and guides upon the intendente's behavior which are exercised by local politicos who have some type of extra-pueblo power. In practice, the intendente is therefore required to be more cautious with regard to displeasing the local gentry than would be expected from an officeholder with the formal power which he possesses. This combination of circumstances has operated in the past so that no intendente has lasted longer than two years in San Luis.[2]

The military affairs of the pueblo and the municipio are entrusted to the local *comandante*, or commandant,

---

[2] This is an interesting example of the accessibility for scapegoating of an individual who, possessing widespread but undefined power, must also assume responsibility for some acts over which he cannot exercise sufficient effective control.

THE SETTING

who has absolute control over the lives of those who are acting at any given moment in a military capacity. Since much of the busy work around the pueblo and the municipio calls for military organization, this power makes the commandant an extremely fearsome individual. At the same time, he too is subject to the immediate and ultimate will of the Jefe Politico.

The military power includes the calling together of work battalions, policing the pueblo with the cooperation of the local paid policeman and unpaid deputies, supervision of military drill, punishment of certain types of criminal offenses, and cooperating with the various branches of the national military and police forces. In more than a figurative way, the power of the commandant involves summary power over life and death. Commandants are reputed to exercise this power in a relatively arbitrary fashion without any noticeable official reprimand.

The military training of the able-bodied men of the municipio involves regular drilling every Sunday for several hundred men, and, on every fourth Sunday, when there is general drill for all able-bodied men in the municipio, supervision of about 1,300 men is entailed. The commandant is aided in his other duties by a group of servants who take turns standing guard in groups of eight, functioning as much to run personal errands for the commandant, and to care for his animals as to exercise any military or police duties. These groups of eight are named by the commandant, and service in them, like in the civil service, exempts a man from the $3-a-year taxes. But even more time than nine weeks a year is put in when on military guard duty.

The commandant is directly responsible only to the Jefe Politico of the department. He is usually a trained military officer, and is ordinarily assigned a temporary rank higher than his regular one for the duration of his command in a given pueblo. He may, however, be moved, without cause or notice, to another post. Unlike the intendente, he may not petition for assignment to another post.

ECONOMIC AND POLITICAL FRAMEWORK

A third chief branch of local government is the administrative, headed by a military officer, skilled in telegraphy, the mail system, and the operations of the telephone. With the aid of one paid and three unpaid assistants, he handles all the collection and distribution of incoming and outgoing mail, telephone calls, and telegrams. His, too, is an appointive post, but unlike the commandant and the intendente, he is very often a local person who has been trained for the task.

The duties of the thirty-one unpaid assistants include traveling on foot forty kilometers to Jalapa, taking turns each day to bring the outgoing mail there for redirection and to pick up the mail for the pueblo. These mailmen also distribute the mail locally, run other errands for the chief mailman, and help take care of the office. The paid assistant assists his chief in all the ordinary line of duties.

The law is strict in San Luis, but its enforcement is often as much a function of the kind of officials as of the formal letter of the law itself. Wide discrepancies exist from official to official, and with the same official from one occasion to another in the conscientiousness with which the law is dispatched. Punishments are meted out in different amounts for the same offense, the criteria varying from person to person being punished and from official to official administering the punishment.

Partly because of these arbitrary and unpredictable variations, there is fear of the law in the hearts of many of the citizens of San Luis. But there is also a concomitant tendency to view the officials and the body of law they represent as people and codes to whom one can go when the occasion arises and be assured of something in the nature of a fair hearing. This view holds far more for the local municipio officials than for those of the department, and is least held with regard to the Jefe Politico of the department, from whom the people have to expect, at best, an idiosyncratic and autocratic type of summary hearing on their complaints.

THE SETTING

The national government tends to interfere in the local scene only at the request of local officials, or at those very special times when a local person is able successfully to attract the attention of some national official. The primary types of situations in which national officialdom interests itself in local matters concern the national elections, the setting of quotas for road work and for military conscripts for a year's training in the barracks in Guatamala City. Otherwise, there is little national interference in local matters, the handpicked military, civil, and administrative officials of the municipio and department being relied upon to observe the codes to the fullest.

The national government, theoretically constituted as a republic, exercises sufficient person-to-person control and vigilance over the local authorities to place such "trust" in their adequate dispatch of duties. Most of the local officials are well aware of the fact that the preservation of their jobs depends on the strength of the national government and its ability to resist and put down the continuously threatening revolutions which seem to be indigenous to Guatemalan political structure.

CHAPTER 2

SOCIALIZATION, EDUCATION, AND RECREATION

EDUCATION in the pueblo is theoretically compulsory for all children between the ages of seven and fourteen. In practice, however, very few children attend school these seven years. The average amount of schooling received by any child varies between one and two years, but many children fail to receive even this much. A primary reason, among others, for the paucity of school years attended is the absence of any available instruction beyond the third year. Some of the wealthier girls repeat the third year as often as three times, since there is no fourth-grade curriculum, and, in the nature of the social expectations for such girls, there is nothing else available to keep them busy. Once every few years a rare child among the upper strata goes to another pueblo to continue on through *colegio*, or secondary school. But this requires far more money than most people in the pueblo can ever muster, since it first requires sending the child away after the third year in the pueblo to continue his primary school elsewhere, so that he shall complete the requirements for entering secondary school.

The official figures for the year 1941 show something of the situation:

TABLE 1

	Registered	Examined	Passed	Failed	Absent
1st grade	49	41	29	12	8
2nd grade	25	20	15	5	5
3rd grade	18	16	14	2	2

A percentage breakdown of these figures reveals that some forty per cent of those registered in the first grade either failed or were absent from examinations, both of which involve repeating the year of instruction. In the second year, approximately the same percentage of attrition was found. In the third year, there is a decline in this rate, due principally to two facts: (1) the natural selection for attendance in the third year of those who are both best equipped and most highly motivated to continue; and (2) the presence in the third-year class of a substantial number of students who have already completed the year and are simply repeating it for lack of anything else to do. As previously mentioned, these consist primarily of girls whose families are relatively wealthy.

The age distribution of first-year students also gives some indication of the rather haphazard and informal attitude which is manifested by many pueblo parents toward the law of compulsory schooling.

TABLE 2

AGE OF CHILDREN IN FIRST GRADE OF SCHOOL

Age	Number
7	16
8	11
9	5
10	8
11	6
12	3

It is quite clear from these figures that there is substantial dereliction so far as observance of the law is concerned. Moreover, there is apparently a substantial number who keep starting school, but also keep dropping out, so that they repeat the first few weeks or months of school in each of several successive years.

The attrition of attendance is directly, though not solely, a function of the early incorporation of the poorer children into the adult division of labor. As an educational problem, this is generally common in rural areas, and San Luis is no exception. For instance, in June 1942, out of a total of 774 possible attendances, there were 151, or about 20 per cent, absences. These include, of course, many multiple absences from a limited number of children, the

EDUCATION, RECREATION

outstanding cases in this regard being those of three children who were each absent 16 times in this one month.

In December of 1942, some six months later, out of a total of 735 possible attendances, there were 223, or slightly over 30 per cent, absences. Again these involve such extreme cases as three children absent 15 times, one absent 13 times, and two absent 12 times.

It may be inferred from the foregoing figures on registration, passing, and attendance, that the various factors of economic necessity, indifferent attitudes, and inadequate application of the law combine to make the formal school system considerably less significant in the lives of the pueblo residents than might otherwise be expected.

Some other important elements which enter might be mentioned here. Important among these is the fact that instruction in the schools is conducted solely in Spanish, despite the fact that a good portion of the Indian segment of the community, though bilingual in Spanish and Pokomam as adults, are primarily only Pokomam-speaking as children. The result is that communication is difficult between the teachers, who know nothing of the Indian dialect, and those children who know almost no Spanish. The failure on the part of such children to learn their subjects and the inability of the teachers to instruct is quite expectable. Unquestionably, this factor is extremely significant in producing an attenuation of motivation on the part of both teachers and pupils, no matter how strong the initial motivation might have been.

Moreover, certain facts about the curriculum contribute to setting the school aside as an enterprise, participation in which does not command much excitement or interest from parents, especially from those who are concerned with their children deriving some "practical" value from their schooling. For instance, an introductory biology course given in the third year is taught in such erudite terms as to be intelligible only to the most advanced and adept of pupils. Even for them, it is mainly a matter of memory work, so that from the best of them one can expect only a glib flow of classifications which seem to have no real meaning for them other than as a display of mnemonic pyrotechnics.

Further, the introduction into the Spanish language itself is on such an advanced level that there is an evident but unwarranted assumption of considerable training beforehand. In light of the facts stated above regarding the inadequate pre-school preparation of Indian children, it is quite clear how disfunctional for adequate learning is such a type of course. Additionally, the courses in manual and liberal arts have almost no reference to the problems which the child is likely to encounter in his pueblo environment. Much of the school year is spent in preparing shows and patriotic demonstrations to be presented on special holidays.

In short, there is little of a nonesoteric and pragmatic nature, other than reading and writing, which the child learns in school, if, indeed, he even manages to learn to read and write. Most parents appear to be fairly well satisfied if their children emerge only mildly literate after their several years of schooling. There seems to be a general tendency, by contrast, to rely on home instruction for adequate inculcation of those values and skills which are requisite to adult survival in the pueblo. For these additional reasons, formal schooling can be said to be of little actual significance in the lives of a majority of people of San Luis.

In contrast with this is the fact that aside from inheriting wealth or a rare case of acquiring money through skillful commerce, there is no basis for social and economic mobility other than education in some specific arts. This is at all times quite plainly evident to the pueblo residents from the fact that the best-paying jobs in the pueblo all entail skills which can be acquired only after some years of formal schooling beyond the three available in the pueblo.

The fact that advanced education does not form a significant part of the life intentions of most pueblo residents appears, therefore, to indicate that genuine social and economic mobility are not themselves significant life aspirations. This absence of motivation helps keep in motion the kind of reciprocal circle of events which has as one of its consequences a decided lack of interest in the school system.

It is most interesting to note, in light of this, that one of the most commonly prescribed recipes for social mobility for the Indians in the pueblo which is offered by the Ladinos is "education." At the same time, for a variety of reasons, Ladinos talk far more than act about the problem of making more and better education available to all people. Matching this is the very commonly expressed belief among the poorest Indians that they and their children are intellectually incapable of handling the school curriculum, no matter how advantageous to them it might be if they were able to do so.

The fact that the formal school system enters so insignificantly into the lives of most pueblo people naturally places great emphasis upon the informal avenues and techniques of education. With regard to the acquisition of adult work skills, the children are placed in a position of almost total dependence upon their parents. One of the predictable consequences is the operation of a generally well-observed pattern of parental authority, diffusing into and deriving from a more general principle of age-respect. The *ad hoc* law-making of the intendente has been known to be exercised in support of this principle, so that young men who have been disrespectful to their elders, especially to their parents, stand in danger of being brought to the intendente for punishment, though no formal laws define the situation.

By and large, however, the right of parents and elders to this respect does not need the support of formal law. For, aside from the role which such elders play as teachers of skills, they also function in more cases than not as the sole source of economic support of the young men and women until the latter have established their own economic roots. This economic independence is difficult to acquire without an initial stake which generally can be gotten only from one's parents. Rights and responsibilities thus tend to find a working equilibrium, so that, within this minor cultural system, tensions and strains remain at a minimum so long as the two sides of the ratio of responsibility and reward are kept functioning. In recent years it has become difficult for parents, especially those without adequate landholdings, to provide a satisfactory initial economic stake for their children. As a result there has been an expectable attrition in the age-respect principle.

There are significant differences in regard to what Indian and Ladino children are taught is proper behavior. It will later be seen how these differences are among the main points of emphasis in the socialization of the child in San Luis. They come to be of special import under those circumstances where social prestige for the dominant Ladinos and social safety for the subordinate Indians are involved.

Cutting across the Indian-Ladino line, however, are certain clearly accepted sex differentia in patterns of socialization. In both groups the girl is ordinarily considered the special concern of the mother and the boy of the father. This means the very early establishment of sex differentia in types of recreation, work, verbal patterns, and general role expectations. There is a clear-cut emphasis on some form of male dominance in making decisions affecting the household. A greater emphasis on equalization of rights in inter-sex relations is to be found in the Indian pattern of socialization, but this represents more a quantitative than a qualitative deviation from the general pattern.

At all times and in all areas of life in San Luis, gossip is an effective technique of social control to which children are very early exposed. There is constant public denunciation of this citizen or that as an *hablador* or gossip, so that children soon learn that it is highly invidious to be so reputed, at the same time that they inescapably

EDUCATION, RECREATION

acquire a sense for the power of judiciously used gossip. In a community characterized as San Luis is by a high visibility of social acts, and one which is additionally so self-conscious and self-concentrated, personal reputation is a matter of a great deal of ego-investment and involvement. Hence, skills in "slaughtering" others' reputations through gossip and defending oneself in turn come to be of considerable significance. Again, here one finds significant, if only quantitative, differences in both the frequency of resort to and the effectiveness of the use of gossip, depending upon the group in which such social action is carried on, and the person gossiped about.

Almost all children are exposed at an early age, sometimes as infants in arms, to religious exercises and training of one sort or another. They join their parents in religious processions, masses, private devotions, and, when capable, are expected to learn catechisms, and, in some cases, to prepare for confirmation. Throughout the entire pueblo, public manifestation of religiosity is the expectable rather than the unique. As a result, children quickly acquire the muscular and verbal patterns of religious worship. Sex differences exist in these regards, too, for the expectation for adults is that the woman, by and large, shall be the main religious functionary in the household. Certain differences, however, cut across this sex line, since among the Indians the male adult is as frequently, if not more often, the religious functionary.

In the main, however, religious behavior acts as a social leaven in this otherwise fairly rigidly stratified social order. In religious processions, masses, baptisms, and related events, there is a far greater tendency toward equalization of the rights and responsibilities of all citizens of the pueblo than is ever found in any other area of social life. The prostitute, the undesired and low-prestige Indian, the barefooted, poor Ladino, the workman and the proud landowner tend to assume equal social proportions in religious affairs. As a result, the socialization of children into democratic community participation is perhaps nowhere so effective as here.

Education in sex relations is informal and tends to take place largely by indirection. The children have examples of sexual concourse among animals continuously visible to them. Moreover, given the pattern of small, undivided houses which characterize lower-economic dwelling conditions, there is ample opportunity for children to observe parents in their sex relations.

Patterns of courtship vary considerably between Indians and Ladinos, but in most cases there is a unitary emphasis on male aggressiveness and leadership in the courtship. Common-law marriages are not infrequent, and the pueblo and its environs contain many children born out of wedlock as well. Some differential prestige inheres in the status of legitimate child, but this is generally insignificant. Thus, formalization of relationships in the shape of an acknowledged union is not unlikely to take place after rather than before pregnancy. Nor is there sufficient invidiousness attached to bastardy to prevent its rather frequent and acknowledged occurrence. Again, since social acts are so highly visible, and those not visible are so quickly and easily learned or rumored around the pueblo, children learn early that there is considerable latitude attached to such matters. It remains undeniable, however, that, relative to other conditions, being a legitimate child, being married by both civil and church authorities, and bearing children at least nine months after such ceremony, brings more prestige than any other combination of these alternatives.

It is equally undeniable that there is a direct correlation between the social value attaching to female pre-marital virginity and the prestige one enjoys in the community. For since gossip is prevalent and social cliquism well structured, it is all too easy to give reasonable grounds for suspicion that virginity has been lost. As a consequence, one finds among the most highly rated inhabitants a high degree of concentration on formal ritual in courtship, and

EDUCATION, RECREATION

considerable following of the Guatemala City pattern of chaperoned meetings between young men and women. Unchaperoned courtship is ordinarily taken as presumptive evidence of lack of morals on the part of the female, and her reputation suffers correspondingly, as does her eligibility for the "best" kind of marriage.

For the male, however, there is considerable permission as well as positive expectation that he shall somehow or other acquire sexual skills and experience before marriage. There is, however, far greater unity of opinion among all people regarding the value and desirability of this type of experience for the male than there is regarding the invidiousness of such experience for the female. As we shall later see, intermarriage is rigidly tabooed, but extramarital miscegenation between Ladino men and Indian women is not generally viewed with shock or detestation. Since it appears, however, to be far more expected than realized, there is the predictable quotient of stereotypes regarding the sexual proclivities of Indian girls and the sexual abilities of Indian boys. One finds this stereotypical pattern rather widely distributed throughout Ladino boys and men.

Direct participation in organized sports among San Luis people is at a relative minimum. Of games involving teams and teamwork, only two are of any significance: basketball for the girls and soccer for the boys. Even these are relatively haphazard and informally structured, so far as expected programs and tournaments are concerned. Moreover, these sports are largely indulged in by adolescents, and almost exclusively confined to Ladino children. Structured in this fashion, they are scarcely significant patterns of participation for the vast majority of pueblo residents. For those few directly involved, however, these sports come to assume considerable meaning, and participation and skill in them is another source of prestige. Whatever skills one can and does acquire in these games is learned informally from older participants. There is no organized program of instruction whatsoever in such activities.

THE SETTING

There is one billiard parlor in San Luis which draws, by way of participant and spectator, a good number of the adult males in town. Actual playing is again almost solely confined to the wealthier Ladinos, by virtue both of the costs involved and the informal social regulations which prevail. But a relatively large number of the most prestigeful figures in the pueblo can be seen almost nightly at the billiard parlor. Conversations about close games, shots missed or made, and related matters form a predictable part of the idle conversation which itself constitutes almost a universal form of recreation in the pueblo.

Small parties are formed by both Indians and Ladinos for hunting, fishing, picnicking, and bathing. These are largely recreational in intent, though there are useful consequences by way of food and cleanliness which result as well. Favorite spots for these sports are matters of discussion, and techniques for improving one's efficiency at securing animals or fish are also matters which evoke considerable public talk and interest.

At the adult level, it is principally the males who participate, with female participation being limited to the picnic parties, which tend to be more scattered and infrequent than hunting, fishing, and bathing. Again, there are differences in the Indian and Ladino patterns of organization of the membership of these outings. But as modes of recreation, they are generally characteristic of San Luis people, rather than being confined to only one or the other of the two major groups.

At the infant level, there are the traditional aimless patterns of play, involving homemade dolls, miniature tools of the shop and the field, and those random objects of nature such as stones and twigs which children have considerable proclivity in incorporating into their invented games.

Games of chance involving betting or economic speculation of any kind are relatively absent except for some very low-stake pool games, and a very occasional poker game. To the best of available knowledge, women do not

EDUCATION, RECREATION

engage in any games of chance; they are not even to be found playing cards of any kind "just for fun." There seems to be no particular moral sanction against such games for women; nor, however, is there any discernible positive pattern of expectation in this regard.

The only times at which there is widespread joint participation of all elements and all age and sex groupings in the pueblo occur at the religious fiestas in spring and autumn, and at occasional pueblo celebrations of national holidays. Fiestas are the occasion for considerable dressing up, spending of money, and consumption of alcohol. Social lines are drawn regarding types of behavior at such times, but there is considerable unity of spirit and involvement.

On national holidays, on the other hand, rather forceful techniques are often required to make sure that all elements of the community are adequately represented. The understanding of the significance of various patriotic rituals, the ability to sing national songs and anthems, and the motivation to celebrate such days at all are differentially distributed up and down the social, economic, and educational ladders. As a consequence, when an intendente desires to have his pueblo "show up" adequately for visiting officialdom, military and other power is often invoked to guarantee adequate attendance. Since such holidays, however, are generally taken as reasons for having secular fiestas, once the official celebration is complete, there is rather widespread participation by hundreds and sometimes thousands of people in whatever random gaieties are available.

Organized playing of music is confined for the most part to the marimba crews, some four of which are available at different occasions and for different prices. The most frequent use of the marimba teams is made at the twice-weekly concerts in the public plaza, an occasion which again brings out many people from all walks of life, either to "take a turn" around the plaza square, or simply to sit and watch others so enjoying themselves.

These concerts serve as occasions for preliminary courtship suits for Ladino adolescents. The practice is for a young man to walk up to a young lady who is "taking a turn," ask permission to walk alongside of her, get gently rebuffed the first time around, press the suit a second time, and then permanently retire from the quest if rebuffed the second time, or feel much encouraged if accepted. These openly observable suits are the occasion for much excitement among the adolescents involved, and there is considerable speculation beforehand as to the likelihood of possible suitors, and afterwards as to their intentions and eligibility. For the side-line observers, these suits also provide much conversation concerning the skills utilized, their success or failure, and the social implications of various temporary arrangements.

Weddings, dances, and baptismal celebrations are the other major occasions when courtship is informally conducted among the young people, and when both Indian and Ladino people of all ages find themselves together with common recreational ends in mind. By and large, however, social participation at weddings and dances is very much regulated according to whether one is Indian or Ladino and wealthy or poor. At baptismal celebrations and at wakes, on the other hand, there is considerably more intermingling among all social elements. This is in the main due to the tendency for various families, rich and poor, Indian and Ladino, to become interlocked through godparental relationships.

All such affairs—weddings, dances, baptisms, wakes—involve a considerable amount of nonutilitarian expenditures of time and energy and are taken to be at least partly recreational and productive of *alegria* or happiness. This holds for some religious celebrations as well, other than the main fiestas. Since almost inevitably these involve the use of some form of music, usually that of reed pipes by Indian musicians, and since they are taken as occasions of alegria, they are formally classifiable as part of the total pattern of recreation which goes on in the pueblo.

EDUCATION, RECREATION

The most constant and pervasive form of recreation engaged in by all people, regardless of characteristic or origin, is participating in street-corner gatherings. Though almost always either exclusively Indian or Ladino in constituency, certain patterns of common participation are noticeable, at least to the extent that there is tacit permission given for the Indians to hang on the fringes of sidewalk gatherings. By and large, however, since housing is fairly well segregated and since, therefore, neighborhood constituencies tend also to be segregated, the street-corner groupings are themselves discernibly segregated. It is important to note, on the other hand, that the absence of regularized and formalized types of recreation makes these street-corner gatherings the most frequent and ubiquitous patterns of leisure-time pursuit which one can discern.

CHAPTER 3

RELIGION, MEDICINE, AND MAGIC

Just as the church stands in the geographical center of the pueblo, so does religion, in more than a figurative sense, occupy the center of the social and cultural life of the town. There is scarcely a major facet of life in San Luis which does not contain some direct or indirect reference to religious matters. In short, though there are some village Protestants, there are no village atheists.

The religion practiced by all but about fifteen people in town is some form of Roman Catholicism. The fifteen exceptions constitute a Protestant island, the results of the proselytizing, over the last thirty years, by an obviously ineffective missionary. These fifteen isolates are, of course, well known to most of the other adults in town, and stereotypes are rather freely distributed concerning their conversion, their "queer" practices, and their possible danger. Generally speaking, however, the fact that they are Protestant does not affect their social relations with others in town in any markedly disadvantageous way.

It was noted above that the religion of all other people in San Luis was some form of Roman Catholicism. This loose construction is deliberate, for there is considerable variation between Indians and Ladinos in certain aspects of their religiosity. These differences are primarily a function, on the one hand, of the acculturation of former Indian pagan religion with Roman Catholicism, and on the other, of the significantly different manner in which religion enters into the emotional lives of Indians as against Ladinos. Certain common patterns of belief and practice do prevail, however, and these may be described.

First, for all but Ladino males, being a Catholic involves regular church attendance, regular participation in religious fiestas, processions, and adorations of various saints; a high positive evaluation of church weddings, baptisms, confirmations, and religious burials; and, for many, the

RELIGION, MEDICINE, MAGIC

investment of at least their vocabularies, if not their actual behavior, with a certain degree of "Christian love."

Many houses are fitted with small altars, decorated richly or otherwise in accordance with one's economic and social standing, and private home worship tends to be frequent, especially during crises of sickness and drought. Public worship as a community is held in the one church in town, which as an edifice dominates all the other buildings, being far taller and measuring some 300 x 50 feet in dimension. A small number of reliquary objects, including the complete statuary representations of various female and male saints, most notably that of San Luis Rey de Francia, the major patron saint of the pueblo, constitute the central points of interest in the church. Otherwise, it is somewhat barren and undecorated. There are a small number of pews, but these are inadequate for seating the many hundreds who attend the occasional masses, so that sitting on the floor or remaining standing is customary for the majority.

Public gatherings in the church are infrequent, primarily because there is no resident priest. The visiting priest usually comes once a month, but sometimes his appearances are spaced several months apart. As a result, weddings and baptisms are often delayed until such a time as they can be religiously sanctified by the priest. His visits, therefore, are the occasion for much activity in and about the church. Since these events also entail considerable social celebration, there is considerable extra-religious activity usually occurring before, during, and just after the visit of the priest.

Various sacred spots in and about the pueblo are marked by roadside altars, to which passersby usually contribute a stone, a flower, or any object which in their estimation constitutes some kind of adornment. The most significant of these spots are covered by lean-to shelters, within which are to be found the crosses. Other religious objects are not usually found at these roadside altars. Notably, there are altars at each of the four cardinal points of ingress to the

THE SETTING

pueblo, corresponding, at least in part, with current beliefs regarding the significance of these points in the realm of supernatural controls of natural events. This orientation to the four cardinal directions also expresses itself in the agricultural nexus, so that the *milpas*, or farm plots, are usually constructed with this orientation in mind, and such magico-religious ceremonies as the sprinkling of holy water upon the milpa are considered most effective when the four cardinal points have been so baptized. Aside from the altars which guard the four principal entrances to the pueblo, each *barrio* or district has its own sacred spot, and Indian religious organization requires a religious official to care for the cross and the shelter, and to provide for its special adornment on the Day of Crosses.

The most prolifically celebrated regular holidays are those of Easter and Christmas. Also of special importance to the lives of the people of San Luis is the fiesta of August 25th, which celebrates the name-day of the major patron saint of the pueblo. A somewhat smaller celebration takes place on September 27th, the name-day of a lesser patron saint. Other holidays which are to one extent or another recognized and religiously feted are the Day of the Dead and the Day of Kings. In addition, there are limited celebrations, the fifteenth and twentieth days of each month, in honor of San Luis and Santa Cruz; of October and March 15th, to celebrate the turn of the planting and harvesting seasons; of the name-days of patron saints of three adjoining pueblos; and, in times of drought, special rain-making ceremonies are engaged in, these usually being led by Ladino women, though otherwise almost totally Indian in constituency. The Ladino women play a critical role since it is believed that prayers said in Spanish, with the facility which some Ladino women presumably possess, are believed to be specially efficacious.

People of all classes in the pueblo make religious pilgrimages to various local or faraway shrines, the most

RELIGION, MEDICINE, MAGIC

notable among these being the annual pilgrimage to the national shrine at Esquipulas, some ninety kilometers away, where the "Black Christ" is located. Water is carried to Esquipulas for special sanctification by the resident priest there. It is carried back to the pueblo, held until March 15th, at which time it is distributed for purposes of sprinkling on the milpa plots and on the household altars. Rights to this holy water are accrued by contributing initially to the cost of transporting the water, having it blessed and having a mass performed at the Esquipulas shrine.

There is a hierarchy of religious leaders in town, but this kind of distinction is mainly characteristic of the Indian segment. Otherwise, such religious leadership as is recognized is primarily a function of continuous and long-time participation in religious celebrations and occasions. Special skills in prayer-making are recognized, but aside from this type of skill and knowledge of ritual and catechism, fervent religiosity is the main criterion of prestige in this area of social life. There are no religious scholars in the traditional sense, nor even any part-time devotees of special problems of textual interpretation. While deviations of the kinds mentioned are recognized and accepted, there are no disruptive deviationist tendencies, aside from the Protestants already mentioned. Everyone tends to recognize the minimum religiosity which is required. Any involvement over and above this minimum is either looked upon indifferently, considered as unnecessary, or viewed with respect as a mark of greater devotion.

As earlier noted, there is little formal religious instruction, aside from the lessons which may be passed on haphazardly from parent to child, or those which can be learned simply by observation. Thus, both the knowledge of church history and an understanding of the origins and functions of the various associated personages and rituals is at best meager. Differential interpretations prevail concerning who and what the saints are, and what roles they presumably play. These differences, however, do not enter significantly into the general round of religious involvement characteristic of such a large part of the pueblo.

Through the lives of most of the people of the pueblo there runs a feeling, sometimes intense and sometimes only mild, of divine guidance, omnipresence, reward and punishment. Even the most reputedly reprobate of people in the town are thus touched. A phrase which expresses the general outlook of all segments is that "without religion, we are not men, not Christians, but animals."

This sense of the all-pervasiveness of supernatural control over human affairs is found in all areas of pueblo social life. As a result, economic enterprises are held to be likely of more success if religiously initiated. Political office is taken only after considerable reference to divine sanction and benediction. Cures for the sick, and unmolested flights of the soul to its heavenly quarters, are taken to be possible only if religiously aided; and evil of any sort is held to be at least in part a function of religious defection.

Notably, Ladino males are least actively involved in this pattern of belief and practice. But equally notable is the fact that they affirm its general theoretical desirability, and do not disapprove of the very active participation of their wives and children. Indeed, it is taken as one mark of the marriage eligibility of a young girl that she is much devoted to religious matters and is a "firm believer."

In actual practice, a good deal of magic is interwoven with religion, so that it is more accurate to speak of the dominance of a magico-religious complex than of that of religion alone. The vocabulary of the average person in San Luis contains, however, a distinction between those affairs which are relevant to the benevolent magico-religious complex, on the one hand, and its malevolent counterpart, locally called *brujeria*, on the other. The latter is a far more awesome topic, and has about it a far greater connotation of "evil," whereas the former is largely orientated toward the "good."

RELIGION, MEDICINE, MAGIC

HEALTH, MEDICINE, WITCHCRAFT

The prevailing notions in San Luis regarding the causes and cures of disease are mainly crude and more often wrong than right. Moreover, there is only one person who has any trained medical skills, and even these are rudimentary. Additionally, the cost of his services, though slight relative to costs in other areas, is such as to prevent any widespread resort to him by the majority of people in the pueblo. Finally, the cost of patent medicines with any demonstrated efficiency is prohibitive for most people. As a result, health conditions may be said to be generally parlous in San Luis, with the consequences of a relatively high death rate and a low life expectancy.

Indigenous to the area is a form of tertian malaria. However, a large number of those afflicted appear to have made both a biological and social adjustment to this, so that the occurrence of the fevers and chills which mark the onset of the attack is taken in their stride in the ordinary course of events. Next to malaria, infant enteritis and various forms of pulmonary affliction appear to be the primary causes of death. This applies relatively equally to all segments of the population. Naturally, however, the wealthier the person, the more resort can be had to such effective secular treatment and medicines as are available.

In the face of constant illness, which is also constantly visible, and in the absence of effective secular cures, it would be natural to expect a high degree of anxiety concerning health. But there is to be found in San Luis one facet of life—the belief in magical forces—which operates to reduce somewhat the expectable anxieties. The securities which belief in magical forces brings are of two kinds: (1) those which are produced by the fact that at least some idea is had concerning the causes of illness; and (2) those which result from the fact that some considerable faith is had in the efficacy of various magical cures. Opposed to these operations, however, are the anxiety-producing consequences which result from the equally firm belief in the ability of diseases to be maliciously induced through black magical arts which are available for purchase from known specialists.

As in any system where reason is not the primary guide, the ideas concerning the relations between magical forces and health in San Luis display some marked inconsistencies. The net result is that the same disease may be held, on different occasions, to be differently caused, the preference for one or another notion depending not on pathological symptoms nearly so much as on the socio-psychological situation of the patient relative to possible hostile acts by himself and his enemies. Thus, for instance, when one feels secure about his good standing with his associates, the occurrence of a pain in the stomach may be attributed simply to overeating. When, however, this pain comes shortly after the patient has had an argument, it is believed that the likelihood is increased that some magically induced force, such as an evil wind, purposively conjured against him, is responsible.

The germ theory of disease is given least credence. Far more belief is invested in various types of magical theories. These include the presumed forces of evil winds (*aires*), evil eye (*mal ojo*), contamination from the dead (*hijillo*), spirits and frights (*espanto*), and other magical creatures and powers, such as small animals secretly placed inside of one, which then grow, and ghostlike creatures of no particular form which simply torment the person.

The specialist in the use of these materials and the control of these forces is called a *brujo*, or wizard, and his art, *brujeria*, or witchcraft. He or she is held to act sometimes on the paid instigation of an enemy, sometimes out of sheer malice, sometimes in retribution for bad things said or thought about him. Generally, the brujo is invested with a degree of omnipresence and omniscience, so that he does not require actual sensory contact with those who wish him evil, but is even capable of fathoming thoughts and dreams which have never been overtly expressed.

The evil winds are presumed to have their own motive

power as well as being capable of being manipulated by brujos for their evil purposes. An apparently harmless gust of air may turn out to be a cleverly concealed *aire* which has been sent on its evil way by a brujo. Most clever and deceptive of all such winds are the sudden gusts of cool air which come up on hot dry days and which, because they are so welcome, are inhaled so deeply. These are held to have special penetrative powers, and are especially effective because they are so apparently desired yet really harmful.

Since the retributive theory of cause of disease is given such ample credence, considerable social control, both of word and of deed, is informally maintained through the fear of suffering evil witchcraft after giving offense. In the actual diagnosis of a disease the wizard hired for this purpose generally conducts an inquiry into the amiability of one's social relations. Questions are asked concerning possible offense given, wittingly or unwittingly, and resort to other possible explanations of the disease is not had until it is firmly established by the patient, his family, and the wizard that no one has been given just cause for bringing black arts to bear upon the patient.

It is interesting, in this regard, that many of the wizards who are held capable of black magic are also considered efficient curers of disease. It is said of them that they are familiar with each others' techniques, and indeed it is believed that since certain wizards specialize in inducing certain types of ailments, they are also the best possible doctors for the ailments. The securing of their services creates the rather ticklish psychological situation of getting the disease-causer to act now as disease-curer. Under those circumstances where all reasonable people would hold that the patient had suffered enough for his malfeasance, whatever it might have been, it is also held reasonable to attempt to get the specialist who presumably caused the disease himself to come and treat his own victim.

Generally speaking, the full range of possible magical

causes is explored before any credence is given to possible natural causes of the disease. It sometimes happens that a sick man will call in the local doctor with his presumably secular patent medicines to treat him, at the very same time that he is also resorting to the service of a local curer, with his various herbs and compounds. An interesting situation arises from the fact that the ingredients of some of the most presumably efficacious magical compounds are purchased by the wizards from the local doctor-druggist, who may himself be fully aware of the intended uses, but is sufficiently secular to go through elaborate pretenses regarding the concoction of these compounds. To the best of available knowledge, no formal working arrangements have ever been established by the doctor-druggist with any of the magical curers in the area.

A typical technique for curing pains, aches, and fevers of various kinds is to "draw" them out of the body. Sneezing powder is often administered with much magical incantation to induce the patient to expel whatever little flies or other animals may have been placed inside him. Evil winds and other forces are drawn out of the limbs by the technique of smearing the affected part with a raw egg, so that the drawing sensation may be felt by the patient at the same time that the magician utters his phrases and draws his hands down upon the limb. Anything which appears to be localized in the intestinal regions is first treated with a purgative which often appears to be as effective in inducing considerable debility in the patient as it is in helping expel whatever congestion, if any, is present. The induction of heavy sweating, through the use of aspirins and warm wraps, is similarly held to be efficient in drawing a fever or a chill out of the body. Throughout all these rites, there are also employed all types of magical appurtenances, too numerous to be cited here, and relevant, in any event, only to specialized studies of such practices.

Of general significance is the constant employment of religious prayer along with magical curing techniques. It is not clear from the evidence available whether it is generally believed that certain magical forces have to be propitiated through prayer in order for the magical cures to be effective. It is clear, however, that considerable supplication of a nominally Christian deity is considered very helpful. It is the wizard himself who more often than not engages in this prayer, usually at the church, usually alone, and with the ritual aid of candles purchased at the expense of the patient.

Probably many of the felt ailments are psychogenetic, especially since there is such widespread conviction regarding the possibility of falling sick because of having done evil. In such psychogenetic disorders, the belief in the efficacy of magical cures undoubtedly helps render these cures more efficient than might otherwise be expected. A typical case in point is the common stomachache experienced so regularly by so many in San Luis, as a sequence to having experienced a fright. The magical exorcism of the "fright" is often sufficient to reduce or eliminate the ache.

It is also widely believed that different kinds of people have different susceptibilities to various types of diseases. Thus, infants are held to be the most susceptible of all people to all kinds of magically induced illnesses. It is therefore also believed that wizards out to do an evil turn are more than likely to concentrate on the infants in the marked household. Since infant sickness and mortality naturally run high for a variety of perfectly adequate empirical reasons, there is much coincidental evidence which can be and is appealed to in testimony to the greater susceptibility of these infants to magic. Hence, special magical precautions for infants are taken, such as the covering of the child's face when in public to avoid any passing "evil eye," and the painting of a cross with a green ointment on the forehead of the baby and on the wall over his bed. This latter is considered especially important at the beginning and end of every month when wizards are presumably most active.

One's milpa and animals are also considered prime objects of magical attention. This makes good sense since one's fields and animals are the most valuable possession of the average individual in San Luis. Harm to the milpa may come through specially induced winds which rip up crops, or through special droughts or excessive rains, or through the magical induction of an excessive number of plant parasites which destroy the produce. Animals are believed subject to some of the same kinds of magically induced diseases which are held to be effective with humans.

It is difficult to determine how much of the average cash income of the local pueblo resident is spent on magic and medicines in any average year. But a brief listing of the cost of various magical and other medical services may give some indication of the extent to which illness is feared as much for economic as other reasons.

The following should be considered against the background of the fact that the average wage is 10 cents a day: The simplest and most diluted aspirin tablet costs 1 cent. "Very efficient" aspirins cost 5 cents. A quinine injection costs 50 cents. A good cathartic costs between 5 and 25 cents. The services of the average curer retail at 25 cents a visit, plus food and alcoholic beverages for him, plus the cost of whatever patent medicines and herbs he employs in the cure. A visit from the local druggist-dentist-doctor costs 50 cents.

In short, then, even the simplest medical needs involve expenditures which can be ill afforded by the average resident. More complex needs, of course, cost proportionately more and are proportionately less supportable. A prolonged illness of any kind, especially where some type of medication is continuously needed, often quickly takes away a lifetime's savings. It is held by many of the people that many deaths could be avoided if people could afford to pay for more treatment.

Over the past few decades there has been a noticeable decline in the number of people who are believed capable of working magic, the number of situations in which it is believed magic is justifiably employed for causing illness, and the proportion of illnesses which are diagnosed as magical in origin. Among the most important factors contributing to this threefold trend are the following: (1) All forms of magic-making have been declared officially illegal. When a presumed culprit is caught, punishment is rather severe. (2) There has been a small but rather persisting shift to a belief in the greater value of secular diagnosis and treatment, due in part to a general secularization of life in San Luis. (3) Some of the former wizards have died without having imparted their special skills to any younger men. Concomitantly, there have failed to appear on the scene any matching number of men who have gotten the "call." The failure to get the "call" is probably at least in part due to the now illegal status of wizard. (4) The circle of magical retribution and counter-retribution appears to have had such obviously unfortunate consequences for so many people, that there seems to have occurred a type of informal consensus to resort to magic only under the more extreme circumstances.

Since the individual who resorts to employing the skills of a magician to cause harm to another requires at least tacit community approval both to justify his action and to render it efficient, the absence of this sanction can and often does act as a restraint upon the employment of magic.

Matching the attrition in magic is a growth in resort to religious devices, primarily prayer and supplication. Prayers may be said to induce evil as well as good, and the extent to which one's prayers are answered is believed to be as much a function of the efficiency of the prayer content and delivery as of the justifiability of the cause involved.

CHAPTER 4

THE PUEBLO: ITS RELATIONS AND REPUTATION

IN SPITE of the marked degree of local chauvinism and pueblo-centrism which one encounters there, San Luis has a reputation in local surrounding areas and in the nation's capital as an unpleasant, uncharming and slow-moving place. In the neighboring pueblos of Pinula and Ipala, one encounters this sentiment frequently; both of these pueblos are considered locally as far more attractive places than San Luis. Merchants from Guatemala City have openly expressed the fact that San Luis is considered a barren and unprofitable place of call. National officials on their infrequent visits tend to share these sentiments. At least some of the more ambitious residents of San Luis themselves join in these feelings.

There appear to be at least some objective reasons for the reputation. Life in San Luis is apparently very undiversified, by comparison with other areas. The standard of living is low. The facilities for outsiders are extremely limited and uncomfortable, and the physical appearance of the pueblo is by no means impressive.

Moreover, communication with the outside world is rather difficult to maintain. The trip to Guatemala City, which is only 146 kilometers away, requires two days of travel, since, in the absence of any train or motor service to San Luis itself, the first day must be spent in reaching Ipala by a 17-kilometer mule-back ride, and then taking a subsequent ride of 25 kilometers on a train which goes to Zacapa, a stop-off point, only once a day. From Zacapa, it takes the train the better part of the second day to reach Guatemala City. No busses or private motorized transportation of any kind are available even as far as the neighboring pueblo of Pinula. The same kind of difficult travel is involved in reaching any of the other nearby pueblos, including Jalapa, the department capital, which

THE PUEBLO

is the nearest place with a life even approximating urban expectations.

Train fare to the capital is itself too expensive to be afforded by any but the most wealthy of the local residents. It costs about the same to ride from San Luis to Guatemala City as it does to go by ordinary coach train from New York to Chicago. For most people, therefore, the trip is clearly out of the question, and for this and other reasons most people in San Luis never have made nor probably ever will make the distance by train at their own expense.

Some of the possible effects of this isolation are alleviated by the fact that many of the men of the pueblo have been brought to the capital at the expense of the government for purposes of military training. Moreover, a surprising number of Indians have made the trip on foot, having neither mules nor train fare. Most of the Indians who have been in the capital city, however, appear to have been so well insulated by fear, ignorance, and the absence of any frame of reference for the meaningful incorporation of their new experiences in the city, that the stay was virtually ineffective so far as opening any new horizons of possibilities are concerned. For the Ladinos who have been to the city, the experience is one which by and large only increases their verbally expressed discontent with San Luis without resulting in any determination or plans to improve the pueblo. In short, encounters with more sophisticated and urban conditions of life by the citizenry of San Luis have not appeared to result in anything significant by way of suggestions for San Luis itself. For all the observable influence they appear to have had, the visits and contact with the capital might just as well not have occurred.

News of the outside world reaches San Luis through four subscription copies of a daily newspaper published in Guatemala City. These are eagerly read and discussed, but only by a relatively small number of people. There are no electric radio sets in town, since there is no electricity available. The one gasoline powered set which is

THE SETTING

owned by the local doctor had long since ceased functioning, at the time of these studies, due to a shortage of fuel. Another source of information is to be found in the word-of-mouth news which is conducted by the local telegraph officer, who passes on choice bits of gossip and news he hears over the wireless. Finally, the daily mails bring with them news from people living outside the area, and sometimes this proves to be of considerable interest and discussion.

The following figures give some indication of the volume of exchange between San Luis and its environs, so far as movement of telegrams and mail is concerned. These statistics are for the entire month of December 1942:

Private telegrams sent: 70 (total of 299 words)
Private telegrams received: 67 (total of 245 words)
Official telegrams sent: 86 (total of 2,094 words)
Official telegrams received: 84 (total of 2,825 words)

Private telephone calls sent: none
Private telephone calls received: 1
Official telephone calls sent: 1
Official telephone calls received: 5

Private letters and postals received: 292
Private letters sent: 58
Private pamphlets and packages received: 131
Official letters received: 149
Official letters sent: 48

The category of "private" is simply nominal, since all phone calls and telegrams are made or transmitted by the local telegraph officer who is also a man of simulated military rank and himself directly subject to the Jefe Politico, and ultimately to the national censorship office. *All* mail is subject to censorship by both local and national officials, so that there is little possibility of any genuinely private communication being carried on through the mails, telephone, or telegraph, especially if there is any ground for political suspicion of any of the parties involved.

The pueblo has no movie houses or legitimate theaters. It has no organized music other than the marimba concerts already mentioned. Running water is found only in nearby rivers and streams and at four centrally located fountains, from which most of the residents get their water. One house, that of the local pharmacist, had battery-powered electric current for a short time, but this was short-lived. There is a nominal airport, located a few kilometers outside town. But except for one arranged landing of a small plane on the day of its opening, the airport has never been used and is now totally grown over with weeds. No organized athletic teams go out from the pueblo or come into it, except for a very sporadic occasional visit of girl basketball players from other pueblos who happen at the same time to be friends or relatives of people in San Luis.

In spite of all this apparent isolation, the Indian men of the pueblo are considerably sophisticated in travel, and decidedly familiar with alternative patterns of life led by people in other pueblos both near and far. This is primarily due to the fact that for the several months each year when the ground is allowed to lie fallow, Indian men and their sons go on sales trips to neighboring areas, following any one of a number of well-established routes, selling various wares, primarily pottery objects made by their wives and straw hats which they themselves make. These trips all are made on foot, and sometimes involve travel over several hundred miles into neighboring Honduras and San Salvador. The trips are viewed both as work and recreation, since they are both productive of income and, on the road back, of considerable pleasure and sport. The trip *to* the places of sale usually involves the carrying of backbreaking loads, and therefore tends to prove too burdensome and wearing to be viewed as anything but a necessary prerequisite to the making of some cash income and the pleasure of the return trip. Due to these trips, it is possible to assert that though the Indian men are relatively the poorest segment of the population, they are also the best-traveled segment.

In addition to these extended trips, there appears to be considerable socially and economically motivated interaction between the pueblo people and the residents of the outlying *aldeas,* or hamlets. San Luis is the central market place for the produce of the aldea farmers, and on market days there is a tendency for considerable social reuniting to take place, with some marked increase in the consumption of alcohol. For the aldea people, therefore, a trip to the pueblo is considered something of an event, though the reverse is not true.

Closeness of relationships with other pueblos, to the extent that it is found, is primarily a function of the existence there of relatives or close friends. There are no organized techniques for acquiring new friends from outlying areas, such friendships as exist having been made at weddings, wakes, or various other celebrations which bring people to and from other pueblos. Relationships are therefore primarily informal, and there are no lines of organized formal interaction among the officialdom or citizenry of any one pueblo with any others.

These informal relationships tend largely to be confined to the Ladinos since, by contrast with the Indians, they tend to have their family lines spread throughout the nation. The Indian group, on the other hand, is almost totally local in membership, dialect, and other features of its culture, so that it is virtually a self-enclaved community. This difference in lines of extra-pueblo connections makes a difference in perspective with regard to the pueblo, so that it is reasonable to say that the Indian is much more closely associated in his own outlook with his local environment, whereas there is a tendency among the Ladinos to look outward and upward to other people and other larger areas for their self-definitions. This difference, in turn, has significant consequences for the adjustment pattern of both groups, as will later be shown.

There is no questioning the varied set of satisfactions available in the local community, so long as one's horizons are limited to their achievement. But the meaningfulness of these satisfactions is limited to those who know little and care less about the outside world, and whose ties to the local area are rooted deeply in local custom, tradition, and meaningful participation. The passage of time has brought with it a marked attenuation both in the variety of satisfactions and the number of people who have a sufficiently stable base in life and a sufficiently traditional orientation to embrace the round of San Luis patterns and be content.

PART II
LADINO-INDIAN SIMILARITIES AND DIFFERENCES

CHAPTER 5

PHYSICAL FACTORS AND THEIR SOCIAL DEFINITIONS

WE HAVE SEEN that San Luis contains two major segments of population. One is called Ladino, and numbers approximately 1,100, while the other, called Indian, totals 2,400 persons. This distinction between Indian and Ladino is neither artificial nor simply nominal. Rather, it describes a line of demarcation between two culture patterns and two world views. It is, in short, a difference of which all pueblo residents are well aware and by which they are importantly conditioned.

Throughout the previous materials occasional reference has been had to differences between Indian and Ladino attitudes and practices. This emphasis is justified by the fact that running throughout all the patterned differences in culture, world view, and the like is a basic principle of social organization which hierarchizes the ratings, rewards, and punishments in the pueblo, and which places Ladinos in the superordinate and Indians in the subordinate status. This stratification system is castelike in character. It will be the principal intent of this section to describe the details of the system, showing how the two castes are fitted into one social system in a type of equilibrium which requires their common participation in many aspects of the social life of the community. Special attention will be paid to the prevailing subjective definitions held by Indians and Ladinos regarding the differences between them and the evaluations they respectively make of these differences and their implications.

PHYSICAL APPEARANCE

The terms "Indian" and "Ladino" have variable meanings in different parts of Central America. It is important, therefore, operationally to define the meanings which are

LADINO-INDIAN DIFFERENCES

invested in these terms in San Luis. No brief or simple definition will suffice, however. For it is only as one knows the details of the distinctions as they prevail in San Luis that one can clearly understand just what is there meant by the terms.

Throughout the pueblo, the notion is widely held that the Indian-Ladino distinction refers, among other differences, to one in inherited physical characteristics. There is some vague knowledge of the separate original proveniences of the Indian and Hispanic groups who came together hundreds of years ago and have remained together since, intermingling their genetic stocks all along the line, to form the present genetically mixed population. That mixture has been so thorough that it is estimated that perhaps no more than five to ten per cent of those who call themselves Ladino, and thus presumably derive from Spanish ancestors, do not have some Indian ancestry. In spite of this mixture and its apparent effects, it is still widely believed that there are distinctive physical differences. Evidence can be selectively mustered at any time to "prove" this point. For it is relatively easy to pick out markedly Mongoloid-looking individuals and contrast them with markedly Caucasoid types, using some of the characteristics of standard ideal-typical racial divisions for this purpose. The ability to do this, in combination with pressing cultural compulsives to keep the two groups separate, leads to a widely held and commonly expressed belief that one can always distinguish any Ladino from any Indian by physical appearance alone.

As would therefore be expected, standard stereotypes prevail regarding the "typical" appearance of members of the two groups. The stereotype of the Ladino thus describes him as tall, fair-skinned, blond-haired, blue-eyed, with wavy or curly hair, and with some observable body hair and beard. By contrast, the Indian is held to be somewhat smaller, much more darkly pigmented, dark-eyed, dark- and straight-haired, and noticeably free of body hair and beard. Reference is also had by the Ladino to the pres-

PHYSICAL FACTORS

ence in the Indian of the epicanthic eye-fold and the so-called Mongoloid spot which from time to time appears in the vicinity of the rump of new-born Indian children. This last item is appealed to as the critical token of identification in cases of doubtful parentage.

Reliable anthropometric measurements on the total population or any sizable portion of it are not available. It is not possible to say with any certainty, therefore, how accurate is the impression of this observer that the prevailing descriptions are more stereotyped than typical, and that the difference in the means of the physical characteristics of the two groups is insignificant.

However, the sense that this impression is accurate is strengthened by the fact that one frequently errs when he tries to identify otherwise unknown persons on the basis of the prevailing physical stereotypes alone. Moreover, when one pays sharp attention to the problem of the number of people in each group who approximate the ideal-type descriptions which prevail, he discovers that these are indeed ideal types and not typical averages.

It became clear, after several months of pursuing this problem of identity, that, all other things being equal, an individual is called Ladino or Indian depending on his known or suspected parentage. Generally speaking, this identifiable parentage tallies with the cultural and linguistic habits of the individuals being identified, so that a composite set of clues is generally employed. These nonphysical clues, whose details will shortly be described, are given priority over physical appearance when the latter does not conform to stereotypical expectations.

From all this, it also became evident that the varieties of skin color and other presumably distinguishing physical features have become so generally distributed throughout the pueblo population that by themselves they are not very reliably differentiating pegs on which to hang social distinctions. But they are often invoked, especially in cases where the other nonphysical criteria are themselves so blurred as to make it necessary to appeal circularly to the

LADINO-INDIAN DIFFERENCES

known or presumed ancestry and from that to justify the decision that there is sufficient distinctiveness of physical appearance to warrant the decision as to group membership.

Similarly, when physical or ancestral clues are too blurred to permit certain identification, any one cultural characteristic or any one linguistic habit of the individual may be singled out as the special and unmistakable mark of the person's group membership. Clearly here, as in cases where no clues are reliable, the person is defined by subjective feeling almost regardless of the objective facts.

It is interesting to note that disputes of identification occur, primarily among Ladinos, as to whether a person is or is not really a Ladino, but not around a disputed claim to Indian status. It is evident from this that Ladinos care a good deal about whether or not a person is a Ladino, as he claims. It is not possible, however, to say whether Indians care about the genuineness of someone's claim to being Indian, since by and large there are no known cases of people claiming to be Indian when they have a chance to claim Ladino status.

So far as sheer physical criteria are concerned, the question of the extent of actual differences between the two groups must remain, at least scientifically, in limbo, until some sound and representative anthropometric studies are made. Inside the pueblo, however, there are few if any important disputable cases of identity, so that by and large everyone agrees on the identity of everyone else, including his own. This then, like the case of the identification of the American Negro, is an instance where the social definitions of group membership include and yet are different from at least some of the physical and biological tokens of membership. In San Luis, as in the United States, the consequences of the social definitions of group membership which are only presumably but not really physically different as groups, force the observer to work within the frame of these definitions and to allocate group membership on the basis of these extra-physical criteria. As a consequence, one is never sure in retrospect whether he was using only physical, or only cultural, or some mixture of physical and cultural cues to identify individuals with whom he was in association.

Nevertheless, in San Luis, no matter what other criteria of difference are employed, physical characteristics are certainly held by many to be importantly differentiating. It seems reasonable to assert, therefore, that many of the people of San Luis invest their social caste lines with certain biological meanings. That these imputations regarding biological differences are not accurate, by scientific criteria of anthropometric measurement, does not any more invalidate their social significance than does the inaccuracy of the Negro-White biological distinctions which prevail in the U.S. invalidate their social consequences.

Indeed, again as with the Negro-White distinctions in the U.S., the data of San Luis force one to the conclusion that the belief in biological difference is a vital support of the social caste distinction, and, as in other such cases, also serves to rationalize those social distinctions which prevail. Moreover, it can be conclusively shown that there is genuine feeling regarding the mixture of bloods, with at least some implication of "contamination" expressed by these fears.

The following materials, relating to answers by Indian and Ladino interviewees to questions regarding the possibility of Indians changing to Ladinos, and vice versa, show some of the importance which beliefs in "inherent" differences assume in San Luis.

REGARDING THE POSSIBILITY OF AN INDIAN CHANGING TO A LADINO:
The Indians said:
Possible in San Luis 18
Possible only where not known 20
Possible only from birth on 3
Possible, but no opportunity 2
Not possible at all 5

LADINO-INDIAN DIFFERENCES

Reasons why not possible:
One can't change his birth.
One is always an Indian even though he may look like a Ladino.
An Indian can never forget his Indian dialect.
One can't change his blood.
Once an Indian always an Indian.
An Indian is always known by his Indian form.
An Indian is always known by his color and face.
One can't change his own nature.
You can always tell an Indian by his two voices he uses to speak Spanish and the dialect.

If possible, how?	*Number of times mentioned*
Become literate and educated	13
Acquire money	13
Change language habits	35
Get material possessions (land, clothes, house, etc.)	98
Marry a Ladino woman	8
Change work habits	20
Live with and like Ladinos	20

REGARDING THE POSSIBILITY OF AN INDIAN BECOMING A LADINO:

The Ladinos said:

Yes	2
Yes, if not known	3
No	14

Reasons why not possible:
One's origins are always known.
Can't change blood.
Once an Indian always an Indian.
One can't change his nature.
You can always tell an Indian by his bad Spanish.
You can always tell an Indian for his spiteful badness.
You can always just tell an Indian.
One can't change his race.
You can always tell an Indian by his skin color.
The poverty of Indians always makes it impossible.

PHYSICAL FACTORS

	Number of
If possible, how?	*times mentioned*
Become well instructed, educated, and literate	4
Acquire Ladino customs, like sleeping in beds, eating at right time, behaving well, adopting whole Ladino life	4
Get good clothes	2
Let children mix with Ladino children	2

REGARDING THE POSSIBILITY OF LADINOS CHANGING INTO INDIAN:

The Indians said:
Possible	20
Not possible	19
Possible only where not known	5

Reasons why not possible:
  Once a Ladino always a Ladino.
  You can't change the difference that exists.
  A Ladino is always known.
  Ladinos can't do Indian work.
  One can't change one's parents.
  A Ladino is always known by his color and face.
  Ladinos are too well dressed, Indians too poorly dressed.
  Ladinos don't want to.

	Number of
If possible, how?	*times mentioned*
Learn Indian dialect	25
Wear simple and torn clothes	9
Learn to do Indian work	15
Marry Indian women	8
Make trips as the Indians do	4
Take off one's shoes and socks	2
Learn Indian customs	1
Live in humble house	1
Live in the pueblo	1
Get acquainted with the people	1

REGARDING THE POSSIBILITY OF A LADINO BECOMING AN INDIAN:

The Ladinos said:
Possible	2
Not possible	13
In customs but not in blood	1

Reasons why not possible:
  Indians won't accept Ladinos.
  No Ladinos want to.

LADINO-INDIAN DIFFERENCES

One can't change one's blood.
One can't change one's race.
It would be too shameful.

If possible, how?   *Number of times mentioned*

Change clothes, put on torn and dirty clothes 2
Make grammatical errors in speech 1
Work like the Indians 1

It is noteworthy that a much larger percentage of the Indians think it is possible for an Indian to become a Ladino than for the reverse transition to take place. By contrast, the Ladinos are relatively consistent in the numbers who felt that such transitions were or were not possible. Three questions immediately suggest themselves here: (1) Why do different percentages of Indians feel one kind of transition is more possible than the other? (2) Why do the Ladinos remain relatively constant in their opinions about the possibilities of both transitions? (3) Why do Ladinos and Indians differ in the percentages of each who consider the transitions as possible or impossible?

(1) It is probable that more Indians think it possible for an Indian to change to a Ladino than for the reverse to occur simply because the former is an alternative which is at least partly realistic in the Indian's own life terms, whereas the latter transition simply is out of the question, as a realistic life possibility, so far as most of them and their thinking is concerned. This is to say that most Indians are familiar, either personally or vicariously, with real or putative "passing" by Indians to membership and acceptance in the Ladino group, whereas none of them has any familiarity, personal or vicarious, with any instances of transition from Ladino to Indian.

Changing to Ladino status by an Indian represents one of the real life alternatives available to Indians, under rigorously specified conditions, as a change from their current fates. But it is correctly felt and estimated by both Indians and Ladinos that no one would want to "become" an Indian once he had acceptance as a Ladino. It seems reasonable to assume, then, that at least a large number of those Indians who thought the transition from Ladino to Indian was impossible meant to indicate that no one would want to make such a change.

One other possible reason concerns the learning of the Indian dialect, which, according to prevailing stereotypes among the Indians, is relatively impossible for a Ladino to accomplish. Since speaking the dialect is an indispensable criterion for being considered Indian, the fact that the learning of the language is considered relatively impossible for non-Indians might conceivably make Indians estimate that the transition from Ladino to Indian was out of the question.

By contrast, Indians have other Indians as examples of people who have learned to speak Spanish well enough to "pass." Moreover, they have the further examples of people who have completed the passage without any real difficulty in other places where their ancestry was not known. The known actuality of this transition would thus tend to make it seem as one capable of achievement under the specified conditions.

(2) By contrast with the Indians, as noted before, about the same percentages of Ladinos feel that both transitions are equally impossible. This, too, makes sense in light of the prevailing beliefs entertained by Ladinos regarding inherent and unalterable differences between themselves and Indians. The typical Ladino explanation for most behavior differences resorts to biological factors. In the case of such wide and observable behavior differences as those between Ladinos and Indians, it is thus almost inevitable that biologically fixed and irremovable obstacles should be cited. Moreover, Ladinos have something of a vested interest in preventing "passing" by Indians into Ladino status, and they would thus tend to reject that transition as much as they would typically consider the reverse as simply nonsensical.

(3) In part, this last factor helps account for the differential percentages of Ladinos and Indians who consider

the two types of transitions as possible. At least some of the Indians have a vested interest in believing that the Ladino status is by no means difficult to achieve, if one "really" desires it. This would tend to make them estimate the possibilities of this transition much higher than would the Ladinos. This type of reasoning fits into what is already well known about the way in which typically some members of subordinate groups tend to minimize the differences between themselves and the superordinate group, whereas the latter tends to maximize the differences and the difficulty of eliminating or overcoming them. For, it is also well known that often the superordinate group tends to view the differences between themselves and their subordinates as more naturally "given" and "fixed" than do the subordinates.

By way of supporting statistics, it will be noted that 43 out of 48, or almost 90 per cent, of the Indians felt the changeover to Ladino status was possible under some condition or other, whereas only 5 out of 19, or some 26 per cent, of the Ladinos thought this was possible. Similarly, 25 out of 44 Indians, or some 57 per cent, thought the changeover from Ladino to Indian status was possible, while only 3 out of 15, or 20 per cent, of the Ladinos agreed with this estimate. One thus can see a marked asymmetry in the view held by Ladinos and Indians regarding these matters. Apparently, the Ladinos have much more psychologically invested in maintaining the differences between themselves and Indians than do the latter; or they actually think the differences are more substantial; or, some combination of belief and psychological investment forms a gestalt which makes them respond so differentially.

An important fact is that the vast majority of reasons given by *both* groups for the impossibility of changing over in either direction refer to "fixed" or "inherent" things, such as blood, skin color, nature, race, form, and ancestry. In this regard, then, both groups share common views on what are the difficulties involved, even though

PHYSICAL FACTORS

they do not tally in their respective numbers making the estimate. One may conclude, therefore, that where it is felt that Indians cannot become Ladinos, or vice versa, it is also felt that this is due to matters of biology as much if not more than to simple cultural features.

If one views the situation of possible attitudes, it is seen that Indians can fall into one of four "types" regarding the desirability and possibility of the transition to Ladino status:

- a. the transition is possible and desirable
- b. the transition is possible but not desirable
- c. the transition is not possible but is desirable
- d. the transition is not possible, nor is it desirable

These four alternatives yield six possible contrasts: (1) a with b; (2) a with c; (3) a with d; (4) b with c; (5) b with d; (6) c with d.

In actuality most Indians fall into categories (a) and (d). That is to say, Indians tend to feel either that the transition is both possible and desirable, or not possible and not desirable. At least one factor importantly differentiating these two groups is the age of the members of each. The older Indians tend to reject both the possibility and the desirability of the transition to Ladino status, whereas a much larger percentage of the younger Indians hold the transition to be both possible and desirable. In short, here is a significant cleavage, along age-lines, on a critical issue in the culture, which reflects a tendency toward change. Thus the traditional homogeneity and stability of the social organization and culture pattern of the Indian group is challenged.

More and more each year, young Indians begin to break away from the habits and customs of their elders and to inquire into the possible rewards and satisfactions to be found in the Ladino way of life. It is clear that the immediacy and high visibility of the Ladinos and their apparent cultural satisfaction can and sometimes do act as real stimuli here. When these are further enhanced by some experience with a cash economy, such as can be had by working for relatively decent wages outside the pueblo, it can be surmised that the potential for social change inherent in the present structure and function of the pueblo is not to be ignored.

CHAPTER 6

LANGUAGE, LITERACY, AND EDUCATION

It will be recalled from the materials of the foregoing chapter that differences in language habits and abilities are often taken as critical marks for distinguishing Indian from Ladino in San Luis. The prevailing rules state that if a person speaks only Spanish he is almost without question a Ladino. But if he speaks either only the Indian dialect or both the dialect and Spanish, he is almost certainly Indian.

Certain marginal cases test the rule. For instance, at least some of the people who are called Indian profess little or no ability to speak the Indian dialect. Others say of them that they are simply pretending and attempting to claim a status which they do not merit. Additionally, an occasional Ladino is reputed, by himself or others, to be able to converse in the Indian dialect as well as in Spanish. When these putative abilities were tested out, it was found that this ability was minimal, amounting to no more than the knowledge of a few phrases.

The manner in which the ability to speak the dialect is critically diagnostic of Indian group membership is revealed in the numerous stories one hears about Indians who are "passing" in other pueblos. Since San Luis Indians travel far with their pottery ware, they encounter along their routes various individuals who were born and raised as Indians in San Luis but who have subsequently moved to other places, as far even as San Salvador and Honduras, in which places at least some of them are "passing." San Luis Indians agree that it is not "right" to reveal the deception to the people in the other pueblos, but they also feel it quite within the game to taunt the "passers" by conversing about them to their faces in the local San Luis dialect, and to enjoy watching the "passers" squirm as they pretend not to recognize the nasty things being said about them. This is held to be an especially funny situation when the "passer" is married to a Ladino woman who does not know his Indian origins.

It is perhaps an index of the superordinacy of the Ladinos in San Luis that Spanish is used exclusively in any interaction between themselves and the Indians. By contrast, in many sections of western Guatemala, where much of folk Indian culture still prevails, Ladinos are often required to learn the local Indian dialect if they are to carry on relationships with the Indians. It seems almost as if in those places where the Indian culture has been preserved, the Indian has a correlative self-sufficiency which forces the Ladino to come to him and yield in certain matters, whereas in the highly acculturated regions, such as characterize eastern Guatemalan Indians, the Indian is forced to come and yield to the Ladino. The latter is certainly more typical of Guatemala as a whole. For, throughout the country, Spanish is the single official language of the government, the schools, and the churches. In this, then, as well as in many other ways, Hispanic culture has assumed and maintained dominance from the outset of its contact with Indian culture.

In San Luis the local Pokomam dialect is used almost exclusively by the Indians in intra-group matters. Naturally, the dialect is liberally sprinkled with Spanish loanwords which, for the most part, are used to refer to matters and materials for which there are apparently no equivalents in Indian dialect. These loan-words, in turn, are given a flavoring of the local dialect in the manner in which they are pronounced and made to follow the grammatical and syntactical dictates of the Indian dialect.

No standard distinctions exist among the Indians concerning relative proficiency in the use of the dialect, except for those one expectedly finds differentiating the child from the adult. One other possible exception concerns the case of priestly prayer-makers, who are held to be endowed with special facility in this craft. But this is more a matter

LANGUAGE, LITERACY, EDUCATION

of sophistication in ritual and theology than of language facility.

Considerable distinction is both evident and recognized, however, in the respective abilities of various Indians with the Spanish language. It is commonly agreed that Indian women are much less facile with Spanish than their own husbands. And it is further understood that young Indian children are unable to speak Spanish long after they are perfectly capable to handle the Indian dialect.

The reasons underlying this difference indicate something about the interaction between Indians and Ladinos. The Indian man's proficiency in Spanish is acquired principally because he has a great many more and enduring contacts with the Spanish-speaking Ladino community than his female counterpart. Indian boys go to the Spanish-speaking schools in greater numbers and proportion than do Indian girls. Young Indian men go off to military service in the barracks, where only Spanish is allowed, and where speaking any Indian dialect is severely punished. No young Indian woman has a comparable experience, except for those occasional girls who take up domestic service in Ladino households.

Moreover, it is the Indian man who goes on sales trips to neighboring pueblos where he is forced to use Spanish if he is to conduct his business adequately with foreign Ladinos and Indians, neither of whom speak the Pokomam dialect. Additionally, it is usually the Indian man who represents his family in any dealing with local officialdom, and who does his stint of "voluntary service" as a servant at the city hall, where only Spanish is spoken. Again, the Indian man is the one who conducts business dealings with the Ladino landlord whom he must ingratiate if he is to secure land for rent.

By contrast, it is rare that the Indian woman needs to use Spanish. Her sallies into public generally consist of going to the fountains for water, or to the markets and stores for produce. At the markets, the Indian dialect serves rather well. In the conduct of business at the stores, a bare type of Spanish serves adequately. At the water fountains where gossipy conversation is a main attraction, the cohorts in gossip are almost exclusively other Indian women, and here again the Indian dialect is primarily employed. On the other hand, there is now discernible a tendency for Indian women to appear in public places far more frequently than in the past history of the pueblo, and as a result of this one notes a concomitant tendency for Indian women to become more proficient in the use of Spanish.

Opposed to all the situations in which Indians use Spanish are those in which the dialect is not only more readily employed, but in which, indeed, there is a strong cultural injunction that it shall be employed. Reference is here had to those typical in-group situations where the use of the local dialect serves as a badge of membership. Some rough classification of these situations is possible, so that it can be said that in addition to all other situations mentioned, Indians tend to use the dialect in the following situations:

(a) when they wish to hold conversations which the Ladinos will not understand;

(b) when they wish to make fun of or curse the Ladino in his presence without incurring his disfavor or the possibility of punishment;

(c) in the conduct of all Indian religious services, the efficacy of which is held to be increased by the uttering of prayers in dialect;

(d) in the conduct of witchcraft, whether benevolent or malevolent;

(e) in courtship situations, which, because they are often semipublic, require the dialect for additional privacy from Ladino ears;

(f) in the conduct of marriage arrangements among the parents of the fiancées and the sponsors representing each family;

(g) in the household, among members of the family.

Most of the above-cited situations fall within the scope

of intra-Indian affairs. At least some of them, however, it will be noted, take place within the earshot or the presence of Ladinos. It can thus be reasonably stated that the dialect serves as a cement for the social solidarity of the Indian group, in that it functions to protect the Indian in his resistances to or reactions against Ladinos, as well as helping to bind Indians to each other in the normal course of their lives.

In the household, for instance, the dialect is used almost exclusively. This has a significance beyond that ordinarily expected, for it means that the dialect is the language of the most extreme affection and anger. Ordinary social relations are thus given their strongest reinforcement in the Indian dialect, a fact of no mean importance in understanding the tenacity of Indian culture in the face of so many pressures toward acculturation. This takes on added significance when it is realized that the child's first orientation into the world of abstract symbols of justice, authority, and morals in general is articulated almost exclusively in the dialect. For, most Indian parents feel that no matter how adversely this practice may affect the child's subsequent ability to speak Spanish, it is important that he be taught only the dialect as his first language. In this manner is it guaranteed that any one generation of Indians will tend to use the dialect more and more freely than Spanish.

It is no accident then that the Ladinos view the use of the dialect as the hall mark of "Indianness." Nor are the Indians adversely affected by the fact that Ladinos consider this an invidious distinction. The many services which the dialect provides them appear to compensate for the dismal view taken by the Ladinos.

Nor is it accidental, then, that both Indians and Ladinos tend to agree that no matter how well tutored an Indian may be in the Spanish language, he almost always speaks Spanish in a way distinguishable from that of a person who has learned Spanish as his first language. Commonly known facts regarding such linguistic differences between native-born and secondary speakers of a language suggest that this view, as held by the people of San Luis, is not fictional. At the same time, the difference tends to be exaggerated by the Ladinos, as would be expected, so that it is not always easy to distinguish between a Ladino and an Indian in terms of his facility with Spanish alone. It is thus by no means always certain that clues other than language —such as clothing, physical appearance, gesture, and previous knowledge—are not being used to identify the individual.

The following table summarizes, in gross terms and percentages, the distribution of the ability to speak Spanish and Pokomam among a sample of 49 Indian and 22 Ladino households.

TABLE 3

Can speak	INDIAN MEN (49)		INDIAN WOMEN (46)		LADINO MEN (22)		LADINO WOMEN (17)	
	No.	Per cent	No.	Per cent	No.	Per cent	No.	Per cent
Spanish	49	100	46	100	22	100	17	100
Pokomam	49	100	45	97.8	1*	4.55	0	0

* The one case of a Ladino man listed as able to speak Pokomam refers to an individual who can handle a smattering of phrases.

Further differences and similarities among the Indians and Ladinos emerge when they are compared with regard to their abilities to read and write Pokomam and Spanish. No one in the pueblo, Ladino or Indian, can read or write Pokomam, since, as a written language, it does not exist. Certain vocabulary lists have been compiled by professional linguists and visiting anthropologists. But so far as local knowledge of them is concerned, they too might just as well not exist. No distinctions can be made, therefore, regarding the relative literacy of Indians and Ladinos in Pokomam.

The matter is considerably different, however, with regard to Spanish. In theory, the chance to learn to read and write Spanish is equally available to all. In fact, however, this chance is differentially distributed so that exposure to

LANGUAGE, LITERACY, EDUCATION

the opportunity is far more frequent for Ladinos than for Indians. The following table indicates something of this result:

TABLE 4

Literacy*	INDIAN MEN (49) No.	Per cent	INDIAN WOMEN (46) No.	Per cent	LADINO MEN (22) No.	Per cent	LADINO WOMEN (17) No.	Per cent
Can read Spanish	16	32.6	2	4.35	16	72.7	13	76.5
Can write Spanish	15	30.6	2	4.35	16	72.7	13	76.5
Can only sign name	1	2.1	2	4.35	3	13.6	0	0
Totally illiterate	32	65.3	42	91.3	3	13.6	4	23.5

* The frequencies totaling greater than N in each case are due to the overlaps in the categories of "can read Spanish" and "can write Spanish."

An attempt was made to estimate statistically the significance of the difference between the percentages for the various groups and subgroups in the foregoing chart, with the following results:

	Reading Spanish	Writing Spanish	Total illiteracy
Indian men vs. Indian women	S.D.*	S.D.	S.D.
Ladino men vs. Ladino women	N.S.**	N.S.	N.S.
All Indians vs. all Ladinos	S.D.	S.D.	S.D.
All men vs. all women	N.S.	N.S.	S.D.

* S.D.—Significant difference (Critical ratio over 3).
** N.S.—Not significantly different.

It will be noted from these summaries that so far as reading and writing Spanish are concerned, the significant differences are to be found between men and women in the Indian group, and between all Indians and all Ladinos (men and women included). From this it may be concluded that chances and/or motivation to learn to read and write Spanish are differentially distributed by caste, and, within the lower caste, by sex.

77

LADINO-INDIAN DIFFERENCES

These conclusions are borne out by the following tabular summaries of the years of schooling acquired by men and women in the Ladino and Indian groups. Expectedly one finds statistically significant differences between the amount of exposure to education of Indians vs. Ladinos, on the one hand, and Indian men vs. Indian women, on the other. The critical ratios in these two cases are far larger than that found for any of the other comparisons previously made.

TABLE 5

Years of school	Ladino men (22)	Ladino women (17)	Indian men (49)	Indian women (46)	Total 134
0	5	5	28	41	79
1 mo. to 1 yr.	0	0	7	2	9
13 mo. to 2 yr.	3	0	3	1	7
25 mo. to 3 yr.	1	3	4	2	10
37 mo. to 4 yr.	1	2	5	0	8
49 mo. to 5 yr.	3	5	0	0	8
6 yr.	2	3	1	0	6
7 yr.	0	1	0	0	1
8 yr.	3	0	0	0	3
9 yr.	0	0	1	0	1
10 yr.	0	1	0	0	1
More than 10	4*	0	0	0	4
Total Years	123	77	60	10	270
Mean	5.59	4.53	1.22	.217	2.01

* This includes 1 at 11, 2 at 14, and 1 at 20 years.

TABLE 6

SUMMARY

Years of Schooling

	Total	Mean
All Ladinos	200	5.12
All Indians	70	.715
All Pueblo	270	2.01
All Males	183	2.57
All Females	87	1.38

As further evidence of differences between Ladinos and Indians, the following records may be offered regarding registration, attendance and absence at school, and success or failure of Ladino and Indian students.

TABLE 7

MALE STUDENTS REGISTERED IN FIRST GRADE OF PUEBLO SCHOOL

Ladinos		Indians	
Age	Number	Age	Number
7	7	7	9
8	3	8	8
9	1	9	4
10	0	10	8
11	3	11	3
		12	3
	14		35

No figures are available as to the total number of Indian and Ladino children between the ages of 7 and 12 for the former and 7 and 11 for the latter who are in the pueblo and are therefore potential school children. But if the estimated total populations may be taken as bases from which to judge proportional representation, it is notable that the Ladino population is represented in the first year of school in a significantly disproportionate amount.

The figures on absences from school, however, do not reveal disproportions of the same variety. In June 1942, out of a total possible number of 540 absences, 110, or 20.3 per cent, Indian absences were recorded. This contrasts with a figure for 41 out of a total possible 224, or 18.3 per cent, absences for Ladino children. In December of 1942, however, there were 148 out of a total possible 525, or 28.2 per cent, absences for Indian children as compared with 75 out of a total possible 210, or 35.7 per cent, absences for Ladino children. If it may be assumed that June and December are representative months, all other things being equal, then no significant differences can be shown between the attendance ratios of the children of the two groups.

Figures on success and failure in school are kept most informally in San Luis, so that the only data available come from random notes and the memory of the school director, who is also teacher of the first grade. He reports that of the 35 Indian children registered in the first grade, 11 failed their examinations and 8 were absent from the examinations, making a total of 19 out of 35, or about 54.3 per cent of the Indian registrants who did not successfully complete the first grade. This contrasts sharply with the figures for the Ladino children, which, according to the director, show that of the 14 Ladino registrants only one failed his examinations and none was absent, indicating that only 7.14 per cent of the Ladino children failed to complete the first year successfully.

No reliable figures are available for registration, attendance, and success or failure in the second and third grades. It is evident, however, from those just reported for the first grade that the attrition rate is markedly higher in the group of Indian children than among Ladino children. This is especially significant in light of the fact that the differences in the proportionate registrations and absences from school do not themselves appear to be markedly significant. A readily apparent explanation—aside from all other possible interpretations—is the well-established difference in language facility of the Indian and Ladino children who enter the first grade. It appears, therefore, as though formal school, or at least a year of it, does not contribute to any substantial reduction in this difference, but rather tends more firmly to establish it as a permanent fact.

The differences in amount of formal education and the derivative language facilities which are shown by the foregoing figures have implications and consequences which extend far beyond the mere possession of certain skills in reading and writing. Five of these may be spelled out in more detail:

(1) Movement into higher skilled white-collar jobs, with their concomitantly higher prestige and income, generally requires some considerable facility in reading and writing Spanish. Even on the local scale, such jobs as teacher, sec-

LANGUAGE, LITERACY, EDUCATION

retary, scribe, intendente, druggist, telegrapher, doctor, and the like, all have a literacy prerequisite which most Indians are unable to meet. It is thus apparent that the differences in education immediately set in process a series of determinants which severely circumscribe the economic alternatives of the Indian far more than the Ladino.

(2) Though Indians are aware of the consequences of the lack of formal education, and though they sometimes tend to deplore their lack of opportunity to acquire that education, it is quite apparent that there is a widespread deemphasis in Indian culture on the value of sending children to school. Indians offer a variety of rationalizations for failing to have their children become educated. None of these, however, seems to explain this failure nearly so well as the fact that there is a strong positive emphasis in Indian culture on the value of teaching children agricultural skills at the earliest possible date so as to be able to incorporate them profitably into the adult division of labor as soon as possible. A contributing factor here is that the subsistence type of economy in which the Indian is involved generally commends to him the necessity of having his male children at work with him, or, if they are female, with their mother, as quickly as muscular coordination and strength permit. It is not hypocrisy, therefore, which compels the Indian to assert verbally the value of an education but in actuality to keep his children from acquiring it. Rather it is simply the preponderance of a traditional value strengthened by sheer economic necessity, as judged by the Indians in terms of those same traditional values.

(3) The preponderance of these traditional values which orientate the Indian primarily toward agricultural work and thus limit his economic horizons stands in marked contrast to the work aspirations of the average Ladino. For, the latter envisions the earliest possible detachment and freedom from the necessity of manual labor. Corollary to this is a difference in evaluation of the worth of manual labor, so that a marked distinction between Indians and

LADINO-INDIAN DIFFERENCES

Ladinos, which is recognized and made explicit by both of them, is the high positive value in Indian culture on the worth of such manual labor and its direct opposite in Ladino culture. As will later be seen, each group takes the attitude of the other toward manual labor as an identifying characteristic, and, as such, as depreciative of the character of that group.

(4) Several factors combine to give further social and political importance to the aforementioned differences in literacy. Primary among these is the fact that Spanish is the language of official government affairs and of most things which command prestige from sources outside the pueblo. The inability of the Indians to deal adequately with Spanish thus gives them a generalized low social rating, on the one hand, and a degree of political incompetence and impotence on the other. For, regardless of the strength of the informal political structure of the Indian group, all Indians are subjects of the general political structure of the pueblo and nation. They are thus largely dependent upon and much subject to the manipulation of Ladinos in these matters. By itself, and all other considerations aside, this makes Indian participation in politics a matter of the most simple and direct forms of persuasion and coercion, divorced from any real ability or inclination to consider the merits of issues or candidates.

It is no accident, then, that Guatemalan politics, and especially San Luis politics, are run by small cliques, who consider the Indian citizens primarily in terms of the ease or difficulty with which they are likely to be able to be persuaded or coerced. This lends further support to the traditional low estimate which Ladinos have of Indians, and to the expectable abjectness of social position which the Indians occupy and tend by and large to accept. Finally, the political impotence and low social rating combine to make of the Indian an ideal scapegoat for the Ladino, with all the expectable consequences of this fact.

(5) The tenure of the prestigeful and politically influential positions by the Ladinos helps cause those In-

dians who are seeking socially to elevate themselves to view Ladino dispensation of favor as prerequisite to their mobility. This has led in recent times to the emergence of a small number of young Indian men who openly preach and practice the virtue of acquiring skills in currying this favor. While almost all Indians tend to be servile and deferential in front of Ladinos, the behavior of this class of favor-currying Indians is noticeably exaggerated in this regard. One of the results of this activity so far has been to produce greater alienation between this group of Indians and the rest. Moreover, while the attempts at ingratiation sometimes result in small favors for the Indians involved, an overall result is the further depreciation of the already low social esteem in which all Indians are held by Ladinos. It is difficult to judge, therefore, whether any substantial gain has been made, even from the value-outlook of the Indians so involved.

These, then, are some five of the principal consequences which arise from the initial differences in amount of formal education between Indians and Ladinos. It can thus be seen that the network of institutions is so closely interdependent in San Luis that direct and wide ramifications in diverse institutional areas are expectable from differences existing in any one such facet of its social life. Thus, any one differentiating factor tends to support the existence or to cause a noticeable elaboration in other aspects. It serves, further, to set aside the group of Indians from the Ladinos as culturally distinguishable segments of the pueblo population.

CHAPTER 7

CLOTHING

THE clothing worn by an individual is one index of group identity which is used by almost all people in San Luis. Differences in this respect are both qualitative and quantitative. For women, there is a distinguishable Indian costume which almost all Indian women wear and which no Ladino ever wears. As for the men, certain minor qualitative differences may be seen. But by and large the real contrast is in the greater variety and cost of the Ladino men's clothes relative to the lack of variety and the cheapness of the clothes worn by Indian men. These differences, which are sharp and distinguishable in people past the age of puberty, are, however, much less noticeable in younger children.

The range of possible dress for adult males in the pueblo stretches from informal evening wear such as might be found at any lower middle-class gatherings in the United States, at one extreme, to ragged, torn, and patched cotton trousers, topped by an equally decrepit cotton shirt, covering homemade long cotton underwear pants, and ungraced by socks or shoes, at the other. By and large, Ladinos tend to approximate the former end of the scale and Indians the latter.

The matter is considerably different for adult women. The vast majority of Indian women wear a costume composed of a cheap cotton "peasant style" blouse, with pique frills at the neck and cuff lines. This is worn tucked into a heavy length of multi-colored, ready-made wool which, stretching to the ankles, is worn wrapped round and tucked into itself at the waist for support. Indian women also almost always affect a headdress which usually consists of braiding their hair with interwoven ribbons and covering the hair with a long shawl, which is usually white, sometimes colored, but never black.

CLOTHING

On their feet they wear either a pair of paper-thin homemade leather sandals, or, more usually, nothing. No underclothing is worn by Indian women. Considerable extra adornment in the form of strings of beads, earrings, and bracelets is considered fashionable. Frequently the necklace is composed of old coins, or sometimes of genuine coral. It thus often results that more money is spent for the adornment than for the basic clothing itself.

Many Indian women have only one complete outfit of clothing. Quite a few, however, have two outfits, a very few have three, and one has four. New outfits are usually purchased once a year, but sometimes three and four years pass before an Indian woman buys new clothing. This is understandable because it costs about $5 to purchase the materials for a complete outfit, and this type of expenditure is not easily afforded by the Indians. At the same time that sheer economic inability may force the woman to go several years without new clothing, a cultural sanction against conspicuous display of wealth makes even those men who can afford it very hesitant about buying more than one outfit a year for the women in the family, and also helps eliminate any "shame" which might otherwise arise in those women who are obviously impoverished.

It has been estimated that about 25 per cent of adult Indian women do not wear the "typical costume." Instead, they are to be seen dressed in very inexpensive cotton European-style housedresses and similar quality slips and undergarments, all of which are as often ready made as home made. Those women who dress in this European fashion also tend to shun wearing the beads, earrings, and necklaces which seem intrinsic to the native costume. However, they retain group identity to the extent of refraining from wearing stockings and shoes. They often share with Ladino women, on the other hand, the wearing of a black rather than a white shawl. The cost of an outfit such as these mildly Ladinoized Indian women wear varies between $1.50 and $3.50. It can thus be seen that it is not economic but rather cultural compulsion which determines that one rather than the other type of outfit will be sported. This judgment is supported by the fact that a large proportion of such Ladino-clothed Indian women consists of unmarried Indian girls who have taken up domestic employment in Ladino households.

By contrast, the Ladino woman never wears anything resembling the "typical costume" of the Indian woman, almost always wears a black shawl, and never a white one, and, when economically possible, wears shoes and stockings. This latter item is in marked contrast with the Indian woman who would not wear shoes or stockings even if she could afford them.

By further contrast, the Ladino woman usually wears the expectable range of underclothing, including some form of slip, brassiere, and underpants. Such jewelry as she may sport, in the form of earrings, necklaces, bracelets, and the like, are always clearly distinguishable from the types worn by Indian women. Additionally, the Ladino woman usually wears her hair bobbed, rather than long or braided.

Comparisons of the amount of money spent on the outfits of Ladino as against Indian women show that the clothes of the former involve a minimum expenditure of $5 for the most simple type of materials, and up to $8 to $10 for the "fairly dressy" outfits. This may or may not include the cost of shoes and purses, items which are never found in the clothing budget of the Indian woman. Moreover, most Ladino women, as will be seen from the figures below, have more clothing than do Indians. This is especially the case with adolescent and post-adolescent Ladino girls who are being courted or hope to be. It is in this age group of 17-25 that one finds the greatest amount of public display of variety and quality of clothing.

There is no comparable phenomenon among Indian girls of this age, for by the time an Indian girl is seventeen she is usually already married, a mother, perhaps several times over, and therefore long out of the courtship period. The Indian girl of this age is closely confined to the household

CLOTHING

of her husband and usually makes only infrequent public appearances, for water at the fountains or goods at the markets and stores. If still unmarried at this age, she is courted in a semiclandestine fashion, at night, or hurriedly and with a minimum of observation during her infrequent sallies out of the house in the daytime.

By contrast, it is during their adolescent and post-adolescent years that the Ladino girls most frequently appear in public. They form the main constituency of dances and other social gatherings. They occupy prominent places in religious ceremonials and processions. They dominate the audience and the teams at the basketball court every afternoon. They are the life blood of picnics and outings of various kinds. In short, they are constantly on display, and, realizing it, make every effort to live up to their roles, a primary characteristic of which is being as expensively and variedly dressed as possible. Their social prestige, and hence their marriageability, hinges considerably on their ability conspicuously to display themselves.

The adoption by an Indian woman of the Ladino style of clothing occurs most frequently, if at all, at puberty, and next most frequently at marriage. In both instances, the pressures exerted by Ladino godparents seem to be very important. One of the rare cases of Indian women wearing shoes occurred, for instances, at the wedding of an Indian girl, when her Ladino godparents purchased stockings and shoes for her and urged her to wear them. Immediately after the wedding, however, she removed the shoes and stockings, never to wear them again, even though she continued to dress in European style clothes. In such cases as these, the Indian community sometimes recognizes the pressures and the probable gain to be derived from conforming to the wishes of a well-to-do Ladino godparent, and withholds the scorn and public mockery which is otherwise meted out to an Indian who is so presumptuous as to wear shoes in public.

With notable and rare exceptions, all children, Ladino and Indian alike, tend to dress alike, sex differences always remaining evident, up until the ages of ten or eleven. For girls, this usually consists of simple little European style housedresses, with a minimum of underclothing or none at all. Certain exceptional Indian girls are dressed in miniature versions of the native costume even before puberty. Aside from these, however, the principal distinction. between Indian and Ladino girls of pre-puberty age is in the jewelry worn, with Ladino girls sporting European-style necklaces, beads, bracelets, and rings, whereas the Indian girls affect replicas of the jewelry usually worn by their mothers.

Most Ladino and Indian boys of all ages tend to resemble their parents closely in their clothing styles, with even less difference between them at the younger ages, since in these years almost all boys, not just the Indian, tend to go barefoot. It is only as they approach puberty and beyond, that the differences in the quality of the clothing and the amount available become more perceptible. Exceptions to this generalization are to be found in the cases of the wealthiest Ladino families who dress even their youngsters in clothing which is conspicuously expensive by comparison with that worn by everyone else, even to the point of having them wear socks and shoes. Finally, it is sometimes possible, according to local estimates, to distinguish between Ladino and Indian men and boys in terms of the kind of straw or palm hats worn, the Indian sporting his own homemade braided hats, while the Ladino tends to purchase and wear kinds which are imported into the pueblo. This difference is more presumptive than real, however, for actual count of the wearing of these hats reveals that no significant differences exist on this score.

As would be expected in the case of the men, the most apparent differences are those which occur at the extremes of the economic ladder. For instance, a sine qua non of attendance at Ladino weddings, dances, public receptions, and the like, is the wearing of a black or navy-blue woolen suit. Only a few Ladinos possess this item of clothing, yet all Ladinos tend to index it as a mark of generic membership in the Ladino group. By contrast, no Indian has such a suit nor would think of purchasing it, even if he could afford it.

It is thus clear that certain clothing differences, no matter how initiated, are now supported by both economic and noneconomic determinants. The same generalization may be applied to such items as neckties, socks, and, above all, shoes. Indeed, the wearing of shoes is most frequently cited by both groups as distinctive of group membership. Aside from whatever economic circumstances enter here, Indians insist that no self-respecting Indian would ever wear shoes, even though at least some of them could afford to buy them, and many have pairs left over as souvenirs of their year of military service.

What may be concluded, therefore, is that out of a relatively limited range of possibilities, differing notions as to right and wrong ways in which to dress determine the kind of clothing for which money will be allocated. These differences operate so as to standardize certain "appearances" as typical of Indians and others of Ladinos. There is, however, considerable overlapping in the distribution of these types, so that in effect one cannot easily distinguish the poor, barefooted Ladino in his ragged clothing from the average Indian by dress alone.

This latter fact is illustrated by a curious incident which occurred just prior to this investigation. The President of Guatemala had decided to hold a celebration in Guatemala City in "honor" of the Indians of the country, and in commemoration of his "freeing" of them from debt servitude. For this occasion he commanded that each pueblo should send a delegation of Indians dressed in "native costume." Typically in eastern Guatemala, and especially in San Luis, there is no such native costume. An ingenious intendente, however, decided that his local delegation would have to show up in some kind of costume which would distinguish them from prevailing Ladino clothes style. He decided, therefore, that the Indian delegates would go to the celebration in their long white cotton underdrawers and shirts. And thus they appeared, with the result that it is now a standard joke among Indians and Ladinos alike in San Luis that this is the way one distinguishes Indians from Ladinos.

From the foregoing it can be seen that so far as clothing is concerned Indian women are far more sharply distinguishable from Ladino women than are Indian men from Ladino men. This difference arises from several noteworthy facts which may here be mentioned.

First, as was earlier noted, there is a prevailing tendency among Indians for the man to be the public representative of his family. His attitudes, behavior, language, and appearance are therefore all more generally accommodated to prevailing Ladino styles than is the case for his female counterpart. The latter is accustomed from the outset of her training to expect quick marriage, early childbirth, and generally close confinement to the self-enclaved areas of Indian life. Her full participation in this pattern is the criterion by which she and others judge her right to the rewards which there inhere. It assures her a place in the community of people and understandings which, by reason of her training, she finds easy to handle adequately and satisfactorily.

Each departure from the customary norms, whether only apparent or real, thus involves for her the breaking of habits and patterns which are rather firmly ingrained in her, and thus entails considerable psychological difficulty. Additionally, any such departures bring criticism and punishment, involving, sometimes, severe psychic suffering. Nor are there compensations to be found, as is sometimes the case with young Indian male deviants, in recognition and reward, no matter how slight, from the Ladino community. Since, therefore, the Indian woman expects herself to be totally traditional, she enhances the customary expectations which prevail in the Indian community and which attract considerable public interest and response whenever she deviates.

CLOTHING

A rather interesting case in point revolves around twelve young Indian women who had been "selected" by an enterprising Ladino intendente to represent the Indian community, as Indian beauty queens, at the name-day fiesta of the pueblo. These twelve girls were accordingly rouged, lipsticked, and beribboned as they had never been before in their lives. They were paraded up and down on exhibition in the market places. There they also danced for the spectators, something never before done by Indians, and, in general, were treated in a fashion somewhat akin to, but much less courteously than, the beauty queens on parade in Atlantic City. Now, each of these beauty queens was of marriageable age. According to rumor, each of them had an Indian sweetheart to whom she was promised. Each of these girls immediately lost her sweetheart after having participated as fiesta queen. In nine months after the fiesta, not one of them had regained her old boy friend or acquired a new one. The Indian men were frank in their opinions. The Ladinos were aware of the opinions. For their departure from the behavior norm, even though it was literally forced on them by the mayor, these girls were simply being ostracized by all available Indian males with marriageable intent.

Some of the Indian sweethearts in question did not directly say so but inferred strongly that for the Indian girl to have been elected beauty queen must have meant that in some way she had secured the favor of the Ladino mayor and his aides, and that in San Luis there was only one such way to secure the favors of Ladino men. An Indian girl generally runs considerable risk of being unmarried and remaining unmarried if she is known not to be virginal. When in addition the putative lover is suspected of being a Ladino rather than an Indian, the chances of her marrying are proportionately diminished.

In short, then, whether aware or not aware of the consequences of their behavior, these twelve girls had made departures from the permitted norm, for which they had acquired a sort of left-handed prestige among Ladinos and

Indians alike. But, inasmuch as their lives have to be made and lived in the Indian community, their loss of potential Indian husbands seems a far greater loss than whatever gain in status and prestige they may have acquired with the Ladinos.

Thus, though any given Indian woman may not be able to foresee the consequences of deviant behavior, it is an overall fact that sometimes very severe consequences do befall them for even appearing to deviate from customary norms. The Indian woman's retention of her native clothing may, therefore, aside from pragmatic reasons such as warmth and modesty, at least in part be accounted for in terms of the fact that this clothing is the manifest symbol of membership in a community of people and understandings in which she feels comfortable and secure.

Several other tangential reasons seem important in explaining why the Indian woman retains her native clothing style, in preference to European clothing style. Among these is the fact that the woman's "native clothing" is definitely tied up with avoidance of evil witchcraft directed against children. One of the most common and popular preventive measures which Indian women adopt in order to save their child from the evil influence of wizards and witches is to wrap the child in the full skirt and tuck him to sleep in that fashion on the nights of the first, the fifteenth, and the last of every month, the nights when wizards and witches are considered most powerful and children most incapable of resistance.

A further consideration involves the desire to distinguish oneself and to be distinguished from Ladino women. This is the corollary of wishing to be identified as an Indian. In this regard, Indian women show an ambivalence similar to that which prevails for the Indian man. For, the Indian woman can also be said to desire to conform to Ladino behavior under certain types of situations, chief among which are those where the initial break from the Indian life style has already been effected. Reference is had here especially to the case of Indian girls who earn

CLOTHING

money by keeping house or watching children for Ladino families. An Indian girl who takes up residence as a maid in a Ladino house almost invariably dons Ladino clothing.

The important thing here is that for an Indian girl to plan to enter service for a Ladino involves an initial break from the Indian life style which recognizes in such Ladino house service the most strong and influential source of contact and acculturation toward the Ladino horizon which an Indian woman can encounter, short of marriage with a Ladino. Indeed, it appears to involve an even more marked break than is initially manifest. For it is well known that once an Indian girl takes up house service for a Ladino and dons Ladino clothing in the process, her chances of marriage with a "normal" Indian boy are too slim to be counted on.

One cannot but wonder, therefore, what the Indian girls who make these ventures into new norms can possibly anticipate by way of consequences for further relations with the Indian community. For, these girls usually end up as part-time mistresses of either the male adults or the male adolescents in the Ladino household, and continue the rest of their lives in a position intermediate between two sets of understandings into neither of which can they fully penetrate, try as they may.

The most spectacular case of this sort was that of a young Indian girl who was a maid in the Ladino household where I stayed during my investigations in San Luis. But unfortunately the intimate data I secured from her is probably not applicable in general, since she intended to and would most surely have married an Indian "radical," my principal informant,[1] if he had not died. My informant was about as deviant an individual as one ever encounters in a peasant or primitive society. He was far more marginal to the Indian community than was the girl to whom he

---

[1] This is Luis Najera about whom I have written in some detail in other places. Since he is mentioned frequently in this text, the reader may be interested in referring to the following citations in the Bibliographical Note: Tumin 1945 b, 1945 c, 1950 b.

was informally betrothed. With this particular girl, then, there was no actual surrender of securities necessary upon her entry into maidservice in a Ladino household. Indeed, in her case there was actually an opportunity for her to recapture a set of securities which expulsion from her paternal household had forced her to surrender.

The acculturated clothing style of the Indian man, by contrast, ties in closely with his general position in the social life of the pueblo and his differences from the Indian woman in this matter. However, it may not be inferred that the Indian man is generally more interested in becoming Ladinoized than his female counterpart. Rather, it must be stated that because the Indian man is far more exposed to stimuli from the Ladino way of life, and is closer to the Ladino in appearance, he has to endure far more ambivalence and its concomitants on this account than ever does the Indian woman.

This ambivalence is marked, outwardly, by the fact that no matter how closely alike are Indian and Ladino clothing, the Indian refrains from that final gesture of acculturation, the wearing of shoes. The general rationalization of the Indian on this score is that he cannot afford to wear shoes. In most cases this is factually true. But it is untrue in a sufficient number of cases to make it quite clear that the matter is more one of attitudes than of money.

The Indian culture has a strong injunction against confusing one's identity. Considerable self-pride in the status of Indian is manifest in both the public words and the behavior of Indians. It is therefore considered a mark of self-shame and shame of one's group fellows to attempt to hide this identity. Privately, however, a number of Indians indicate a vague sort of preference for the Ladino way of life, involving the wearing of shoes along with other things. It is thus readily apparent to the inquirer that the matter of maintaining self and group identity is sometimes not as clearly and unequivocally supported as it appears to be.

In this regard it is noteworthy that the Indians have

CLOTHING

elevated to the status of a relative culture hero one particular young Indian, named Miguel F., who speaks Spanish with great ease, who is particularly noted for his facility at curing illness, and of whom it is proudly cited by most Indians that he wears shoes. Of him it is asserted by the Indians that he sufficiently distinguished in other things to claim the social status which entitles him to wear shoes. In these types of observations one notes a tendency of the Indians to think in terms of categories of social status, hierarchically organized, for which different types of behavior and appearance are appropriate. However unexpected it may be, Indians tend to rank themselves low in this hierarchy relative to the Ladinos, no matter how high they otherwise rate themselves on such scores as "basic human dignity," "religious fervor," and the like. This sense of the appropriateness of various types of appearance and behavior to various levels of social status permeates the thinking of Ladinos and Indians alike. There are, however, marked differences in their respective evaluations of the reasons for and the consequences of being so differentially rated.

Especially noteworthy in recent years has been the tendency of some young Indian men who have acquired their own incomes from working on nearby banana plantations to sports clothing which is neither distinctively Indian nor Ladino, but which represents a bad and clumsy approximation of the latter. These outfits include white shirts and white duck trousers which are clearly more expensive than the white cotton underpants and shirt which also double for outer garments for other Indians. It also includes imported ready-made sandals with heels which are known to be uncomfortable on the feet of Indians who are accustomed either to no shoes at all or only to a flat, heel-less sandal. These young men also typically sport a loud-colored bandana, worn either around the neck, or allowed to droop conspicuously out of a pants pocket. For a hat, these acculturating Indians deny the traditional home-braided palm and instead express a preference for ready-made hats which cost from three to five times as much as their home-made counterparts. The final touches to this somewhat gaudy costume are colored strands of straw or palm, or colored feathers in the band of the hat, a small black cheroot which is allowed to dangle jauntily from one corner of the mouth, and, finally, elastic arm-bands which are worn no matter how short sleeved the shirt may be.

The typical behavior of youths dressed in this fashion is to saunter, usually on Sundays, to the more prominent corners of the pueblo, and there to lean against walls during the long afternoon, laughing in apparently self-conscious ways about nothing in particular. They are viewed with contemptuous amusement by Ladinos who address them as "Counsellor" and "Doctor" and "Engineer"; and they are looked upon by many Indians with a sense of shame and sadness for what they apparently represent. For it is true that they do represent only clumsy and crude approximations at Ladino appearance. The sandal with heels is the closest they can come to shoes without wearing shoes. The red bandana has the same meaning so far as wearing ties are concerned. The arm-bands are strictly Ladino in origin. The store-bought hats again mark them off from the traditional Indians. It is no wonder, then, that the Ladinos laugh at them and the other Indians shake their heads.

Their appearance, however, is undeniably expressive of a sentiment held by some Indians that one can acquire some of the prestige and standing that Ladinos have by purchasing the outward symbols of membership in the Ladino group. How untrue this sentiment is relative to the real situation of social approval and rejection is evident in the fact that the most intense scorn and contempt of the Ladino is apparently reserved for those who manifestly attempt to secure membership in the Ladino group, but are clumsy and therefore unsuccessful in their efforts.

From observing the various modes of clothing which

CLOTHING

prevail in San Luis, one can detect correspondence between differences on this score and other prevailing differences of attitude and position. Thus, it has been shown how the distinctiveness of the Indian woman's style is closely correlated with other known life attitudes which characterize the Indian woman's position in the pueblo, and how, similarly, the same type of correlative exists so far as the male is concerned. It has further been seen how the male characteristics in clothing are generative and supporting of ambivalences regarding his own social position and the possibility of altering it. Of special importance in this regard is the ambivalence concerning maintaining group identity at all cost, at the same time that considerable effort is exerted by some to get themselves ranked differently.

The following tables and accompanying explanations summarize the actual differences in kinds and amounts of clothing which are to be found between Indians and Ladinos in San Luis:

TABLE 8
MEN'S CLOTHING POSSESSIONS

Garment	Indian men (49)	Ladino men (21)
Homemade cotton shirt	88	0
Ready-made cotton shirt	119	54
Homemade cotton pants	114	7
Ready-made cotton pants	111	75
Under shirt	0*	74
Drawers	0*	86
Cotton jacket	55	42
Wool jacket	2	25
Wool pants	2	31
Shoes	2	39
Sandals	71	7
Socks	3	67
Neckties	1	65
Felt hats	1	6
Straw hat	22	21

LADINO-INDIAN DIFFERENCES

Garment	Indian men	Ladino men
Palm hat	89	16
Handkerchief	107	66
Other**	0	10

* The zero frequencies here are due to the fact that the homemade cotton shirts and pants function as the underwear for the Indian on those occasions when he puts other types of trousers and shirts over the simple cotton cloth he is already wearing.

** The category of "other" includes, for the men, such things as suit vests, sports shirts, bathing clothes, military uniforms, and pajamas or nightgowns.

TABLE 9

WOMEN'S CLOTHING POSSESSIONS

Garment	Indian women	Ladino women
	(43)	(14)
Housedress	1	58
Street dress	0	19
Blouse (Indian)	107	0
Skirt (Indian)	89	0
Slips	2	61
Brassieres*	13	32
Drawers	0	49
Stockings	1	42
Shoes**	1	30
Sandals	33	2
Black shawl	1	18
Other shawl	80	0
Other items†	0	15

* The brassieres which are listed for Indian women are in reality camisoles which are worn around the house in place of the blouse, and are also used for bathing and as nightgowns.

** The single instance of housedress, stockings, shoes, and black shawl, and one of the two instances of slips, listed for Indian women, all belong to one woman, a Ladino, who was living in common-law marriage with one of the Indian men, and, as such, has her possessions listed as those characteristic of women in the Indian households. This instance of miscegenation is unique in the history of the pueblo, and further details may be discovered by referring to Melvin Tumin, "Some Fragments from the Life History of a Marginal Man," *Character and Personality*.

† The category "other items" includes such things as purses, hats, coats, bathing clothes, pajamas and nightgowns, aprons and corsets.

CHAPTER 8

HOUSING: QUALITY, STYLE, AND LOCATION

In San Luis it makes sense to talk of the distinctively superior location and quality of Ladino houses relative to those of the Indians. With regard to location, superiority implies nearness to the central plaza. With regard to quality, such obvious distinctions are made as those between houses constructed of more and less expensive and more and less durable materials.

On the map of San Luis (see end of book), it can be seen that the central plaza lies at almost the precise center of the western boundary of the pueblo. The Rio San Luis and the main automobile road leading to the neighboring pueblo of San Pedro Pinula flank the pueblo at this boundary, both appearing almost immediately behind the town hall. The largest houses in town, the church, the government buildings, and the largest stores are part of the boundaries of the plaza itself, immediately adjacent to and visible from it. Also to be found in and about the plaza are the schools, the basketball court, the main water fountain, the park, and the bandstand. Because these sites are so located, the central plaza is the place of most concentrated and enduring public activity and interest in the entire pueblo.

Without exception, all the houses within a radius of one block and immediately tangential on all sides to the plaza are owned and occupied by Ladinos, and, generally speaking, are of better than average quality in their materials and construction. There is not a single thatched-roof house to be found in this area, and, with the exception of one house on the northeastern side of the plaza, about one half block distant, all houses have brick floors at least in the main room of the house and, in some, in other rooms as well.

An overall view of the plaza can be had from the top of

the church, which commands, in its height, a dominance over almost the entire pueblo as well. This view reveals that all the houses within a block of the plaza have more than one room. In typical Hispanic fashion, these rooms are built around courts or patios, in which, depending upon the status of the family, flowers and trees are grown, or grain, corn, animals, and other utilitarian objects of field and home are stored.

As one moves from the center of San Luis, characterized by the larger, better built, more expensive Ladino houses, outwards toward the periphery, he begins to encounter in increasing numbers the houses of the Indians. Relative to those of the Ladinos, these are smaller, of poorer construction, with fewer rooms, smaller yards, and generally less desirable and comfortable living quarters. Finally, close to the outskirts of town, one finds almost all Indian dwellings, and only here and there an occasional rundown Ladino residence. It is reasonable to say that if gradient lines were to be drawn from the center of the plaza to the outskirts, in all directions except due east there would be steady progressions along these gradients of increasing frequency of Indian houses and decreasing size and worth of the dwellings themselves. This fact is widely known, and it is this knowledge, plus its local embellishments, which makes it possible for the local people to talk in terms of the "Indian quarter," "where the better people live," and the like.

The vague historical records available indicate that the occupancy of the center of the pueblo by the Ladino and the peripheries by the Indians has involved gradual succession rather than sudden invasion. The typical process appears to have involved the relatively recent entry into town of Ladino families who bought centrally located sites from Indian occupants, whereupon the Indians moved closer to the edges of town, and, in many cases, outside the pueblo limits and into a neighboring aldea or hamlet. It is this tendency and its virtual completion which underlies the stereotype existing among Ladinos that the Indians

HOUSING

are people of the hamlets while the Ladinos are the more urbanized people of the pueblo. Factually, of course, this is not true, since the pueblo still consists of about 2,400 Indians and 1,100 Ladinos, and about the same proportions are to be found in the hamlets. But because the Ladinos and their residences tend to be most highly visible to that vast majority who circulate in and through the plaza every day, the impression that the pueblo is Ladino in its constituency is very strong.

The entire pueblo is divided into seven barrios or districts, as the map indicates, and these, too, tend to be known and recognized as either predominantly Indian or Ladino. Thus, the barrios of Los Isotes, Santa Cruz, La Bolsa, El Llano, and San Sebastian are known primarily as Indian in constituency, while El Calvario, and above all El Centro, are known as primarily Ladino in membership. El Centro is the barrio which embraces the plaza and the area immediately adjacent to it, while El Calvario mostly includes the area due east of the plaza extending to the eastern boundary of the pueblo.

This ecological distribution of Ladinos and Indians into distinguishable areas of residence makes it possible for the Indians to maintain considerable in-group privacy from the Ladinos, a condition which they mostly desire and prize. At the same time, it makes the Ladino houses and affairs highly visible and conspicuous to all, a fact which is as prized by the Ladinos for some purposes as is privacy by the Indians. In this significant way, then, housing location functions to satisfy the demands of contrary basic orientations existing in the two culture patterns.

The residential isolation of the Indian has further advantages. For, since he is continuously subject to being drafted for "voluntary work" in and about the pueblo by a number of government and military officials, his residence in the more obscure quarters of the pueblo tends to reduce his visibility and hence his accessibility for such labor.

Moreover, the isolated character of Indian location functions to permit in-group norms to maintain an effectiveness beyond that which would be possible were the Indians in more continuous interaction with the Ladino segment. It permits the greater and freer use of the Indian dialect and thus gives to it a strength-through-habit which might otherwise suffer attrition. It further allows the Indian to function during his daily and nightly routines with a sense of psychological security and ego-intactness which greater exposure to the Ladino, and the concomitantly necessary servile behavior, might otherwise undermine. For these, and other reasons, the separation of the Indian places of residence from those of the Ladino helps to reinforce the general social separation which is institutionalized in the value systems of the two groups.

By contrast, the central location of the Ladino houses allows for the reinforcement of the sense of dominance over the pueblo which is part of the Ladino outlook. It permits the Ladino to feel, and not simply act as though he were, the lord and master of pueblo affairs. It unquestionably helps to reinforce his sense of right regarding the treating of the Indian as a humble and servile creature. With the Indian's distinctiveness reinforced by his isolation in his quarters, further support is given to the stereotypes existing in Ladino vocabularies concerning the appearance, the behavior, and the social worth of the Indian. In all these ways and more, then, the separation of the houses contribute significantly to the on-goingness of the status quo.

Most of the judgments just rendered regarding the functions performed by separation in the location of houses are impressionistic. Certain facts, however, point to the probable adequacy and accuracy of these impressions. Primary among these is the difference between the behavior of an Indian when in the company only of other Indians and when he is with Ladinos. This contrast is nowhere more sharp than in the difference between the general behavior of the Indians who live in the pueblo and those who live in an all-Indian aldea called El Camaron.

HOUSING

El Camaron is less than twenty kilometers distant from the pueblo, but the Indians of that aldea have only occasional and unenduring contact with the Ladinos. The most frequent liaison is had by the lone Indian selected as official representative of the aldea to the pueblo government. He comes into the pueblo on the average of once a week for new orders, instructions, and supplies. Otherwise, it is only an exceptional occasion which induces El Camaron Indians to come into San Luis.

The Indians of El Camaron give an observer an immediate impression of being far more outgoing, expressive, and free from restraint than the pueblo Indians. They talk much more freely in front of the observer. They sing and joke with much more verve and spontaneity than do the pueblo Indians. Their internal relations appear to be far less fraught with anxiety and apprehension than do those of the Indians of the pueblo.

To be sure, these are again only impressions, and the available data do not permit their accuracy to be conveyed or measured except in the terms just described. Yet, this impression is itself so unavoidable that one feels considerable reliance upon it.

QUALITY AND STYLE

It was earlier noted that as one proceeds from the center of town out to its boundaries, a change is noticeable in the kind of occupant and the kind of house. The change in occupant is primarily from Ladino to Indian, and, in house, from well-appointed to poor and humble dwellings.

It is safe to assume that many of the differences in the quality and style of the houses are in large measure due to differences in wealth. The better looking and better built houses are the more expensive ones, since they consist at least partly of manufactured materials, while the poorer houses are built of hand-hewn materials personally secured from the nearby fields and woods. Moreover, the more expensive houses are usually built with hired skilled

LADINO-INDIAN DIFFERENCES

labor, while the poorer houses are more likely to have been constructed by the occupant and his friends.

With reference to this last item, it is interesting to note that Indians have a tradition of mutual aid in house building while Ladinos do not. An Indian has a right to notify his friends that he will be starting to build a house on a certain day, and to expect that a good number of those whom he notifies will be present to help him build. In turn, he is expected to provide the materials and have them ready, to feed the helpers, and to report for work when he in turn is called upon to help build the house of any who have so aided him. Both the expense and the time required of any given Indian for constructing his dwelling are thus diminished. Since no such tradition exists in Ladino culture, any Ladino house, if only of the same quality and style as an Indian house, costs the Ladino much more to build.

The basic building material is a clayish dirt which, when mixed with water and grass, is locally called "bajareque." It is differentiated from adobe, which has essentially the same ingredients, in that it is not cut and shaped into blocks. The technique, therefore, is to pat the bajareque into the interstices of an already constructed sapling frame and to allow it to dry and harden in that fashion. Building with adobe first requires the manufacture of dried blocks of dirt and grass which are then superimposed upon each other and cemented.

The simplest building material, or more properly, wall covering, consists of dried cornstalks which are woven and matted into a frame of home-cut saplings. The matting is sufficiently thick so that it is relatively weather proof, but it is far less durable and attractive even than bajareque. The most expensive building materials used for the walls and foundations are professionally treated and cut lumber, bricks, and reinforced cement. Only in the wealthiest persons' houses, however, does one find such materials. Generally speaking, all houses in San Luis range between the

HOUSING

simple cornstalk type of wall and one which is made of adobe, with plaster coating inside and out.

The following tables show the distribution of the use of these materials, by Ladino and Indian. The figures speak for a sample of 411 households out of a total of approximately 800 in the pueblo:

TABLE 10
INDIAN

Wall type	No.	Per cent	Per cent of all houses
Cornstalks	81	27.30	19.75
Bajareque	191	64.30	46.40
Adobe	22	7.40	5.30
Adobe and plaster*	3	1.00	.75
Totals	297	100.00	72.20

* Adobe and plaster refers here to an adobe base which has been thinly plastered inside and out, for both esthetic and protective purposes.

TABLE 11
LADINO

Wall type	No.	Per cent	Per cent of all houses
Cornstalks	1	.90	.24
Bajareque	39	34.20	9.56
Adobe	32	28.00	7.80
Adobe and plaster	42	36.90	10.20
Totals	115	100.00	27.80

The foregoing figures refer to houses which are primarily of one type of building materials rather than another. It is frequently found, however, that houses have one or two walls of bajareque construction and the others of adobe, or, even, one or two walls of cornstalk and the others of bajareque. It is most often the case, however, that the houses are uniform in their composition.

It will be noted that there are significant differences in the percentages of Indian and Ladino houses which involve the different types of construction. This difference is

LADINO-INDIAN DIFFERENCES

again generally known and acknowledged, so that there is some factual basis for talking, as San Luis people do, of the typical kind of Indian dwelling as contrasted with the Ladino. On the other hand, there is considerable overlapping in the distribution of house-type by the two groups, so that the assumed difference as generally formulated is more radical than is borne out by the data.

In two other facets of house construction significant differences are to be found. These refer to the materials and construction of the roofs and the floors of the houses. With regard to roofs, the varieties possible include (a) thatched roof (usually of straw); (b) manufactured tile on rough sapling support; (c) manufactured tile on sawn-lumber support; and (d) a totally boarded roof, covered by tile. Again, the variations actually found tend to distribute themselves along lines of economic differences, and these, by and large, tend to coincide with Indian and Ladino differentiations.

The following tables on distribution of roof type show something of these differences:

TABLE 12

Roof type	No. Indian	No. Ladino
Thatched	15	0
Tile—rough	33	8
Tile—sawn	1	14
Boarded	0	3*

* Though there are only 22 Ladino houses in this sample, the Ladino total here includes 25 frequencies. This is due to the fact that 3 of the Ladinos had one room with a boarded roof, in addition to the roofing on the other rooms of the houses.

Somewhat sharper differences emerge when a comparison is made between the floor construction in the houses of the Indians and Ladinos. The variations possible include (a) dirt alone; (b) brick and dirt; (c) brick alone. The distribution of these types is shown in the following table:

HOUSING

TABLE 13

Floor type	No. Indian	No. Ladino
Dirt	46	0
Brick and dirt	3	3
Brick alone	0	19
Totals	49	22

It is again evident that considerable factual basis is present for the widespread belief that the Indians live in much simpler and poorer types of dwellings than the Ladinos. Ladinos speak of Indians as the kind of people who have only dirt floors and inadequate walling and roofing. The facts just presented verify this in part. It is also clear that there is a sharper difference in the distribution of floor types than in either the wall or roof types, as between Indians and Ladinos. This is understandable in light of the fact that walls and roofs of a more durable and pleasant construction take priorities over floors, both among Indians and Ladinos.

Ladinos tend to infer from the predominance of dirt floors in Indian houses that Indians like to live in dirt, are dirty by nature, and so on. Expressed preferences of the Indians, however, clearly indicate that the desired type of floor is one made of brick. Whether or not Indians translate this desire into actuality when they can afford it is another matter. For, as in so many other regards, the verbal horizons of the Indians appear sometimes to have little relationship to what they actually do when they are in a position to implement their desires.

It is unquestionable that a number of Indians who can afford brick floors have not had them put in their houses. One of the standard rationalizations offered in explanation of this fact is that "we are too poor." Basically, this refers not to the economic ability to construct a brick floor, but rather to the ability to purchase those other symbols of status which in the prevailing definitions are natural concomitants of brick floors. When the Indian, therefore, insists that he is too poor to be able to afford something which in fact he could afford if it were to be his *only* purchase, he really refers to the fact that he has no "right" in terms of his total economic status to think in the terms implied by "brick floors." This sentiment generally prevails throughout the Indian groups, and it is reinforced at all points by the invidious view Indians take toward those among them who pretend toward wealth or social status as measured by conspicuously consumed items of display. It requires a great deal of courage on the part of any Indian to flaunt this convention and to bear the consequences.

CHAPTER 9

ECONOMIC ACTIVITY AND ATTITUDES

It is generally believed in San Luis that a principal difference between Indians and Ladinos lies in the extent to which each group is willing to and actually does engage in manual labor. It is held that the Ladino abstains from such labor wherever possible, while the Indian does almost nothing but work with his hands.

In point of fact, the real work habits of each group show some deviation from these presumed norms. For, a considerable number of Ladinos are required to work manually in order to survive, and a substantial number of Indians earn at least part of their income from nonmanual work.

Some rough estimate of the actual conditions can be had from the following figures which describe the principal sources of income for a sample of 49 Indian and 22 Ladino heads of households.

TABLE 14

Source of Income	NUMBER	
	Indians	Ladinos
Manual farm work for self	49	6
Braiding hats	48	0
Hired farm hand	43	6
Pottery sales trip	38	0
Wife's work	36	11
Nonfarm manual work	7	10
Commerce	1	8
Storekeeping	—	5
Clerical work	—	1
Professional work	—	5

The arrangement of occupations above is in terms of the decreasing frequency of the occupation as a source of income for the Indians. The lack of correspondence of this order for the Indians with that of the Ladinos is easily noticed. It will also be noticed that both Indians and Ladinos tend to have several sources of income. This accounts for the total number being much larger than the number of Indians and Ladinos in the sample interviewed. The proportional contribution to total income from each of the occupations listed above will be roughly described in the following pages. It should finally be noted that income from leasing of lands and renting land to tenants, sharecroppers, etc., is not listed here. The specific importance of these income sources will be dealt with at some length in subsequent pages.

Certain of the categories described above require clarification. By "manual farm work," reference is had to actual farming of the land. All those listed in this category do such work on land which they either own or rent.

"Nonfarm manual work" refers to any kind of manual work other than farming, including such things as tile-making and leather craft, but not including any of the other specialties listed above. "Hired hand" refers to the work which most able-bodied Indian males are required by law to do, namely, to work on other people's farms a specified number of days a year to a total of 150, in ratio to the amount of land one personally owns and/or rents.[1]

This rule presumably prevents the landless Indian from becoming vagrant. Aside from the fact that hunger and a strong work ethic are quite adequate to keep the Indian busy when there is land available for him to work, it should be noted that the rule actually functions to provide a steady source of farm hands for the wealthier landowners. In eastern Guatemala, where the average landholding is relatively small, the availability of labor is not a serious problem. But in western Guatemala, especially in coffee-producing areas where the landholdings are relatively large, the so-called "vagrancy law" functions effectively for the ends of the plantation owners.

[1] John Gillin, *Ethos and Cultural Aspects of Personality in Middle America*: Introductory Remarks, Paper No. 3, Viking Fund Seminar, August 1949, pp. 7-8.

ECONOMIC ACTIVITY

By "professional work" reference is had, so far as Ladinos are concerned, to such occupations as druggist, doctor, musician, and teacher. Regarding the Indian, it was noted previously that some of them also engage in quasi-professional work. Of primary importance here is the roster of magic makers and magical curers who earn a relatively high income from these practices. But, since magic in any form is prohibited by law, these occupations never show up in any census. However, it is generally well known that about twelve or more Indians earn their living at least partly out of magic.

"Commerce" refers to the buying and selling of primarily agricultural goods. The category "pottery sales trips" refers to the traditional Indian occupation of visiting nearby areas to sell products made by the Indian women. Listed in the class of storekeepers are only those for whom stores are a primary source of income. This includes the druggist, whose pharmacy is relatively highly profitable.

Braiding palm hats is principally an Indian male occupation, though some Ladino women are skilled at the trade and earn a subsidiary income in this fashion. "Work of wife" refers to the fact that a substantial portion of Ladino women do incidental work of various kinds, including teaching, sewing, and the like, and most Indian women make pottery objects which their husbands sell. In the case of the Indians, the return from the sale of these objects forms an important part of their cash income. Finally, "clerical work" here refers to the one bookkeeper in the Ladino sample, a young man who works for his brother. Otherwise, most clerical work in the pueblo is done either by the storekeepers themselves or by the few clerks who work in the government offices.

From the foregoing figures it appears that the vast majority of the Indians earn their incomes primarily from work on their own land, from hiring out as farm hands for others, and from the sale of hats and pottery. By contrast, almost half the Ladinos earn their incomes from some form of nonfarm work, which comprises any one of the many specialties and skilled jobs earlier described. At the same time it must be noted that more than one-fourth of the Ladinos do their own farm work; and a similar proportion hire out as farm hands. By contrast, one-seventh of the Indian sample do some kind of specialized nonfarm work as a source of income.

It is thus apparent that the Indian is not just a farmer and the Ladino not just a businessman or professional. The overlap in the categories of work shows that the ideas in San Luis concerning who does what kind of work tend to be somewhat unreal. At the same time, the actual tendencies are definitely in the directions described by the prevailing stereotypes.

It was earlier noted that the law requires the registration of all able-bodied men in the pueblo and their classification into various categories. The major distinction in the classifications of occupations is based on the amount of land owned by the registrant. The two principal divisions are between the terrateniente, or landowner, and the jornalero, or day-worker. A subcategory under landowners —that of obrero, or worker—takes up whatever registrants do not clearly fall into either of the first two categories.

The day-worker classification includes those men who do not own enough land to be self-sufficient from its produce. Jornaleros are therefore required to work for others a specified number of days a year, ranging from 100 to 150, and to show records of such work performed in their *libretas*, or work books, which all must carry.

The records for the municipio show that 1,341 of the total of 1,535 registrants were classified as jornaleros, and of these 91 per cent were Indian and 9 per cent Ladinos. Since the population distribution is approximately two-thirds Indian and one-third Ladino, it is apparent that the differential distribution of land is statistically significant.

The remaining 194 registrants were classified as follows: 63 landowners devoted to agriculture, 37 landowners devoted to commerce, and 94 workers. Of this total of 194, only 15 or 7 per cent were Indian, while 179 or 93 per cent

ECONOMIC ACTIVITY

were Ladino. In the pueblo itself, some 690 males were registered. Of these 150 were classified as landowners (including obreros). Of these 150 only 14, or about 9 per cent, were Indians and 136, or about 91 per cent, Ladino. Statistics on the actual size of landholdings give further dimensions to this general picture. The following data summarize the distribution of land among 49 Indian and 22 Ladino heads of households interviewed. (All figures are rounded out.)

INDIANS

8, or 16.3 per cent, owned some land.
Together they owned 106 acres.
The individual holdings range from a high of 73 acres to a low of .23 acres, with the median at 5.8 and the mean at 13.2.
If the highest single holding of 73 acres is omitted, the average landholding for the remaining 7 Indians is 4.7 acres.
If the largest single holding is again omitted, the average holding for all Indians interviewed is .69 acres.
Including the highest single figure, the average holding for all 49 Indians interviewed is 2.2 acres.

LADINOS

12, or 54.5 per cent owned some land.
Together they owned 687 acres.
The individual holdings range from a high of 346 acres to a low of .57 acres, with a median at 13.2 and mean at 57.3.
If the highest single holding of 346 acres is omitted, the average holding for the other 11 Ladinos is 31.4 acres.
If the largest single holding is again omitted, the average holding for all Ladinos interviewed is 16.4 acres.
Including the highest single figure, the average holding for all 22 Ladinos interviewed is 31.2 acres.

To these differences in actual amount of land owned must be added the further difference that Ladino lands are considered far more productive and hence far more valuable than Indian lands. Since such property ownership is one of the few major sources of income in San Luis, it is apparent that significant differences exist between Indians and Ladinos in their economic status.

LADINO-INDIAN DIFFERENCES

Moreover, the majority of service occupations, involving specialized skills and higher rewards, are performed by Ladinos rather than Indians. The carpenters, tailors, tile-makers, saddle-makers, butchers, storekeepers, innkeepers, druggists, doctors, dentists, teachers, government officials, and so on, are, with certain notable exceptions, Ladino. The exceptions are the very infrequent cases of Indian artisans (masons and tile-makers) and the very frequent cases where Indian women are the merchants in the outdoor markets. Otherwise, such hiring of labor as goes on in the pueblo almost always involves a Ladino master and either Ladino or Indian employees. Such commercial transactions as take place almost always involve the Ladino as the owner of the goods or services and Ladinos and Indians as the purchasers. And, finally, such landlord-tenant relationships as exist operate between Ladino landowners and Ladino and Indian tenants.

From these data it appears that while the division of labor is so organized as to necessitate the joint participation of Ladinos and Indians if both are to survive, the social organization is so arranged as to make the Indian almost always subordinate and the Ladino superordinate in that joint participation.

This hierarchy shows up in three aspects of the reward system attached to work: (1) income, (2) working conditions, and (3) prestige.

INCOME

The most accurate figures obtainable indicate that the average Ladino family earns about $150 a year, including the value of the food products raised, while the average Indian family earns about $75 a year. With roughly five members in the average family, these figures reduce to $30 a year per capita for Ladinos and $15 a year for Indians.

There are considerable individual exceptions to these averages. The wealthiest Indian, for instance, earns about $600 a year. This is most unusual since the next wealthiest Indian interviewed earned only $300 per year. By com-

ECONOMIC ACTIVITY

parison, the wealthiest Ladino estimated his income at about $1,000 a year, and a considerable number of Ladinos report between $300 and $500 a year average income.

In an economy such as that in San Luis, $75 a year makes an important difference in potential life habits and the public consumption of prestigeful goods. If one adds to this objective difference the increment accruing from the negative emphasis in Indian culture on any type of display of wealth, and its converse in Ladino culture, it becomes apparent that Indians and Ladinos are sharply distinguishable in those aspects of life where money and what it can buy makes a difference.

This difference in income emerges as the result, in part, of daily wage scales as well as property holding. Thus, it is generally true that the average Indian works harder and longer for less pay than the comparable Ladino worker. Hired farm hands receive 15 cents a day and food if Ladino, but only 10 cents a day and food if Indian. (A more curious contrast yet is afforded by the fact that it costs 20 cents a day and feed to hire a mule.) This type of differential holds for all classes of workers and all employers, with notably rare exceptions of Indian employers, who pay equal wages. Otherwise, differential pay rates obtain even though some of the Indian workers may be more skilled and productive than their fellow Ladino employees.

CONDITIONS OF WORK

It has been shown how the distribution of property operates so that almost always Indians work for Ladinos and almost never do Ladinos work for Indians. Prevailing in-group feelings and out-group definitions are such that no Ladino employee of a Ladino employer is treated with the same disrespect and harshness as that accorded the most ill-treated Indian. Correlatively, no Indian employee receives quite the beneficent kind of treatment accorded the most-favored Ladino employees. As an average rule, it is also true that most Ladino workers get better treatment than do Indians of the same status. Indians are reprimanded more harshly, expected to do harder and longer work, and are more peremptorily ordered about.

These generalizations hold for official government employees as well. The Ladino aldermen are treated with far more deference by the mayor than he ever accords to the Indian aldermen. The difference sometimes reduces itself simply to one between requesting the Ladino helpers to do something and ordering the Indians to do the same thing. In dealing with the unpaid Indian sirvientes, for instance, no Ladino official feels it fitting to request something politely.

Certain differentials are also apparent in the conditions of work for Ladinos and Indians who are self-employed. The average Indian milpa, for instance, is usually several kilometers farther from the pueblo than the Ladino milpa plots. This involves an extra expenditure of time which is unrewarded. Moreover, as has been stated, Ladino lands are by and large more productive than Indian lands, and hence Indian farmers show less return for man hour of labor, under the same technological circumstances, than do Ladinos.

A further comparison of interest arises from the fact that a much larger number and proportion of Indians have to go out of the pueblo to work than the Ladinos since the latter are proportionately more engaged in trades and commerce within the pueblo itself. The proximity to home, the ability to eat a freshly cooked meal at noon, the ease of return in case of inclement weather, and other such related factors, add up to a disproportionate psychic income for the Ladino relative to that of the Indian. To this type of psychic return may be added the factor of the presence of others for diversion in the pueblo, whereas work on the milpas, at some distance from the pueblo, is lonely and solitary. Since both Indians and Ladinos place considerable emphasis on the pleasure one derives from the company of others, this would seem to be a factor which is rightly added to the differentiated conditions of work and the rewards therefrom.

ECONOMIC ACTIVITY

PRESTIGE

While there is general agreement among Indians and Ladinos as to what are typical occupations, there is considerable disagreement as to the worth of various types of work. For it is generally true that Ladinos view manual labor with considerable disdain and give positive prestige to conspicuous freedom from such labor. By contrast, the Indians tend to view manual labor as the most basically worthy type of occupation, especially when it is agricultural. A man's worth in the Indian group is thus measured by the conspicuousness of his involvement in this type of work.

These general types of evaluations do not, however, preclude other marginal possibilities. For, in each group one finds deviants who are accorded prestige along lines of compensatory criteria. Thus, the poor, hard-working Ladino is praised by other Ladinos as virtuous and self-respecting, though unfortunate. Additionally, skilled artisans are likewise esteemed, though their work is manual. Similarly, among the Indians, certain specialists, notably in medicine and other types of witchcraft, receive considerable prestige, even though they notably do not engage in manual work. Indeed, perhaps the most prestigeful Indian at the time of these studies was a young Indian magical-curer who was conspicuous by his lack of engagement in any form of manual labor at all.

These marginal cases do not, however, vitiate the general ideal theme which runs throughout each group's definition of the worth and meaning of various kinds of work. Indeed, the fact that these exceptions are locally defined as deviant tends to prove that the ideal is as described, and each of these cases requires a partial redefinition of the ideal norms.

Ladinos express attitudes of general contempt for the Indian work norms, and tend to see them as indicative of the "natural inferiority" of the Indians. Thus, when they have Indian employees, they frequently complain of their inefficiency and ineptitude, and then justify their harsh and impolite treatment of these workers in terms of this "natural inferiority." They appeal to the "facts" that Indians are natively more stupid than Ladinos, worse-charactered, and hence generally deserving of less consideration. They further assert that one simply has to deal firmly with Indian help or else get nothing accomplished.

Still others impugn the honesty of Indian employees. Other characteristic descriptions by Ladinos of Indians take the form of: "people without sense," "badly raised people," "like children," "shameless and conscienceless," "not deserving of any respect."

In infrequent cases Ladinos express a high regard for the trustworthiness and diligence of their Indian employees. This is, however, a minority viewpoint, and is so infrequent as to command surprise when expressed. It is not possible from the available data to type the Indians and Ladinos or the situations involved here except to note that these seem to be cases involving highly particularistic relations between the Ladinos and Indians concerned.

Since the Ladino cannot generally gain prestige by unskilled manual labor, but rather by its opposite, he tends to apologize for, and explain away, such work when he finds himself forced to do it. It is a matter of "temporary embarrassment," or the working out of some "bad luck" which some "malicious scoundrel" has wreaked upon him. But it is never the natural condition of which he is deserving, nor is it in any way desirable. However, if it appears that it is likely that he will have to continue to work hard and manually for some time to come, the Ladino is inclined to develop a set of evaluations by which he is enabled to view himself as an unfortunate one, who has considerable "spunk" and "character" and "virtue" because of the way in which he handles his adverse luck.

The Indian, by contrast, views manual labor very differently. He sees his own involvement therein as expressive of certain natural conditions in the universe, and does not depreciate or derogate the status into which he falls. On

ECONOMIC ACTIVITY

the contrary, manual labor is for him the mark of true worth in a man, and freedom from it is viewed with suspicion and distrust.

Nor does he generally think of changing his status, even if it were possible. Of 49 Indians questioned, some 29 stated they would always want to continue making milpa, no matter what other type of activity they might pursue. This contrasts sharply with the fact that all 6 of the Ladino *milperos* questioned vigorously indicated they would like to stop making milpa as soon as possible.

On further questioning, the Indians, moreover, assert that this pattern will continue so far as they are concerned, 44 out of 49 saying that they prefer the same pattern for their children, with only 4 indicating a desire for a change. By contrast again, of the 22 Ladinos questioned, 15 indicated that they themselves would like some other type of work (always in the direction of more income and prestige); 6 said their children would do the same as they are doing; and the remainder indicated that their children would certainly do different work.

When Indians are posed the further question of what they would do if they had enough money to do with their lives as they wished, they characteristically answer that such a situation is unthinkable, and that even if it were to come to pass, they would always continue to do what they are now doing. By contrast, the Ladinos tend to envision a future in which large sums of money are available and which they use to free themselves conspicuously from any sort of hard work. Since many Ladinos do have to work hard, however, it would seem that one should find—and the actual materials bear this out—that Ladinos are by and large more subjectively discontented with the division of labor even though, by contrast with the Indians, they are objectively the most favored.

It is perhaps anomalous, but still true, that the objectively favored group should be more discontented than the objectively subordinated and exploited group. Perhaps it is more anomalous still that the Indian group is able to find its situation so satisfactory as generally to reject thoughts of possible alteration. The complexity of the matter is increased when it is realized that Indians are by and large aware of the fact that Ladinos seriously depreciate them for their lack of "ambition" and for their willingness to continue a traditional round of life.

What resolves the apparent anomalies is the fact that the Indians and Ladinos simply do not accept or operate with the same values regarding the meaning of human worth. Because the Indians tend to reject Ladino values, the invidious social treatment which they receive from the Ladinos is not nearly as effective a stimulus to change as it might be. Nor does it tend to induce an otherwise expectable sense of felt inferiority. To be sure, Indians customarily tend to depreciate themselves. But this self-depreciation is far more a function of a cultural compulsive toward modesty and inconspicuousness than it is a reflection of their view of their social reputations as refracted through the eyes of the Ladinos.

Viewing themselves as natively different from the Ladinos, and being in their own definitions self-contained as a community unit without relations beyond the pueblo limits, Indians have much less of a basis for disturbing comparisons. On the other hand, the prestigeful Ladino view of life has as its horizon the cities far beyond the pueblo and the "known" luxury, ease, and social reputation of life in those cities. By contrast with such city Ladinos, with whom the San Luis Ladinos form a value-community, the latter often see themselves as "poor relations" whose local positions are a function of the depression of the local area rather than of any objective fault of their own. It is no accident, then, that they tend to blame the "backwardness" of San Luis on the lack of ambition of the Indian, and similarly to scapegoat the Indian on a number of other counts.

Regarding the meaning of limited versus expanded horizons, Gillin has noted as follows: "The typical Ladino . . . lives in a universe considerably more expanded both

ECONOMIC ACTIVITY

in space and time. His notions about the great world beyond the limits of his own community may be uninformed and naïve from the point of view of modern science, but he does not believe that the world ends at the limits of his township or local region. . . . The Ladino's strivings or drives are seldom entirely restricted to his local community, but are also oriented toward goals whose locus is in the larger outside world. In fact, the major rewards of life, from the Ladino point of view, are to be found in the provincial capital, the national capital, or even in the United States or Europe. What one achieves in his hometown is merely a steppingstone to further achievements outside."[2]

By contrast, "The Indian universe is spatially limited and its horizon typically does not extend beyond the limits of the local community or region. . . . According to the Indian scheme of things, life goes on in a timeless present, it has been this way as long as anyone knows, and one will be content to see the pattern continue indefinitely. The object of life is to keep the scheme going according to expectations."[2]

The facts expressed in these observations, in combination with those earlier asserted, are perhaps sufficient to explain away the apparent contradiction involved in the objectively most favored group being subjectively most dissatisfied.

[2] *Ibid.*, pp. 6, 7, 8.

PART III
TENSIONS AND EQUILIBRIA

CHAPTER 10

THE GODPARENT COMPLEX

The materials in the foregoing section have shown certain areas of substantial differences between Indians and Ladinos which are noted and used by both groups, though sometimes in different ways, to rationalize the distance which they keep from each other. These differences are, in most part, observable by outsiders as well, and, as earlier stated, help to delineate the areas of cultural separation of the two groups.

If it is true that partly because of these divisive forces the prevailing tone of relationship between Indians and Ladinos is that of mutual distrust and a mutual desire to keep away from each other, it is also true that certain mechanisms are present which tend to bring the Indians and Ladinos into closer relationship. Some of these function not simply to maintain an effective division of labor but also to reduce social discord and disharmony. Primary among such mechanisms is the institution of "godparentalism." Some of the basic features of the godparent complex are those traditionally associated with this relationship wherever found: simulated familism, mutual concern and support, and an increase in the number of persons to whom one extends the prerogatives and responsibilities of particularistic privilege.

In San Luis, however, the godparent complex has acquired a number of subsidiary features and functions which are explicable and understandable in light of certain cultural urgencies which have arisen from the operation of the divisive forces previously outlined. It will be recalled, in this light, that the Indian's primary orientation is to the land and it is in the land that he finds his basic securities. It will also be recalled that the continuing loss of landownership by the Indian has tended to produce certain marked disruptions in traditional Indian family life and certain observable patterns of felt insecurity.

TENSIONS AND EQUILIBRIA

In cultural response to these generated tensions, the Indians have begun to add to the already existing pattern of godparental ties with Ladino families a function which it has never before served to nearly the same extent, namely, that of exacting from one's Ladino godparental relatives a sense of obligation to provide privileged rights of rental of milpa land.

Renting land on which to raise one's milpa has become, over the years, one of the alternatives the Indian has chosen as an answer to his lack of land. This is an expectable consequence of the loss of land, for it deviates less from older patterns than does such an alternative as seeking cash employment elsewhere. But with an increasing number of Indians seeking to rent land, competition for rental rights has become relatively intense. As a result, if one can establish a privileged position with a landowner, one is more likely to have enough land from which to derive a living. The recognition of this fact has induced Indians to call upon their Ladino godparental relatives to recognize this obligation as inherent in the relationship.

The pattern of using Ladinos for godparents is itself not new to the Indians. For a long time it has been recognized by the Indians that a Ladino godparent for oneself or one's children is a handy thing to have. For if an Indian dies, he knows that his children will have a patron who is likely to be able to help his children. Or, if an Indian gets into trouble with Ladino authorities, an influential Ladino compadre (i.e., the parents of one's godchild) or godparent can prove to be very useful. One can also generally count on one's Ladino compadre or godparent to provide a good baptismal present of clothing to the newborn, and to continue such generosities at infrequent later intervals.

That some of the motivation for seeking a Ladino godparent for one's children is secular does not make less significant the fact that the godparental relationship is sealed by religious affirmation and ritualization. Once assumed, therefore, the godparental status is considered by

THE GODPARENT COMPLEX

all parties as obligatory, and it is held to be shameworthy if one is derelict in the duties which are defined into the godparental role. As a corollary, the assumption of the status, especially if one's compadres are poor and deprived, is considered a mark of worthiness of character. It is no accident, then, that as a result of the combination of these various reasons the wealthiest and most influential Ladinos in town claim to and probably do have over a hundred godchildren each.

A distinguishing feature of the godparental relationship which unites Indians and Ladinos is that it is the one such relationship in which there is some equality of social standing of the parties concerned. The fact that a person is your padrino, or the godparent of your children, gives him the right to expect from you cordiality, politeness, and concern for his welfare. In part, the fact that the relationship is religiously ritualized and sealed accounts for this defined mode of interaction, since it is generally true of religious interaction in the pueblo that one finds there the greatest suspension of social rating and the derivative behavior. This equalitarian type of interaction is institutionally prescribed, and is generally followed, all other things being equal. To be sure, the caste barriers against commensalism and connubialism are almost never voided, not even between compadres, but more of the caste social distance is breached by godparents than in any other formally defined situation of relationship between Indians and Ladinos.

This appears to have very significant consequences for the stability of the existing caste situation. For what it does is to allow each Indian who has a Ladino padrino or compadre—and twenty per cent of the Indians do have such—to feel and to know that there is at least one Ladino family from whom he can expect reasonably polite and respectful audience when he so desires. It gives each such Indian, in short, a particular privileged basis in the society of Ladinos and thus helps to attenuate the general isolation of the castes from each other's affable company, an isolation which otherwise prevails.

In addition to these features of the godparental relationship, and the other benefits described above, another advantage for Indians lies in the general accessibility of the Ladino godparent's house and some of its utilities. Thus, Indian women may and do come to draw water from their Ladino godparents' fountains, and they may and do stop to chat and pass an equalitarian sort of "time of day" with the Ladinos. It is impossible to decide how truly significant this kind of thing is for the Indians, but the fact that it is often mentioned favorably by Indians would appear to indicate some appreciation of its value on their part. All in all, the godparental relationship with a Ladino family is one which seems to be mostly advantageous for the Indians concerned.

Given this trend of particular privileged position relative to one's padrinos, it is understandable that the Indian, in his crisis of land deprivation, extends an already operative principle by seeking privileged position vis-à-vis rental rights for milpa land. Again, unfortunately, conclusive data are unavailable concerning the distribution of rentals by godparental relatives and otherwise. But the frequent citations by Indians of this privilege lend support to this notion, and no known social forces contradict its possibility.

The extent to which Indians need to rent land in order to grow food products essential to survival has previously been shown in Chapter 9. There it was seen that, using a sample of 49 Indian heads of households as representative of the Indian community, approximately only 5 per cent of the Indian community own enough land to be self-sufficient while 95 per cent require rental land, either owning only small portions which are not sufficient or not owning any land at all. When the impact of these facts is added to the facts concerning the central importance of land to the stability of the Indian culture, it can easily be recognized that a secure guarantee concerning the availa-

THE GODPARENT COMPLEX

bility of land is indispensable to the economic stability of the pueblo.

This includes the Ladino portion of the pueblo, as well, for a variety of reasons. In the first place, if Ladinos are to maintain their cultural emphasis on the value of conspicuous leisure and freedom from manual labor, it is important that they have a population devoted to a contrary principle and who find enough life satisfactions in the area to remain and be productive. Secondly, so long as the area remains primarily agricultural, it is important that enough goods be produced sufficiently cheaply to allow the Ladinos to drain off the surplus return in order to sustain themselves, either by consumption of the product or of the returns from the sale of the products. Finally, the stability of the security pattern of the Ladinos depends on their being in the superordinate position in the caste society, with the Indians available for continuous and institutionalized deprecation as a means for ego-inflation of the Ladinos.

The orderliness of the caste relationship, as envisaged by the Ladinos, thus depends on the Indians remaining servile and acquiescent. This in turn requires the preservation of a traditional pattern of life among the Indians. For, with every departure from this pattern, there is subversion of the orderliness of the status quo. This occurs since Indians can and do accept the external caste position so long as they have their own internal sets of satisfaction and life guarantees flowing from their traditional patterns of religious affirmation of the situation. Thus, so long as the Indians can be kept effectively satisfied in the pattern which has land use as its center, the Ladino superordinacy is fairly securely guaranteed.

For these three principal reasons, among others, it is urgent, for the stability of the society, that some equilibrating mechanism be devised to reduce the tensions and insecurities generated among the Indians by their loss of land rights. The privileged position relative to rental of land from one's Ladino compadres is just such a mechanism. It does operate apparently effectively to regularize the availability of land. It does give the Indians a feeling of being vitally integrated into the network of social relationships prevailing in the pueblo. And it does enable the Ladino to feel superior to the Indian and to derive the satisfaction of doing "noble" things for the underprivileged.

This last is important, for to be *de servicio* to unfortunates is considered a worthy attribute of Ladinos. Moreover, it is relatively inexpensive, and carries no lengthy obligations which are not easily discharged. These are the ideal attributes of charity or concern for the underprivileged in San Luis. The character reference is vital, since in San Luis, where so few people have any material possessions about which they can boast, social appraisal and evaluation depends much on "family" and "reputation." As a result, there is considerable vying in petty matters of genealogy, on the one hand, and community service and personal "good-doing" on the other. If one were to go literally by the verbal protestations of some of the Ladinos, it would seem that they did nothing but spend their entire time and incomes in doing good.

In effect, most such claims are untrue. What is true, however, is that a considerable number of Ladinos have one or more Indians partially dependent upon them for favors, some of which—such as land rental rights—are rather basic to survival. Thus a substantial number of Ladinos can claim that they are always engaged in doing good for underprivileged Indians. Naturally, little or no mention is made of the return in share crops or land rent which accrues to the Ladino landowner. Nor is mention made of a fact about which Ladinos may or may not be aware, namely, that acting as godparents for Indians and doing other such small favors pays off substantially in psychic income. Since this type of psychic income is so relevant to the social emphases in the pueblo, it would be hard to demonstrate any overall loss on the part of the Ladinos from their "good-doing," and thus to support

THE GODPARENT COMPLEX

their contention that it involves costly sacrifices on their part.

Moreover, the situation in general is structured so that no significant caste expectations are violated. Thus, the Ladinos can and do virtually control the entire relationship; they can and do maintain superordinacy throughout the situation; they can and do preserve their essential prerogatives over Indians and continue to treat them as inferiors throughout.

The following brief summary of the general features of the relationship amply testify to these contentions:

1. Ladinos serve as godparents for Indian children, at the request of the Indian parents, in a fair number of cases.

2. Ladinos never ask Indians to serve as godparents for Ladino children, and there are, therefore, no discoverable cases of this relationship.

3. The Ladino godparents, and whichever Ladino friends the godparents care to invite, usually attend the baptismal party given by Indian parents for the newly-baptised child.

4. At these parties, Ladino men may and do dance with single Indian girls, but no Ladino woman, single or married, ever dances with an Indian man.

5. When not dancing, the Indians tend to keep to one side of the house and Ladinos to the other, so that for all intents and purposes the separateness of the two groups is clearly marked and preserved.

6. Except in the case of the Indian girls who are asked to dance by the Ladino men, all the observable merry-making is engaged in only by Ladinos.

7. When the time for serving food arrives, the order of eating is as follows: Ladino women, Ladino men, Indian men, Indian women. There have been no observed cases at any time of joint eating. Nor does this separatism get broken in the case even of the Indian parents of the child.

8. One other aspect of the situation is worth describing. But since it refers largely to the "tone" of the situation as impressionistically interpreted by this observer, it is of-

fered here not as incontrovertible evidence, but only as additional data which may give a more rounded picture of the situation. The tone appears to be that of the Ladinos "taking over" the baptismal party, as though it were simply an excuse for getting free food and drinks and having a marimba paid for, to which they may dance. The Indian contingent, by contrast, fades into insignificance as far as merrymaking goes, and usually is to be found either running around fulfilling "requests" of the various Ladinos, or out in the backyard watching the Indian women cook. The Ladinos always seem ready to remind the Indians that they are, after all, doing them a great honor and service by consenting to have a Ladino couple serve as godparents, in the first place, and consenting to grace an Indian house with Ladino presence, in the second.

The evidence for points (1) and (2) above is seen in the following tabulations of the distribution of godparents:

Ladinos (22 male heads of households)

Had Ladino godparents	22
Had Indian godparents	0
Had Ladino godchildren	10
Had Indian godchildren	16
Wife had Ladino godparents	15
Wife had Indian godparents	0

Indians (49 male heads of households)

Had Ladino godparents	9
Had Indian godparents	41
Had Ladino godchildren	0
Had Indian godchildren	23
Wife had Ladino godparents	9
Wife had Indian godparents	36

These figures show that more Ladinos have Indian than Ladino godchildren, but that, by contrast, no Ladino has Indian godparents. Moreover, no Indian has Ladino godchildren, while 18 out of 88 Indians (husbands and wives taken separately) have Ladino godparents.

The attitudes underlying this situation are revealed in

THE GODPARENT COMPLEX

the following figures which describe how Ladinos and Indians feel about asking members of the outgroup to serve as godparents:

Ladinos (22 male heads of households)

Might ask Indian to serve as godparent	3
Might ask Ladino to serve as godparent	19
Would never ask Indian to serve	16
Would never ask Ladino to serve	0
Thinks it possible for Indians to serve for Ladinos	9
Thinks it impossible for Indians to serve for Ladinos	11

A rough content analysis of the reasons Ladinos gave for never asking Indians to serve as godparents for Ladino children reveals the following:

Reasons given	No. of Times Mentioned
"The people would make fun and criticize"	10
"The people would say one is a fool"	3
"The people would say it was shameful"	2
"One doesn't want to lower one's category to that of the Indians"	1
"The people would say that one didn't have friends he could have asked"	1
"The Indians are disrespectful; they address one as 'vos' [highly familiar or highly formal, depending on the situation, but in the case of the Indian, simply a function of ignorance] instead of 'usted'"	1

As reasons for why they thought it impossible for Indians to serve as godparents for Ladino children, the Ladinos offered the following:

Reasons given	No. of Times Mentioned
"We don't ever ask them"	5
"The Indians are looked on as lesser people"	5
"It's not the custom"	3
"I don't know why"	2
"It's the custom"	2
"For their class"	2

Reasons given	No. of Times Mentioned
"Because the castes are divided"	1
"Indians are 'apart' "	1
"The Indians don't like to"	1
"The Indians don't understand the affair"	1
"One's godparent should be able to substitute for one's father"	1
"The Indian *caste* [my emphasis] is looked on as lesser"	1
"The Indians are less civilized"	1
"Ladinos always ask Ladinos, they understand"	1
"We are better than they"[1]	1

As for those Ladinos who said they might ask Indians, or thought it possible for Indians to serve as godparents for Ladino children, the following are some of the necessary conditions which they imposed.

Three said that it depends on the friendship one has with an Indian.

---

[1] The answer of one Ladino interviewee is richly enlightening. He is among the five wealthiest men in town; is considered by most of the Indians as one of the five best friends of the Indians; is held by the Ladinos to be among the five most important men. From all indications during his interview and before and after it, I take him to be a magnificent liar. But I quote verbatim his remarks on the godparental business. The reader will note where, though not explicated, a question from me had been put. "Yes, it is possible for an Indian to serve as godparent for a Ladino; many have so served; they are all Christians and have the same rights; but they don't like to serve, and they wouldn't serve. It isn't their custom; they don't have the facilities; they would have to refuse; they don't have the money. It is possible because there is much affection between us [i.e., between Indian and Ladino]. But they have other customs; a godfather is a second father to a child; if they raised a child of ours, it wouldn't be very seemly; they don't have aspirations; even if a Ladino is poor, he won't live in a ranchito like they do. At least a Ladino will rent a decent house. They live like animals. They don't have aspirations for a good house or a bed or to eat well. Rigoberto? [My note: this was the Ladinoized-Indian secretary (former) of the pueblo.] No, I wouldn't ask him. You see, an Indian with a little aspiration thinks he's a great person; but the Indian always has to be a little below. God help us if they were above us; the torture would never stop. Naturally, I have aspirations to visit the United States, for instance; the biggest spot you have there, I would like to go to. But the Indian? No, they don't have aspirations."

THE GODPARENT COMPLEX

One said he would ask a well-educated and well-dressed Indian if he wanted him.

One said that if an Indian had a bachelor's degree (only two people in town had bachelor's degrees; the interviewee in question himself had had only two years of school, could read only printed letters and could only sign his name), he might ask him, if he were friends with him; the people wouldn't make fun then.

One said he might ask an Indian if he had the preparation and the honorableness.

One said he might ask an Indian if he were "good type."

One said that it is possible because poor Ladinos will sometimes ask wealthy Indians, even though he knows of no cases yet that had happened.

These figures should be contrasted with the comparable figures for the Indian group:

Indians (49 male heads of households)

Might ask Indian to serve	49
Might ask Ladino to serve	47
Would never ask Indian to serve	0
Would never ask Ladino to serve	2
Thinks it possible for Indians to serve for Ladinos	4
Thinks it impossible for Indians to serve for Ladinos	42

In addition, the Indian interviewees were asked one question which was not asked of Ladinos, namely, whether they thought it was *better* to have Ladino or Indian godparents for Indian children. The answers were as follows:

Better to have Indian godparents	29
Better to have Ladino godparents	12
No preference	8

Note that a far larger portion of Indians (47 out of 49) might "theoretically" ask Ladinos to serve than the comparable proportion of Ladinos (3 out of 22) who might ask Indians to serve.

In answer to the question as to why they thought it was impossible for them to serve as godparents for Ladino children, the Indians answered as follows:

TENSIONS AND EQUILIBRIA

Reasons given	No. of times mentioned
"Ladinos don't ask; I don't know why"	13
"Ladinos don't want Indians"	8
"Ladinos never ask Indians"	6
"Ladinos don't ask us because we are poor"	3
"Ladinos think they're better"	2
"They are Ladinos and we are Indians"	1
"The Ladinos are more lively than we are"	1
"We are Indians, they say"	1
"That's the way it is; that's our custom from old"	1
"It doesn't please the Ladinos"	1
"That's their custom"	1
"Because one is an Indian"	1
"Because Ladinos are ashamed to ask Indians"	1
"Because of the difference in clothes"	1
"Ladinos don't ask because they're Ladinos"	1
"Ladinos don't ask and we can't offer"	1
"Because we do not have enough money to handle matters"	1
"Because we are Indians"	1
"Because we don't mix with Ladinos"	1

In answer to the question as to why they thought it was better to have Indians serve as godparents for Indian godchildren, the Indians answered as follows:

Reasons given	No. of times Mentioned
"That's the custom"	7
"There is less expense involved"	7
"We have the same customs"	5
"Indians give advice to godchildren about the customs"	3
"Because we are Indians"	3
"Indians treat their godchildren better"	2
"For the religion"	1
"One has more confidence in them"	1
"We can speak together in the language"	1
"Indian godparents help out all during one's life"	1
"There are some who don't like to speak Spanish"	1

THE GODPARENT COMPLEX

Reasons given	No. of Times Mentioned
"That's my taste"	1
"Our customs are different"	1
"The Ladinos have a different law; it's not the same"	1
"It's better among the same kind of people"	1
"Indian godparents help out fathers and mothers in need. Ladino godparents do not help out their compadres"	1
"When one is poor, one always asks an Indian to serve"	1

In answer to the question as to why they thought it better to have Ladinos serve as godparents for Indian children, the 12 who thought so offered the following reasons:

Reasons given	No. of times mentioned
"If one gets orphaned, he gets better care from Ladinos"	4
"Because Indians talk a lot and make false stories"	3
"Indians live in a funny way; they are backward"	1
"Because the customs are different"	1
"Ladinos clothe their godchildren well; Indians do not"	1
"It is more gallant to speak Spanish"	1
"Ladinos can teach their godchildren what Indians do not"	1
"Ladinos teach their orphaned godchildren Spanish and send them to school"	1
"They are of other customs; are not so sensitive; one can greet them better and more easily on the street"	1
"Ladino godparents give you good advice, Indians don't. Indians tell you not to beat a wife, but what should one do with a bad wife who drags you off to the mayor?"	1
"You can borrow money from Ladino compadres; you can't from Indians because we are poor"	1

Now it will be noted that almost without exception the Ladinos explain the separatism between themselves and the Indians on grounds which speak invidiously of the Indian. These grounds can roughly be classified as follows: (1) shame to lower oneself; (2) fear of ridicule; (3) inferiority or some other undesirable attribute of the Indians; (4) differences in custom which speak poorly of the Indians and/or urge one to "seek his own kind."

By contrast, the Indian confines his explanation of the separatism principally to reasons of plain difference or "greater comfort," i.e., one can speak the dialect with fellow Indians but not with Ladinos. In a few instances, it will be observed, the Indians offer reasons which deprecate the Ladinos. These refer to the belief that the Indians treat their godchildren better and that one has more "confidence" in Indians. "Confidence" here can mean several things, and it is difficult to decide which reference is intended. It could mean "trust" of the kind one extends only to those of whose affection and respect he is sure. Or it could mean an equivalent of the "comfort with one's own kind" idea expressed above. By and large, however, the Indians tend to view the differences between themselves and the Ladinos far less evaluatively than do the latter.

What is in operation here, then, is a system of reciprocal rights and obligations which, *for different reasons on each side of the line of relationship*, makes the relationship sufficiently satisfactory to both sides to keep them both participating.

This asymmetry might ordinarily be assumed, a priori, to be a source of tension, conflict, and potential change. But it is evident that the force of tradition present in the Indian culture induces a general indifference on the part of the Indians to the invidious views in which they are held by the Ladinos. The term "tradition" here is a grab-bag word which contains, most importantly for our present purposes, a set of values at marked variance with those of the Ladino. The fact of the nonsharing of values is, in short, what makes it possible for the Indian to be insulted

THE GODPARENT COMPLEX

by the Ladino, as the Ladino sees it, but not as the Indian sees it.

It is important, however, to realize that many Indians know that the Ladinos think poorly of them. But this "knowledge" is different from the "awareness" which implies recognition plus sensitivity. It is the kind of knowledge which is present when the Indian knows that other groups of people have different ways of life, which do not involve continuous hard work, poverty, and illness, but he cannot see these ways as alternatives to his. Throughout most of his life the tradition-bound Indian, thus, tends to see his actual life fate as a natural and inevitable consequence of his values.

It could reasonably be argued that these forces of traditionalism, with the derivative insulation from external stimulus, help to perpetuate the underprivileged position of the Indian, since they recommend to him the unquestioning acceptance of the status quo. It must be realized, however, that the Indian finds what is for him a fairly satisfactory type of life within the limits of what he considers possible. What strikes the observer as an underprivileged and deprecated situation which "ought" to stir discontent is viewed by the average Indian as a life position which is unavoidable and which has many satisfying aspects to it.

The Indian becomes discontented precisely at that point where he begins to be able to see other ways of life as possible alternatives to his own. This occurs, most simply, when the Indian is virtually forced to view other ways of life as possible alternatives to his own. This in turn occurs generally only when the Indian is demoralized to the point of being marginal to his traditional culture stream. The demoralization is itself a consequence of the inability to match aspiration and achievement. Social and cultural change are thus initiated in San Luis in part by those individuals who are cast off the main currents of the culture by its inadequacies and/or their own.

The contrast between Ladino and Indian marginality

is instructive. For, the marginal Indian has the Ladino way of life as an alternative into which he, as a discontented Indian, can partially fit. On the other hand, the marginal Ladino has nowhere to go except to pick up stakes and try elsewhere. But the very conditions which make him marginal to the mainstreams of San Luis almost guarantee his probable failure in any other locale. In this sense, then, the Indian is far better off than the Ladino, as far as adjustment to basic dissatisfactions is concerned.

CHAPTER 11

THE DIFFERENTIAL STRUCTURE AND FUNCTIONS OF RELIGION

IN CHAPTER 3 reference was made to some of the overall patterns of religious and magical behavior in San Luis, and to some of the more obvious differences between Indians and Ladinos in these two areas. Since religion and magic are so central to the life of the pueblo, it is important that these differences and some of their implications be spelled out in some detail.

Of primary significance here is the fact that it is impossible to understand the internal social structure and supporting attitudes of the Indians without an understanding of their religious and magical behavior. By contrast, much of the Ladino life cycle, both in its formal and informal aspects, can be understood without reference to its interconnections with religious and magical ideas and practices.

In part this difference in the degree of significance and interconnectedness of religion with the rest of the institutional framework parallels similar developments in other acculturating communities: the more urbanized and secularized the community, the more disorganized its central body of meanings and the less cohesive its institutional structure. Analogously viewed, the Indians are the folk and the Ladinos the urban approximates on the continuum.

It may truly be said of the Indian community, for instance, that if one were to pull out of its culture the body of religious ideas and practices which characterize it, the culture, as a differentiated body of behavior with an organized set of meanings, would without question collapse. Some of the evidence for this contention may be offered.

RELIGION AND ECONOMICS

The economic life of the Indians of San Luis is focused so firmly upon the milpa that all other kinds of work can be said to be relatively unimportant. In the Indian's view, however, the milpa itself is more than his plot of land. It constitutes the core of his self-definition. For, as he sees it, his role as milpero is integral to his entire way of life. In turn, a vital part of that milpero role is its tie-in with Pagan-Christian beliefs and practices which define its metaphysical significance, allocate it its place in the world of possible economic activities, ritually circumscribe and sanction various changes of seasonal activities such as planting and harvesting, and, finally, give a sense of fundamental security which no other activity or possession can nearly hope to approximate.

Thus, for instance, the Indian says of himself that he is fundamentally a hard-working, poorly paid agriculturalist, but that both the hard work and the poverty are themselves sanctioned by Divinity. For, he reasons, if Divinity had not so intended it to be, how could one explain why it was then so? The facts of poverty and hard work are therefore taken as a natural accompaniment of the role of milpero, which, itself, according to the Indian, is the role which Divine Providence intended for him. Indeed, the more sophisticated thinkers among the Indians mythologize the milpero role to the extent of reciting the story of creation in which the primary activity is the raising of corn and beans, the Lord Jesus is a milpero of rather dark skin, and the pursuit by his enemies who are seeking to kill him takes place through various milpas "nearby," "just over the hill," somewhere not far from where the "papa santissimo," the Pope, is now located. This mythological rationale for the present role of the Indian parallels in its intent and function what one finds generally true of myths of creation throughout most primitive and civilized groups in the world. It should not, therefore, in any way be considered as a special piece of ignorance or stupidity on the part of the San Luis Indians.

Hard work and poverty, taken by the Indian to be natural and intrinsic to the milpero role, are also evaluated by him as the mark of a worthy Christian. In the Indian's

RELIGION

estimate, a man who does not work hard for a living cannot hope to be considered as virtuous as the man who earns his bread, or, more properly, his corn and beans, by the sweat of his brow. Being a hard-working and poor milpero is what a good Christian essentially *is*. The Indian sums it up by saying, in one breath, "If one is not a believing Christian, what then is he?" and adds, in the very next breath, "If one does not have his milpa, what then does he have?"

There is no discernibly separable number of gods in current religious ideology among the Indians. Yet there seem to be at least some remnants of what may have formerly been a differentiated pantheon. For, separate and special divine types of control and power are ascribed by the Indian to various portions of the agricultural nexus in which he is involved. An analysis of the oral prayer texts of one of the local religious leaders, for instance, shows supplications to the God of the Rain, God of the Planting, God of the Harvest and related deities. It is not clear, however, that separate gods are intended, for the only names which are invoked are those of Jesus Christ and San Luis Rey de Francia, the major patron saint of the pueblo.

Perhaps the most crucial fact about these prayer texts, for our present purposes, is that they reveal so clearly the extent to which the Indians believe in divine control over the most significant turns of events. It is necessary, for instance, according to Indian belief, to sanctify the planting of seed and insure its fruitfulness by sprinkling holy water in the four corners of the milpa. This water has been transported from the local pueblo to a distant shrine at Esquipulas and there blessed at a special mass paid for by contributions of the local Indian gentry. In turn, all those who contributed to this payment are entitled to receive enough holy water for the sanctification of the four cardinal points of their milpas, and for use in the household shrines, especially at times of illness. The return of the religious procession from Esquipulas is marked with more religious fervor on the part of a majority of the Indians than one sees at almost any other time during the year.

Similarly, just before the fall harvest a religious fiesta is held at which there is distribution of the first products of the harvest to the various religious principals, and wholesale prayers of blessing of Divinity for the providential harvest are uttered. A matching celebration is held at the opening of the spring planting season to guarantee success to the crops. Finally, throughout the year, monthly religious reunions of various confraternities, called *cofradias*, are held for reciting, through long nights of prayer and music, the thanks of the pueblo to its patron saints and to Jesus for safekeeping and adequate return from the milpas.

Throughout the interconnections of religious and economic behavior there run intertwined threads of magical beliefs and practices as well. Thus, Indians typically believe in certain magical omens which help them foretell the probable success or failure of a day at work or of an entire crop. It is believed, for example, that if one starts out for work in the morning and sees a woodpecker, one ought immediately to return to his house, since some calamity is sure to befall him in the milpa. Cases of individuals who did not heed the omen, and smashed their fingers, or lopped them off with their machetes that ominous day, are cited to prove the point. Again, formations of clouds, the crossing of one's path by animals, the barking of dogs, and many other such omens are heeded to one degree or another by the Indians.

In addition, the milpa and one's work animals are considered by the Indians, along with their children, to be the most likely subjects for evil magic on the part of a *brujo*, or magician, hired by an enemy. It is of more than passing interest that the milpa and work animals are singled out as objects most likely to be attacked: these are, after all, along with one's children, one's most valuable and indispensable possessions.

Again, omens are also consulted regarding the propitious times to plant and to harvest. These, however, are

RELIGION

relatively unimportant by comparison with the religious deities, and, moreover, are far more diffuse and far less uniform. It is generally true, indeed, that so far as the Indian is concerned, religious ideas and practices are far more standardized and uniform than are the magical. This is at least in part a function of the fact that any form of magic is necessarily conducted sub rosa, while one secures prestige by the openness of his religiosity.

By contrast, the Ladino man is relatively an irreligious person. For, while it is true that one can scarcely find an atheist or acknowledged agnostic in town, it is also true that almost no such detailed connections between economics and religion can be said to obtain for the Ladino. So far as actual religious practices are concerned, these are confined, in the Ladino community, primarily to the women and children. All Ladinos are supposed to be devout believers, but, in general, only the Ladino women feel it necessary openly to ritualize their beliefs.

By contrast with the attention to religious details which the Indian manifests, the Ladino seeks a general, covering kind of insurance of his well-being and that of his economic enterprises by affirming his belief in a Christian deity and approving his wife's and his children's religious activities. But he does not seek any particular and detailed guidance or sanction for specific enterprises. The phrases "God willing," "In the name of God," "For God's sake," and like utterances are an integral part of the vocabulary of the Ladino male. But they do not appear to have nearly the emotional investment nor significance of the same phrases when uttered by the Indians, or, for that matter, by the Ladino women.

Ladino males confess to distrust and suspicion of the sincerity of the frocked priests who occasionally come to perform masses, baptisms, and weddings; and they mock the extreme open religiosity of the Indians. They take the Indian confraternity reunions to be marks of the ignorance and superstitiousness of the Indian, even though, as some of them well know, religious confraternities are *de rigueur* among the social elite of the Ladinos in the nation's capital. Further, the Ladino man tends to convert all holy days into holidays, making carnivals and trading times of the religious fiestas in celebration of the patron saints' name-days, and using other fiesta times as excuses for sometimes licentious drinking and cavorting. In a relative sense, then, it may be said that religion does not enter significantly into the economic life of the Ladino, while it is inextricably intertwined with that of the Indian.

In and of themselves, these differences in the functional significance of religion for the economic life of the two groups do not necessarily imply other consequences. But some such connections do actually emerge, and, on analysis, they prove to be critical.

In our earlier discussion of economic activities, it was noted that though the Indians are objectively the subordinate and ill-favored group, they nevertheless show up as the satisfied and integrated segment of the society, whereas the Ladinos, though objectively favored, show many more marks of psychological dissatisfaction and disorganization. The key to this subjective difference lies on the one hand in the Indian's belief in the divine sanction of the rightness and virtue of his way of life—no matter how objectively ill-favored it may be; and, on the other, in the inability of the Ladino to superimpose upon his round of economic activities those or comparable supernaturally given value judgments.

For, as was noted earlier, the work the traditional Indian does is central to his total life definition which itself embraces a conception of a divine plan. Thus, the activity is not simply instrumental, nor simply a mark of his social prestige. Rather, it is seen as a fulfillment of his destiny. It is self-consummatory. He is a worthy man because he does this work, hard and unrewarding as it may be by objective standards. In doing his work he lives in conformity with the natural principles contained in the divine plan.

It is this which in part enables him to take the abuse and the derogation which the Ladino metes out to him,

RELIGION

and to ignore it, or so devaluate it that it loses much of its possible psychological sting. Moreover, because he takes his fate as "given," the Indian is able to keep his aspirations pitched to local pueblo horizons, ignoring the temptations present in the different way of life of the Ladinos and of the various groups through whose territories he passes on his various trips. It is only through some such psychologically insulating device that one can account for the failure of different culture patterns, to which the Indian is continually exposed, to be effectively stimulating and challenging. His horizons, limited as they are by his ignorance and low-pitched aspirations, are lowered even more by the insulating effect of this belief in the divine sanction of his own way of life. He therefore does not invidiously compare himself with the Ladino or with other Indian groups, and does not therefore generally aspire after their satisfactions, material or otherwise.

By contrast, the Ladino, having no such insulation against the effectiveness of outside stimuli, is continuously touched by them, continuously stimulated to aspire after those which he views as superior to his own, and therefore tends continuously to express his dissatisfaction with his own lot. But because he does not have the necessary intellectual equipment, training, or skills which would make it possible for him to move on to other fields to conquer, he is forced to stay put. Whipped as his ego is by comparison of himself with others who get more rewards of the kind he desires, it is no accident that the Ladino turns with scorn and derogation upon the Indian, and inflates his own sense of importance by taking a dismal view of the worth of the Indians.

It can thus be seen that a saving grace for the traditional Indian is his belief in the permeation of all his activities by a divine spirit and plan which sanctifies whatever he does, no matter how unrewarding it may otherwise be. So long as the Indian holds to this belief, he may truly be considered as a traditional Indian. For one finds a relatively constant correlation between this attitude toward

TENSIONS AND EQUILIBRIA

Divinity and those other attitudes which tell the Indian that the old way of life is best. By contrast, one finds in those younger Indians who have begun to engage in other than milpa economics the most sharp and poignant expressions of dissatisfaction with the traditional status quo and of the clumsy and evident efforts to become like the Ladinos.

It is in this latter group of Indians that the seeds of social change are planted. These are the Indians who, more than others, reject the age-respect principle which governs Indian social behavior; attempt to dress like the Ladino; do not assist their fathers in familial religious rites; go out of the pueblo for several weeks or months every year; mock some of the traditional leaders for their "ancient" ways; and court the company and acceptance of the Ladinos, neither of which do they receive in any but a most unrewarding fashion.

In short, in this group of Indians one finds the nub of tension and disequilibrium in Indian social structure. For they do not have the insulation against insult, mockery, and general social depreciation which the Ladinos express with regard to Indian behavior, nor do they have an alternative satisfactory pattern. As noted earlier, it is this insulation and the ignorance of alternatives which enables the traditional Indian the better to ignore and reject the significance and consequences of the Ladino's scorn.

ECONOMICS, RELIGION, AND SOCIAL CONTROL

The growing pattern of rejection of the traditional way of life among some of the Indians has further important implications for internal social control, and for the general stability of the overall caste situation. It may first be noted that while both Indians and Ladinos are subject to the rules and regulations of the formal governmental structure of the pueblo, department, and nation, much of the social order which one perceives in the Indian community is maintained by certain internal devices and principles which are not shared by the Ladinos.

RELIGION

Primary among these is the principle that age demands and commands respect and obedience. As interpreted in the most traditional Indian circles, this is taken to imply that any older person may reasonably expect respect and obedience from any younger person. It is recognized, however, that the fullest right to expect these things from younger people is had by parents with respect to their children, and by older siblings with respect to their younger siblings.

This principle is by no means unique, for it is found in a rather wide assortment of variations in societies without writing and written traditions, and in which, therefore, socialization of the young into adult skills required for survival depends on oral transmission by the elders.

With such a monopoly of highly desired scarce goods, it is expectable that the elders are able to maintain firm control over the behavior of their children. In San Luis, this principle in its secular aspects is reinforced by the adjunct monopoly over skills in religious ritual, the performance of which is considered by traditional Indians to be indispensable to individual and social well-being. This finds the peak of its expression in the religious leadership of the community. For the religious leaders, or *principales* as they are locally called, are in effect the traditional political leaders as well, and are among the oldest men in the pueblo.

It is apparent from the remains of the older system that the principales formerly functioned as justices of the peace and of matters for higher tribunals as well, officiating at the most important of Indian secular and religious ceremonials, and acting in any capacity which required communal authority and sanction. But the system as formerly operative is highly attenuated today. This is evident from the fact that it is most difficult for a representative sample of Indians to agree on the details of the structure of this leadership. There is considerable disagreement, in effect, among various Indians as to how many principales there are, what are their duties and rights, how they accede to their positions, and just who, particularly, the principales are at any given time.

This disagreement arises in part from the fact that there is differential resort to the services of the principales on the part of various Indians and differential participation in religious rituals at which they preside. These differences in turn are reflections of other differences in the socialization patterns of various groups among the Indians, so that some of them have grown up knowing little and caring less about the principales, while others have been raised in the most orthodox fashion, including unquestioning affirmation of the important role of the principales.

The secular government of Guatemala incorporates Indian self-government to some rough degree by allocating internal community responsibility for peace and order to some of the principales, and by having some of them serve as "official representatives" of the Indian community when the occasion demands it. This is evidently more of a token gesture than a sincerely intended action. For, by testimony of Ladino officials and Indian principales, the latter serve more as rubber stamps rather than as a decision-making body of Indian representatives. Yet, in traditional Indian circles, government and God go hand in hand, as is evident from the kinds of secular power which are assigned to the principales by virtue of their positions of religious leadership.

The coexistence of two possible tribunals of justice sets up a potential for conflict in the Indian community. In the event that two traditionally orientated Indians get involved in a dispute, there is some considerable likelihood that they will resort to adjudication by one or more of the principales. But in the event that a traditional Indian becomes involved with a more secular Indian or with a Ladino, or indeed, distrusts the particularistic leanings of a principal-judge, the dispute is likely to come to the attention of the Ladino officials.

It is generally felt among the Indians that it does not do anyone much good to bring a dispute before the Ladino officials, since both parties are likely to receive some form of punishment, no matter what the equities of the case. But it is becoming increasingly apparent that the Ladino government has the formal power to enforce its decisions, once rendered, whereas the decisions of principales carry only such weight and force as may be subjectively invested in them by the parties to the dispute. This always leaves open the possibility that there will be a reneging on an agreement mediated by the principales with the subsequent resort to the Ladino officials for a new and perhaps different decision.

Ladino officials make it clearly known that they in no wise appreciate the existence of a dual tribunal. Their distaste for the internal settlement of affairs among Indians is made evident when an Indian who is dissatisfied with a ruling by a principal brings his complaint to the Ladino court. Under such circumstances it is not unlikely that both parties are rebuked for not having resorted to the official channels from the outset.

Unfortunately, more precise data regarding the attrition in the frequency and types of cases brought to the principales over a period of time are not available. It seems unquestionable, however, that each additional year in the history of the pueblo sees a decreasing importance attaching to the opinions and decisions of the principales. For, the structural basis of their power lies in the age-respect principle which itself, as has been noted, has begun, though only on a small scale, to degenerate. The reliability of these contentions is partially vouchsafed by the complaints of the old men themselves and in the obvious attitudes of some of the younger men toward the restrictive expectations still extant.

It is unavoidable that the attrition in the secular aspects of the age-respect principle should spread to the sacred or religious aspects as well. In a sense we have here a self-reinforcing circle of events. The breakdown of the secular power and influence of the principales destroys the symbolic value of age and its traditional connotations. This in turn weakens the religious leadership roles of these same principales. At the same time this is abetted by the general processes of secularization and the consequent decrease in religiosity. This is reflected in the inability of parents to socialize their children into traditionally religious ways of belief and life. This weak link is further weakened by the abstention of the young men from attendance at the cofradias where ritualization of religio-political-economic ties is performed. The failure periodically to ritualize and thus to strengthen these ties sends its effects through the entire interacting circle, and the secularization goes on.

The consequences of these processes of secularization for the traditional Indian family are readily apparent. Every refusal to resort to the principales as justices of the peace implies a correlative decrease in the willingness to consider age, and therefore one's parents, as legitimate sources of power and authority.

The traditional respect for parents is dependent at least in part on the fact that the economic norms among the Indians dictate that children shall work for their parents until they achieve their majority. At this time, the parents are supposed to have saved enough money and acquired enough land to endow both their daughters and sons with adequate dowries of both land and money, to make an independent start in life for themselves once they secure a mate.

Thus, the young people of the society have been traditionally dependent on their parents for a start in life. Their very ability to get married, indeed, depends on the parents' ability to provide the beginning wherewithal. In traditional days and ways, no other alternatives were possible. Desertion of the pueblo was simply too far-fetched an idea for any but the most marginal and dissident of individuals. Rebellion against parental authority found no support in any moretic structure. Finally, it has heretofore been relatively impossible to secure income by

RELIGION

any means other than working on the milpa for one's parents and, later, for oneself.

With the alienation of the Indians from their base in land, to the extent reported earlier, it has become decreasingly possible for parents to provide each of their children with either gainful work on their milpas and/or enough land, when they reach their majorities, to begin their own life enterprises as married adults. This situation has literally forced Indians to seek cash employment on the milpas of others; or to take up subsidiary trades; or to leave the milpa for some or many months of the year, to work on banana plantations of the United Fruit Company, where the average rate of daily pay far exceeds anything the pueblo can offer. Though the idea of working for anyone but one's parents, and the idea of leaving the pueblo, even for only a few months, to seek gainful employment, were and are simply anathema to the traditional norms of the Indian group, sheer force of circumstances has brought about the condition whereby this has become unavoidable.

As a result, several new facts have become a constant part of the social atmosphere of the Indian community. There is first the fact of the weakened source of parental authority through the parents' failure to be able to provide the traditionally expected reward for the traditionally expected obedience and conformity. As a correlative of this, some Indian youths now find it possible to make an economic start of their own without relying on their parents for nearly as much help for as long a time as has heretofore been traditional. They thus have fewer things for which to be grateful and obedient to their parents, and more ways by which to refuse to accept such authority as the parents may still feel their right to assert and impose. This combination of circumstances has most unhappy results so far as the stability of the traditional way of life is concerned. The milpa, the family, social control and God, being traditionally interlocked, as closely as they have been, all show the effects of these new combinations of facts. Thus, a simple economic kind of pressure has given rise to a multifarious chain of events which threatens the basic structure of the culture pattern.

Yet, lest the extent of the danger be overestimated, it needs to be asserted that this is by no means the dominant pattern. To the casual eye, things remain much as they have been for many years past. The predominant occupation of Indians is still the milpa. The predominant mode of dress remains that which is determined by low income, inconspicuous consumption, and the other cultural emphases earlier mentioned. More often than not, parents give their youngsters their economic start in life by endowing them with land, though small in size, and with enough of the other goods of life to enable them to make a beginning. More often than not as well, the parents are asked to engage in the traditional rituals of marriage arrangement, with the principales serving as adjudicators and brokers. More often than not, the Indian goes to church, prays to his house figurines, lights his candles, participates in the major fiestas, and occasionally attends the cofradias. The principales remain the most respected and revered men in the Indian community. Sharp divisions of labor along sex lines continue to prevail. In short, much of the former traditional pattern remains, at least superficially, intact. Withal, the tension is there and mounting, and the security and stability of the traditional way of life are in definite danger.

CHAPTER 12

THE DIFFERENTIAL STRUCTURE AND FUNCTIONS OF KINSHIP

THE FAMILY is a basic principle of social organization in San Luis for both Ladinos and Indians. No other social grouping within either of the castes is so pervasive as the family in its conditioning of behavior. Nor does any other agency even threaten to compete with it for the first rank of influence. For the family group is the central agency of socialization into values, education for adult skills, economic cooperation, religious instruction and devotion, allocation of power and privilege, ascription of status, and exchange of affection and loyalty.

The importance of the family is based on a number of reasons. Primary among these is that there is little specialization of function, by occupation or otherwise, within the pueblo. This applies with equal force to both Ladinos and Indians. Nearly everyone is primarily concerned with the production and sale of a limited number of agricultural crops, most especially corn and beans. Since most selling and exchange occurs within the pueblo, and since prices are extremely depressed locally by comparison with other centers even in Guatemala, the amount of capital for investment is minimized. Small-scale industries employing two or three craftsmen do exist, but these are marginal to the economy proper, and, in most cases, do not represent the chief source of income of even these craftsmen themselves.

The low level of income and investment capital joins with the low horizons concerning occupational diversification to result in the occupational sameness so characteristic of the pueblo. These in turn are supported by an undiversified kind of consumer-demand psychology. This itself is part and product of the pervasive ignorance concerning alternatives and the inability to implement alternatives even when they rise to the point of effective desire. Moreover, at all times the people are forced to devote most of their productive time and energy eking out a bare subsistence from the depleted marginal lands on which they raise their crops.

This lack of diversification and of surplus capital results in the inability to maintain a leisure class of specialists in nonutilitarian occupations. This dearth of specialists is maintained by the absence of any effective demand for them, and the consequent lack of training of any reasonable number to perform such functions.

The absence of diversified functions results in a dearth of secondary organizations, voluntary or otherwise, such as one finds in a developing heterogeneous society. The lines of possible organization are limited to those bases of loyalty already existing within the unspecialized frame of social and economic life. This has the result that no clubs, unions, or social or fraternal organizations of any significance are to be found in the pueblo. Such organizations as do exist are temporary collocations of individuals for rather immediate political purposes. Even these are minimal in number and frequency of reunion due to the hazardous character of political activity in Guatemala.

The Indians have their cofradias, or religious confraternities, which meet once a month for religious purposes. It is true, of course, that these cofradias also serve as sources of community integration for the Indians. But they are not subjectively conceived as such and their functions do not ramify into the more explicitly secular areas.

Ladino women also form temporary unions around Christmas time in order to allocate rights and responsibilities regarding the religious services they perform for the holiday. But these unions are highly temporary and are abandoned yearly after the holidays. One may truly say then that formal secondary organization is at a minimum in San Luis.

Previous observations regarding the school system have shown that the schools scarcely reach the majority of the children in the pueblo and are highly limited, in terms of

KINSHIP

time and effect, in their impact on those who do attend. No organizations connected with the schools are to be found. Nor do the parents of the children find this common parental role sufficient basis for an enduring organization. There is a local school board of sorts, but this, like most such other organizations, exists more on paper than in fact.

The schools are in session only a relatively few hours a day, and, by comparison with other school systems, a relatively small number of days a year. Absenteeism runs high. Effectively, schooling ends for most children after the first year or two. It would thus be far from the truth to claim the schools as a secondary instrument of socialization in any significant sense of the word.

The church, as a center of organized religion, does have its effects on town life, but not nearly to the degree that one would expect in a community so highly devoted to religious belief and practices. There is no resident priest, no secondary organizations of any lasting kind associated with the church, no Sunday school, no formal religious instruction of any regular kind, and no adult or child auxiliaries of importance. Religious instruction, like religious worship, is carried on primarily in the home.

To sum up, one may say that all the forces in San Luis lead to the retention by the family of the basic functions traditionally associated with the family, and no secondary organizations exist to compete with the home for the performance of these functions. It is most nearly accurate, therefore, to insist that the family, as an organized group of kin, with its attached functions extending beyond those of reckoning descent, is the single most pervasive and important social agency in San Luis.

Genealogical chartings of the relationship systems in San Luis impress the observer with the way in which kinship bonds weave in and out to relate wide numbers of individuals into extended kinship groups. Among the Indians, the peak of this extension is reached in a small hamlet, called El Camaron, where the entire community of almost 400, with but few exceptions, can be described,

TENSIONS AND EQUILIBRIA

kinship-wise, in terms of three family lines and the various conjugal ties among them. In the pueblo of San Luis itself, kinship ties are not nearly so extended among the Indians. But they are sufficiently far-flung to make these ties the most widely binding. Among the Ladinos, a similar condition exists, except that the extensions are not so wide.

Both Indians and Ladinos recognize second and third cousins and, since they come face to face with them frequently, relationships of this order are defined and maintained. Vertical extensions of more than three generations, however, are difficult to find, not because they are not socially recognized where they exist, but because of the early age of death of the average person in the pueblo. Conjugal ties add to the consanguine bonds a dimension of defined relationship, and to these the godparental and compadre relationships previously described add people who are considered kin in one way or another. A further source of quasi-kin relations stems from the presence in various families of illegitimate Indian children who are the offspring of Indian mothers and Ladino fathers. Formal ties are not recognized in these cases, but the community does recognize the rightness of the maintenance of some special relationship between the father, the child, and the mother. This special relationship may consist only of privileged access to the household of the Ladino parent for small favors, but it is considered proper and fitting that this should be so.

For instance, the Ladino druggist, in describing his family, noted that his father had had some eighty children, only three of whom were legitimate, but that he always expressed concern in one way or another for his various bastard offspring. The druggist himself had a dossier of more than a dozen women by whom he claimed to have had children. But it is not certain that he felt any special obligation to all of them. Bastard offspring of Ladino men and Indian women invariably take the names of their mothers and move inside the Indian world. But their continued presence in town, and the continued face-to-face

KINSHIP

meeting of partners in cohabitation makes this quasi-kinship institution more significant than would otherwise be expected.

Among the wealthier Ladino families one finds occasionally an old retainer and possibly some bastard offspring who are considered integral parts of the household. Their possible relationship to the present or past master of the house is often a subject of rumor but one cannot easily ascertain the exact nature of the relationship, if in fact any does exist.

In the house in which this writer lived, for instance, there resided an old woman cook, a young woman who helped in cooking, shopping, taking care of the children and the laundry, and a young girl of thirteen or fourteen who assisted the two other women in all their duties. All three occupied positions above that of servant, but not quite that of family member. They did not address the members of the household in kinship terms, but their relationships with them were far more privileged than one would ordinarily expect. This condition is not widespread. But one encounters it often enough, especially among the Ladinos, to recognize that between ordinary contractual relationships and well-defined kin bonds there is a sliding back and forth in the ties which are recognized among San Luis people. These tend to complicate the kinship picture, but they force the observer to recognize them as a dimension of relationship which is important for the people of the pueblo.

Orphaned children are frequently adopted, without any legal formalities, and, in some cases, children of parents yet alive are taken into other households, there to live as full members of the household. This sets up special ties between the biological and the adoptive parents which defy description in ordinary kinship terms and which act as a still further extension of the relationships one expects to encounter.

Within the Indian community one gets the impression that kinship has become somewhat watered down over recent generations. For instance, when one young Indian girl was asked about her relationship to her husband's brother, she called him "my husband." When I asked her why she called him this, she said "Because he is my husband." Sensing that this was a clue to a possible fraternal polyandrous situation, I tried to get her to elaborate, whereupon she turned and fled, and avoided me ever after. When I used this clue in kinship inquiry with others, they told me the girl was obviously mixed up, that no such practices existed, that they had never heard of any such thing before. Yet, the girl was so insistent that she called her brother-in-law husband because he was her husband, that I could not do away with the feeling that some form of fraternal polyandry did exist. However, no other such clues were ever turned up.

To be sure, this is skimpy evidence on which to assume the formerly general existence of a condition now no longer operative. But other suggestions lead one to believe that kinship is becoming less effective and extended. Thus, for instance, one hears increasing dissension on the part of young people with the assumption that older brothers may act *in loco parentis.* "He's not my father, he's only my brother" is heard often enough to make one aware that since the traditional expectation is that the older brother does stand as surrogate parent to younger siblings, kinship bonds, as formerly defined, are tending to disappear.

The continuity of importance of kinship in San Luis is nevertheless vouchsafed by the fact that the pueblo is small in its makeup, geographically and demographically speaking; that it is relatively isolated from the outside world; and that, as a result, the number of possible alternatives to traditional patterns is extremely small. It is easy, therefore, to identify any given individual with his relatives and ancestors, and to allocate to him the ratings held by his family. Status by ascription is by far more significant and widespread than status by achievement.

Moreover, the smallness of the society results in the high visibility of acts at any given time, and in the high recall value of family reputation, once established. The relative isolation from the outside world, plus the paucity of diverse social activities inside the pueblo, serve to focus attention on local matters to a high degree of intensity. The dearth of alternative possibilities of life involvement tends to restrict any generation to the lines of occupation and social activity of their progenitors, and thus to reinforce already existing reputations.

The essentially agricultural nature of the community, given its lines of caste organization, and the values which cohere with it, additionally force a lowering of social and economic horizons. This operates so that, given the negative emphasis in Ladino culture on manual labor, and its opposite in Indian culture, there result really only two principal ways in which the different peoples can and do acquire prestige. For the Ladino, the prestigeful dossier consists of a conspicuous history of leisure and luxury, or, in rare cases, some distinction in military or governmental services. For the Indian, the prescription is one which calls for a conspicuous history of hard work and religious ardor.

It thus makes considerable sense to equate personal with family reputation in San Luis. For it is only the rare individual who does something by way of work or other kinds of accomplishment which is distinctively different from what his ancestors did. By and large, the opportunities for diversification are so limited that the really different-minded individuals must seek to exploit their new horizons outside the pueblo, and thus tend to be lost, so far as visibility of their deeds is concerned, to the local area.

It is here that one sees an additional "advantage" which the Indians have over the Ladinos. For, given the Ladino values on leisure and luxury, and conspicuous consumption thereof, it is most difficult for any new generation of Ladinos to reestablish a waning family reputation by dint of hard work and the further accumulation of material resources requisite to a life of leisure and luxury. Their own values, in short, in combination with the declining character of the agricultural economy, force them into a position of maintaining a bold though patently shabby social front to cover an increasingly decrepit interior.

It is perhaps this above all which makes the Ladino appear to be far more sensitive to matters of lineage and genealogy than the Indians. There is little way other than in manifest attitudes for new generations of Ladinos to validate their right to the traditional prestige vested in their family names. One gets the impression from Ladino conversations and attitudes that here is a small-time and small-scale aristocracy which has become rather washed out over the years, with its current members living more on the reputation of their ancestor rather than on present-day achievement. An analogy with decadent Southern aristocracy in the United States would appear to fit.

Among the Ladinos, for instance, one finds family feuding, a practice not discoverable among the Indians. This feuding is as often as not a carryover of hostilities developed generations back in time, with each new generation reinforcing that hostility by further acts, without provocation equal to that which initiated the hostility. Even where years go by without any open fracas between families, when an incident does occur it tends to be interpreted in terms of this one's long-standing reputation for evil or that one's equally ancient and established reputation for maliciousness. The family feud sets the social frame of reference within which the members of the respective feuding parties tend to view each other's acts, so that things otherwise considered as trivial and irrelevant tend to be interpreted as acts of implicit if not explicit insult and hostility. It is all too easy to arouse the ire of a Ladino by reflecting, if only by subtle indirection, on the soundness of his ancestors.

As a precaution against and preventive of mutually destructive hostility in this highly limited but charged social atmosphere, the Ladinos have carried on a traditional pattern of light and deferential social patter which smooths social intercourse, so that it is not unusual for two people

KINSHIP

whose families are known to hate each other to greet each other with "At your service, Don Fulano," to be responded to with "Your wish is my command, Don Pedro." One would not expect so much of this patter, nor such high sensitivity to insult of one's family name, in a society where family was of secondary importance, or where individuals had techniques for acquiring reputations other than those socially inherited from their kin groups.

The Ladino thus shows, by his behavior in these regards, how ambivalent the functions of family can be. At one time, his family may serve as a source of pride and prestige, as a unit in which he is proud to claim membership. But by the same token, his family may also serve as the point of initiation and maintenance of conflict with opposing kinship units, and may render him all the more suggestive and susceptible to insult and the subsequent hostility than he otherwise might be.

The Indian in turn not only need not be, but is not in fact, nearly so concerned with his family's reputation. To be sure, each individual tends to be viewed as a constituent unit of a family in whom characteristics are presumably uniformly distributed. But it is eminently possible for a son to be considered far more religious and hard-working than his father, or, indeed, to reverse the expectation, so that while his father acquired a good reputation, the son is in turn losing it. In short, the Indians may be said to consider each other far more as individuals than do the Ladinos with much less general ascription from the large kin units of which they are members.

Both for Ladinos and Indians, it is true that there are no secondary associations, voluntary or otherwise, which are of any real significance as status-giving mechanisms. There are political and social clubs of an impermanent and weak nature among the Ladinos. But these tend to collect membership more along already existing lines of family reputation than by any criteria of individual achievement. Thus we may say that Ladinos by and large stand or fall in their reputations in terms of their families, while

Indians tend somewhat more to rate among their fellows in terms of what they themselves have done or give promise of doing.

In a sense, this differential function of family reputation violates our expectations. For, in the normal course of events, one would expect to find kinship of greater importance for the more folklike Indians than for the more secular Ladinos. This case serves to illustrate, therefore, that the concept of "importance of kinship" covers a diverse number of aspects which do not by any means distribute themselves in consonance with each other. It is thus important to examine these other facets.

One of these which adds up to the "importance of kinship" is that which refers to the extent to which people feel bound to their family ties and feel secure because of their membership therein. Here, too, one finds significant differences between the Indians and the Ladinos.

Among the Ladinos, for instance, one frequently encounters publicly known and openly conducted disputes among siblings. Among the Indians this would be and is a rarity. The reason is simply that in the Indian culture older siblings substitute for the parents in their absence. In traditional Indian family circles it would therefore be as unthinkable for a younger brother to disobey an older brother as it would be for him to disobey his father. This principle suffers attrition in inverse ratio to the age-separation of the siblings, so that the closer in age the siblings, the less applicable the rule. Substantially the same reasons which support the relationship of deference and obedience between children and parents are transferred to the siblings and support it there.

Among the Ladinos, however, young men's eyes are increasingly turning in partial dissatisfaction upon pueblo life, and in unrealizable anticipation upon life outside the pueblo. As a result, the monopoly of skills and goods held by the elders is losing the binding effects it previously commanded. This is ample evidence that the monopoly is not itself sufficient to engender voluntary respect and deference. Rather, only in combination with a number of other attitudes will the system operate as an effective principle of social organization. Without the traditionally commanded respect, born of unquestioning involvement in a total round of traditional life, the monopoly of the elders acts not as a principle of support, but rather as a restraining influence, throwing up tensions between parents and children, allowing neither the satisfactions inherently possible in the situation nor the full expression of the dissatisfactions. The secularization of attitudes among the Ladinos, without their implementation in satisfactory social action, thus results in the family's becoming a genuine source of conflict and hostility.

Because of these factors, and in reciprocal support of them in time, there is found among the Ladinos the expressed desideratum of breaking from dependence on one's family as soon as possible. But insofar as no concrete programs of training for this independence are available to the Ladino youth, this attitude acts less as a source of pleasurable anticipation than as a source of tension.

The desired procedure for Indians, by contrast, is for the newly married boy to build a house on a plot immediately adjacent to his father's, if possible, and to fit himself, his wife, and her family back into the larger kin organization in which he grew up. This has become decreasingly possible for all children to do, and the lack of alternatives tends to create marginal youth who are dissident and nonparticipating in traditional Indian culture. There is general agreement, however, even among the marginal youth, that the traditional pattern is the more desirable one. Thus, the Indian boy, faced with the same lack of alternative opportunities as confronts the Ladino, is nevertheless able to secure far more effective support from his kinship structure.

The continuity of training in the Indian family from its inception accounts in part for this phenomenon. From the earliest years the Indian child is expected to repeat, microcosmically, those functions which he will later be called on to perform as an adult. Unlike Ladino children who are allowed to wander about, the Indian child is kept close to the home and finds his parents and siblings continuously available for diversion, security, and affection. When his mobility and strength are considered adequate, he is slowly graded into a round of responsibilities as well as into the rights of free play. Little Indian girls are very early to be seen carrying their younger siblings around on their hips, as do their mothers, and little Indian boys can be seen trudging off to the fields with their fathers. Their toys are miniature replicas of the household and field utensils and tools which they will later be expected to wield with proficiency. By the time they are twelve or thirteen years old they are considered to be nearly fully equipped, by way of skills and attitudes, for adult responsibilities.

By contrast, infancy and childhood irresponsibility are far more prolonged among the Ladinos. The orientation toward conspicuous consumption of leisure and luxury is inculcated early in life, so that Ladinos can and do derive additional prestige from their children's, as well as their own, participation in these patterns. If only a minority of the Ladino families are able to engage in these patterns with any élan and effectiveness, it is primarily because of their inability and scarcely if at all because of their lack of desire to do so.

These different orientations to life lead to and reciprocally support different patterns of authority within the family structure of the two groups. The Ladino family may be said to be, at one and the same time, both far more permissive and far more authoritarian in its general relationships than the Indian family. The latter is characterized more by principles of cooperative responsibility, both between and within generations. It may seem that the generalizations concerning the Indian age-respect principle are here being contradicted. In fact, however, there appears to be a fundamental compatibility between the prescribed respect and deference for parents and older siblings on the one hand, and genuine efforts at cooperative family living on the other. For, there is a strong cultural prescription that rights are to be balanced with responsibilities. Thus, though the father tends to be the public head and representative of the family, he is not expected to make important decisions for the family without consulting with his wife and, if feasible, with his growing children.

There is a sense in which the Indian family is a more organic whole than the Ladino family. It is the sense which one gets from watching the Indian family at work and at rest—since they do not play—and noting the easy fitting into a total organization of the discrete members who constitute it. One does not get this sense from the Ladino family under comparable conditions. At least part of the reason for the difference appears to come from the more spontaneous and habitual sharing by the Indians of a common lot, without each member considering himself as a discrete unit. One suspects that the cooperative management of the family is responsible in part for this.

The Ladino family, by comparison, gives one a sense of a unit held together more by contract and restraint than by spontaneous and willing sharing of enterprise and fate. And again, it is the pattern of authority and management which probably plays a role. The Ladino family tends to vary in its treatment of its members from extreme permissiveness to extreme and unreasoning authoritarianism. That is to say, the extremes of loose and severe discipline are invoked apparently far more frequently than in the Indian family.

Discipline seems to run to such extremes, by contrast with the Indian family, at least partly because the traditional definitions of relationship among familial members are by no means so standardized and mutually accepted as among the Indians. This is itself a reflection of the disorganization present in the total Ladino social pattern, and at the same time it is one of the factors which keeps that disorganization occurring. For if one takes it as axiomatic that stability or instability of a social organization is guaranteed in the patterns of socialization of the children, then it follows that the Ladino family, being indecisive in its cultural transmission, is undergoing such attrition. One sees the beginning of this kind of thing among those segments of the Indian community which have departed most from their traditional patterns.

Without traditionally dictated lines of rights and responsibilities, the family tends more toward anomie and less toward solidarity. This condition approaching anomie is all the more insupportable for the Ladino because of the great emphasis which his social criteria place upon family, its continuity and its obligations. And since there are no secondary organizations of any significance as status-giving agencies, the family's cracking appears to cause considerable stress throughout Ladino culture. In a real sense, the oncoming generations of Ladino youth face significant social disinheritance and alienation.

It is in this sense then that one may speak of the greater solidary character of the Indian family. For it continues to serve, far more efficiently than the Ladino family, some of the basic functions of kinship units which we have come to recognize as indispensable to the organic solidarity of a large family.

CHAPTER 13

WHERE THE PEOPLE MEET

EVERY social system represents an equilibrium between responsibilities and rewards which accrue to the members of that system. Those rewards and responsibilities are built into the definitions of status and role which prevail, so that, for the most part, the average citizen of the average society knows very well what is expected of him by way of duty and what he may in turn expect by way of return for performance of his duties.

In San Luis, small and isolated though it may be, the round of rewards available to the citizens of the pueblo embrace about the same categories as one finds in larger and more heterogeneous societies. Thus, it may be said that all people in San Luis strive, though in different ways and to different degrees, for prestige, income, health, education, power, diversion, mobility, and security.

It is important to realize, however, that Indians and Ladinos tend to desire these things from life in different ways. They do not define the expected rewards in the same way. Finally, they do not react in the same way to deprivation when they encounter it. If one judges the reward situation in a society from the viewpoint of the felt satisfaction of the people, it would be necessary to say that the Indians probably feel more satisfied with life than the Ladinos.

But if we view the matter in terms of absolute amount of return for amount of contribution, the Ladinos have much the better of life in San Luis. Relative to the work they do and the services they provide which are functional for the community, Ladinos get a disproportionately larger share of the available income, education, power, mobility, deference, formal prestige, perquisites and health facilities. The situation is therefore fairly labeled as highly exploitative of the Indian. The Ladino community tends to live off the Indian's productive labor; uses his military manpower for his own ends; exercises rights over his women which he in turn does not permit with his own women; forces social deference wherever possible; minimizes the cost of education by systematically discouraging the Indian from desiring education; excludes him from his social company wherever possible; forbids marriage between himself and the Indian; refuses to allow Indians to eat at the same table, play on the same fields, share the same public facilities, earn the same income, join the same social events; and, generally, will not share visits back and forth or maintain friendships of any significance.

Throughout all this exploitation, the Indian expresses only incidental and inconsequential resentment. It has been shown how the culture has become molded so that the Indian defines himself as a poor man, a sick man, a hard-working man, and all this because that is the way God intended it to be. He defines himself, in short, in terms of his actual social condition and attaches to that manmade condition a divine sanction which commends the rightness of it to him. The Ladino too feels he is only doing what is right, and he therefore feels it perfectly right that the Indian should work for him, run errands for him, be his house-servant, defer to him, give him prestige, keep a certain distance from him, and throughout "stay in his place."

The mutual support which these two sets of attitudes give to each other is apparent. Dissension on the part of the Indian, or even mild resentment; continuous uneasiness on the part of the Ladino; arguments between them— any of these would and do occasionally disrupt the stability of the situation.

Additionally, other facts can and do enter from time to time to upset the traditional equilibrium. The cumulative disfunctional effects of the land-grabbing practices of the Ladinos, depriving the Indians of their essential source of felt security, have already been described. Also, occasionally Indians do get from their travels suggestions about a better life outside. Further, idiosyncratic variations in life histories sometimes throw selected individuals off the beaten track in the pueblo. And, again, some of the Ladino attitudes, especially their dissatisfaction with the smallness of San Luis, help to create dissidence and disturb the stability of the status quo. But by and large the round of life continues relatively undisturbed, and people go about performing their traditional roles in traditional ways, receiving their expected rewards and reacting to them in predictable fashions.

Essential to this continuity of the pueblo round of life are the prescribed patterns of social distance and avoidance of Indian by Ladino and vice versa, so that they meet, it seems, only under specified conditions and with defined rules of intercourse, and, otherwise, they tend not to share in each other's lives. This pattern of avoidance—maintained primarily at the insistence of the Ladino and the willingness of the Indian to "keep his place"—reduces the possibilities of conflict to a bare minimum.

For one thing it reduces the number of times that the Indian and Ladino are actually physically face to face. For another, it helps the Indian avoid being ordered around at whim and fancy, without reason, and further helps him to avoid being "drafted" for the most unpleasant and thoroughly resented kinds of "public voluntary duty." Moreover, it provides the Indian with the possibility of an internal community life within which he is his own master and within which all men are equal, or at least are differentiated in terms indigenous to the Indian conception of life. Further, it keeps the Indian from continuous exposure to the surface charms of the Ladino way of life. This operates especially with regard to the women who are almost never in Ladino company and who are an extremely conservative influence upon their males, checking their acculturation before it even starts. Again, this avoidance pattern enables the Indian male, upon return from work, to assume a dignified and prestigeful status in the privacy of his own home, undisturbed by any other reflections and secure in his power as pater familias. Additionally, it enables the Indian dialect to be taught first, quickly and easily, to Indian children. This provides the Indian community with a contra-acculturative technique which the Ladino rarely if ever bothers to estimate as important and hence does not try to understand so that he may penetrate more into the mind and the heart of the Indian.

For the Ladino, no such compensatory or contra-acculturative devices are necessary, since the pattern of avoidance is as much of his making as possible, and thus represents the fulfillment, without undue tension, of his own expectations. Since it has, as a correlate, the deferment of the Indian to him when they do meet and the construction of all situations of joint activity so that the Ladino is superordinate in all, the avoidance pattern, as it operates, is most effective for him.

Equally essential to the continuity of the status quo are some of the activities in which both Ladinos and Indians engage jointly. It will later be seen that by and large these instances of togetherness are confined to situations which demand the interaction of both groups if the desired end is to be achieved. In some instances, this end is the production and distribution of goods and services. In other cases, it is apparent compliance with formal law. In still other instances, it is involvement in institutional activities which serve as drains of tensions generated by the stratified social arrangements. Finally, it is the ordinary routine of life which must unavoidably be performed and in the course of which definable interaction between Indian and Ladino takes place.

Whether by witting device or historical accident or some combination of both, the situations of joint and separate activities for Indians and Ladinos are devised in such a way that they interact where it is needed if the pueblo economy and social order is to continue. And they stay away from each other at just those points where they most desire to be separate from each other. It would seem therefore that over the years of history of the pueblo the people have worked out, unconsciously but efficiently, a system whereby they get done what has to be done to keep them going in the way they consider proper. And, at the principal points of possible tension, they have evolved avoidance mechanisms and compensatory devices which minimize the potentiality of these tensions.

In questions such as these, one sometimes gets involved in trying to decide which is the chicken and which the egg. Was the world outlook of the Indian such that, on confronting the rigors of the Spanish conquest, he was able easily to adapt himself to a subordinate, castelike, exploited situation? Or did those rigors compel this kind of adjustment, forcing a change in the world outlook and the searching for compensatory devices? Apparently something of both situations occurred in the development of the present pattern among the Indians of San Luis. But it is also true that the pattern had to be worked out in such a way as to be sufficiently satisfactory to the Indian for him to be willing to socialize his children in each successive generation into those defined roles which make his present accommodation possible.

We have at the present time, therefore, an adjustment which represents a balance between satisfaction and dissatisfaction, aspiration and achievement, responsibility and reward. The social system can be seen, then, as an equilibrium of these competing tendencies. It is therefore important to describe that equilibrium, to show in what different ways Ladinos and Indians interact in different situations so that the continuity of the society is guaranteed and to point out those weak points in this social chain of recurring events which are most susceptible to wear and rupture. Throughout the previous chapters something of this has been attempted, making it possible now to typologize the situations of avoidance and interaction between the two groups.

By way of a major generalization, we may say that those situations in which Indians and Ladinos jointly participate are characterized by at least one or more of the following conditions:

TENSIONS AND EQUILIBRIA

1. Ladinos and Indians are mutually dependent for the success of the effort about which the situation is constructed.

2. One of the groups needs the other and profits from its participation without the latter incurring any loss or feeling especially "used."

3. Both groups are compelled by a force or custom external to and compulsive upon both of them to participate jointly.

4. The joint participation is unavoidable and of short duration, even though it may be regular in its occurrence.

Characterized primarily by the first condition are the situations of joint economic participation: (a) employer-employee; (b) seller-buyer; (c) landowner-tenant.

The second class of situations includes: (a) the godparental system as initiated and maintained by the Indians; (b) relations between Ladino men and Indian prostitutes.

Characterized by the third condition are those instances of joint participation in (a) Ladino religious affairs; (b) political matters; (c) the educational system.

Included in the fourth class of meetings are those encounters on the highways, the public streets and plazas, and inside the public buildings.

Much descriptive material regarding several of these situations has already been given. This was unavoidable in the presentation of the general round of life of the pueblo, one central feature of which is the division of functions between Ladinos and Indians. It remains, therefore, only to fill in the details of those situations not yet considered at any length. These include (1) the relations between Ladino men and Indian prostitutes; (2) political affairs; (3) some further features of the educational system; and (4) the incidental and accidental public encounters.

1. PROSTITUTION

The relations between Indian prostitutes and Ladino males is not of the formalized commercial character one encounters in urban prostitution. Rather, it is believed, and there is some evidence to support it, that a variety of Indian women, mostly young, can be secured for the proper price. Rumor has it that they are as often married as unmarried. The absence of their husbands from the pueblo during the day while away at their milpas gives them a mobility which makes possible brief and clandestine relationships with Ladino men who are generally in the pueblo the entire day. The standard price of ten cents, which is equivalent to a day's wage, obviously would be an attraction hard to resist so long as the mores also permitted, tacitly sanctioned, or at least did not too strongly frown upon, this kind of interaction.

Apropos of this, the Indian sexual mores would be considered by an American as somewhat "relaxed" by comparison with our own. Illegitimate children, extra-marital unions (primarily for men), and pre-marital experimentation (for both men and women) are all deplored less and apparently occur more commonly than in the United States. This does not, however, take the stigma off prostitution to any greater degree than one finds it removed here. But there is apparently less indignation and moral righteousness expressed at the idea of temporary or semi-enduring extra-marital cohabitation in which the male contributes partly to the support of the female. This extends, within the Ladino community, to those women who have been known to have been or to be the mistresses, part- or full-time, of one or the other men of the community. They are not totally excluded from "society," though, of course, neither do they occupy prominent positions in the community. One may say then that, generally speaking, there is a relatively benign view taken by the culture to the practice of quasi-commercialized sexual cohabitation. The real stigma is stamped only upon those women who engage in this practice as their main livelihood, which, apparently few if any do.

Given this permissiveness of the sub-rosa mores, one of the expectable blockages to the practice is removed. By way of positive inducement for the women, the money obviously plays an important role. For the males, the prostitutes serve on the one hand to reduce those tensions generated by a system of monogamous marriage, and on the other the cultural pressure to demonstrate virility through sexual prowess. Such consequences for the satisfaction of the demand for sexual variety as are present in resorting to prostitutes who are not "really" prostitutes are apparently also attained in this relationship.

Moreover, using Indian women for this purpose allows the Ladino males to pretend to themselves and to others about the greater "decency" and "character" of the Ladino women. No statistics are available concerning the number of Ladino as against Indian women who engage in commercialized sex relationships, so that it is not possible to say whether this practice is disproportionately distributed. One may hazard the guess, however, that since the sexual mores are less prohibitive for the Indians, and the economic situation less fortunate, the likelihood is that Indian women do engage in this practice disproportionately. Statistics are not available, either, concerning the number of Indian men as against Ladino men who resort to these women. But the depressed economic condition of the Indian male, his absence from the pueblo most of the day, and the general pre-marital availability of women on a noncommercial basis—unlike among the Ladinos—would suggest that the Indian man is far less likely to resort to these quasi-prostitutes. In one sense the Indian male is more fortunate in this regard, since one may see the situation as one in which he gets free what the Ladino male has to pay for.

Genuine love relationships of any enduring quality do not ordinarily arise out of these situations. At least, if they do, they are never spoken of, and no one knows about them. What does happen sometimes, however, is that children result from the union of Ladino men and Indian women, and everyone in the pueblo knows of cases where very respectable Ladino gentry contribute partially to the support of such children, especially if the woman remains unmarried. Even where married, the relationship may be "regularized" by the Ladino male acting as godparent for the child and thus bringing within the moretic expectations a defined responsibility which he would otherwise have to ignore or to assume covertly and without official sanction. Some Ladino wives even know about these bastard offspring of their husbands and do not appear to resent the relationship so long as their own welfare is not neglected as a result. Some of the Ladino males are not reluctant, under the proper conditions, to boast of these progeny.

One may say, then, that the principal positive consequence for Indian women is an extra source of income, plus some presumption of special relationship with the male in question. Since, however, this special relationship is not highly culturally estimated, one can scarcely reckon this as a genuine cultural gain for the women. Nor is the relationship considered the essence of rightness. But there are enough satisfactions on both sides of the line for the practice to remain in force and to continue as an example of relations between two groups who otherwise keep their distance.

2. POLITICAL AFFAIRS

Here reference is had to the joint participation of Indians and Ladinos in the political management of the community. Thus, all Indians have voting privileges on an equal basis with Ladinos. And, theoretically, Indians are equally qualified to hold office, as citizens of the Republic, along with Ladinos. Indeed, in previous administrations, and still today in various parts of the country, specific rules command the proportionate representation of Indians in various government offices. Such rules also apply in San Luis, but the manner in which they operate results, in the net, simply in a perpetuation of Ladino power and Indian political subservience. Recent reports indicate that even when political power was genuinely offered to the Indians, they themselves demurred from accepting it on grounds of inadequate preparation. One suspects this as a rationalization to cover the real feeling, bred for so long in the culture, that it is simply dangerously unwise for an Indian to "get out of place." The net result, then, at least as of the time of these studies, may be summarized somewhat as follows:

a. No Indian has an active civil or military position which enables him to give orders to Ladinos. There are a few Indian reserve officers of higher rank than many Ladinos, but they are either confined to inactive status or are given posts where they command only Indian troops.

b. None of the paid offices in the pueblo is at present in the hands of the Indians. Thirty years ago a partly Indian man was mayor of the pueblo. And in relatively recent times two Indians have served short terms as secretary of the pueblo. But it is reported that these two Indian secretaries did not generally give orders to their Ladino subservients and that when they did they were usually not heeded. Such a situation may be contrasted with the present one where the Ladino secretary is able in an indirect manner to order even the mayor.

c. The unpaid political offices involving the greatest nuisance value and most loss of time are uniformly assigned to Indians. The yearly draft of "volunteers" for military training is almost uniformly composed of Indians.

d. In assigning of duties to the higher unpaid officials, the paid officials generally reserve the most arduous and degrading jobs for the Indian employees.

e. Ladino higher officials treat Ladino lower officials with a respect which, even at its minimum, is greater than that shown to any Indian employee. No Indian employees, in effect, are shown any respect. Whatever attempts are made by Indian officials to assert themselves usually end up in trouble for them.

Certain exceptions must again be noted. Indians serving as policemen are sometimes ordered to arrest an erring Ladino. Secondly, Indian officials sometimes issue orders to Ladinos, but in such instances they are acting on direct mandate of the mayor or secretary and never on their own initiative. Indian citizens sometimes effectively cause trouble for a Ladino official by petition to higher officials. Indians have devised many techniques for being conveniently absent when they know they are going to be called on for "voluntary service." Indians lie and cheat for each other when one of them gets into trouble with an official. Most Indians do all they can, when not serving as officials, to hinder the prosecution of the law when it affects someone close to them. When serving as officials, they tend to enforce the law in an apologetic manner when it affects another Indian. In virtue of apparent or real stupidity and ignorance, Indians often break the law and are sometimes not held culpable. These and a host of other small exceptions give less reality to the compulsiveness of the law and serve in part to mitigate the discrimination in positions of prestige and material reward.

Some pretense is made at catering to a vestige of former Indian self-rule. There is an occasional instance when the local Ladino officials call in a committee of Indians to plan, "jointly," a pueblo celebration. In effect, such committees are almost purely rubber-stamp and exercise no power. Whatever Indian self-rule does remain is informal and resides in the willingness of Indians to resort to their own wise old men for arbitrations of disputes and to abide by their decisions.

All but one of the Indians interviewed indicated that they would not serve for the mayor or the commandant or the mailman if they could possibly escape the service. All but one indicated that they disliked the military drills and would stay at home if they possibly could. They further stated that it was the fear of punishment which brought them to military drills (three days at hard work for every drill missed). All but one who were named aldermen said they had tried to get excused from the service but could not. Only one Indian was allowed to escape service as alderman, and he only because he managed to stir up enough trouble with a petition to national officials that the local officials thought it best to let him go free rather than go through the complicated routine of answers to petitions and subsequent investigation.

All Indian roles involve their taking orders and giving none. Yet it is not so much the subordinancy of the role as the loss of time and the general "bother" (*molestia*) involved to which Indians object.

In summary, then, the Indians and Ladinos alike are compelled by the force of law common to both of them to participate jointly in the government of the pueblo. The particular roles they play in this government are determined in large part by Ladino custom, Ladino dominance, Indian fear, and the differences in education, training, and "connections" which in part give rise to and in part sustain the custom, the dominance, the fear and the self-same differences. For there are proportionately fewer Indians than Ladinos who are capable, by criteria of education and training, to handle government jobs. Moreover, there are very few if any Indians who have the "connections" needed to secure government appointments. But there are many Ladinos with such "connections."

These factors account for some of the differences. But there still remains the fact that though there are Ladinos who could take over the more subservient and arduous unpaid roles, these roles are traditionally assigned to the Indians by the Ladinos who have the power to do so. Two factors bear on this: (1) Ladinos feel that only Indians should be assigned such work. This feeling arises from the Ladino conception of the Indian as an uneducated, untrained (and perhaps untrainable), and "uncultured" person. (2) The second factor is twofold: (a) If a Ladino official or unofficial "advisor" attempts to name a Ladino to a post traditionally assigned an Indian, he runs the not insignificant risk of incurring considerable trouble for himself if the Ladino so named should attempt, through his connections, to "correct" the situation. Almost no Ladino, no matter how humble, is without such connections. Almost no Indian has such connections. (b) A Ladino who is named to such a post can almost always appeal to a more powerful local Ladino "protector" to get him out of the situation. Almost no Ladino is without such a protector. Almost no Indian has a protector who will intervene in such matters.

The maintenance of social distance and the general caste relationship is thus evidently present even within this situation of joint participation. We have here, then, another instance where the formal definition calls for relative equality and the informal construction results in marked inequality. The maintenance of political power in the hands of the Ladinos obviously is very functional for the preservation of their social and economic power in general.

3. EDUCATION

The laws of Guatemala provide that all children between the ages of seven and fourteen shall attend school. But the enforcement of this law is at best haphazard. It is therefore not the law but apparently a different compulsion operating with relatively equal force on Indians and Ladinos alike which results in Indian and Ladino children attending school together. This, combined with the fact of the schools not being divided, except by sex, ensures the joint presence of Ladinos and Indians.

This compulsion is upon both Ladinos and Indians to the extent that there is a combination of jointly shared custom and positive evaluation of literacy. A third factor enters, however, which specifically refers only to Ladinos. This is the fact that for most Ladino children, unlike Indian children, there is almost nothing they can do during the school years other than attend school.

Both Ladinos and Indians have the same teachers, curricula, and formal criteria of success and failure. But there are considerable differences in the orientation of the schooling, the adaptability to the curricula, the administration of discipline, and, in some cases, the individual care they receive at the hands of the teachers.

a. Ladino boys are sent to school in the hope they will receive enough education to go on to secondary school, and from there on to lucrative work, preferably with the government. Indian boys, however, are sent to school almost always with the understanding that they will be taken out after a year or two. It is hoped that during this time they will learn enough to read simple words, write their names and simple phrases, and learn how to count in Spanish so as not to be cheated by tradesmen.

Ladino girls are sent to school to get "finished" and to become more eligible marriage partners for educated Ladino boys. Indian girls are sent to school, if at all, to acquire a modicum of literacy, without any reason for acquiring this other than "it's very nice."

b. Most Indian schoolchildren have far greater and more numerous difficulties in school than Ladino children because many of them have to spend one and sometimes two school years simply learning Spanish, a difficulty hardly ever encountered by the Spanish-speaking Ladino children. The fact that no teachers speak the Indian dialect makes this experience, for at least some of the Indian children, not only trying but traumatic. Despite these difficulties, however, it is not too unusual to find Indian schoolchildren at the top of their classes. This may in part be due to the fact that they do not have to unlearn any ungrammatical Spanish. The schoolteachers note that this job of unlearning is a very difficult one for many of the Ladino children.

c. None of the teachers is long on patience and understanding, and the shortness of their tempers appears to find its first outlet on Indian children, who, in their greater difficulties with school work and with understanding anything the teacher says, seems to bring discipline on their heads more often and more harshly than do Ladino children. But only casual observations and the hearsay evidence of Indian children and parents is available to prove these statements.

d. Individual attention by teachers takes the form of grooming students for participation in school dramas and pageants to be given on national holidays and fiesta days. In all the school shows witnessed by the writer, only Ladino children filled the speaking and the leading parts. Indian children were used only for the less prominent and less important roles, involving no speaking. This situation persists even though schoolteachers said, and the final marks conclusively showed, that there were enough bright Indian children to have played at least some of the more prominent roles.

Other differences may be mentioned. There is the fact, for instance, that most Ladino children who attend school have literate parents and siblings to help them with school work, whereas most Indian children do not. There is the further fact that the congeniality of home surroundings for the performance of home study is far greater in most Ladino houses and families than it is in Indian houses. It may further be noted that most Indian children are expected to be busy with chores from the time school lets out to bedtime, whereas most Ladino schoolchildren are allowed leisure for play and study if they wish.

All of these contribute in some measure to differences in the net result of the education of Ladino and Indian children. But there were no means available for measuring the extent of the influences which these factors exerted.

With regard to attitudes toward each other on the part of schoolchildren, there is evidence from observed behavior and hearsay from schoolchildren. It was observed that during recess Ladinos played with Ladinos and Indians with Indians. In the schoolrooms themselves, Indians tended to sit next to and study with fellow Indians, and Ladinos tended likewise to keep to themselves. After school, it was clearly observed that Ladino schoolchildren tended to play together whereas Indian schoolchildren almost immediately made their ways to their separate homes to perform their chores. Talks with a few Indian schoolchildren brought occasional comments to the effect that Ladino schoolchildren tended on occasion to make fun of the more ragged clothing of the Indian schoolchildren and to make fun of them in class for their difficulties with pronunciation of Spanish words.

4. PUBLIC ENCOUNTERS

With the exception of encounters in the park on the evenings of the twice-weekly marimba concerts, accidental meetings between Ladinos and Indians are essentially "touch and go" contacts. There are certain rules of behavior, however, which are known and observed by both Indians and Ladinos in such meetings. The most general rule is that when Indian and Ladino come toward each other on the narrow sidewalks of San Luis, the Indian steps off the sidewalk to allow the Ladino to pass by. Most Ladinos expect this and most Indians observe this. Every time a Ladino encounters an Indian who does not conform there is trouble. This writer never witnessed an incident in which a Ladino stepped aside to let an Indian pass. This applies without any qualifications to encounters between Indian women and Ladino men, Ladino men and Indian men, and Indian men and Ladino women, no matter what the ages of the persons involved.

Similarly, on the highways, where there are usually preferable stretches over which to ride, a mounted Indian is expected to and usually does rein his animal aside to let a mounted Ladino avail himself of the good stretch of the road. No Indian was ever observed to fail to do this, nor was any Ladino ever seen to move aside for an Indian. Again, this applies to both sexes and to people of all ages.

When an Indian encounters a Ladino at the time that both want to enter a store, a house, a government office, or the church, the Indian steps aside to let the Ladino pass. Again, no Indian observed ever failed to do this, no Ladino observed ever moved aside to allow the Indian to pass first.

When an Indian and a Ladino come to a market-place vendor at the same time, the order of priority of Ladino

WHERE THE PEOPLE MEET

over Indian is observed. When an Indian and a Ladino come to the counter of a store for service at the same time, the Indian withdraws to allow the Ladino to be served first. Again, no infractions of this general rule were ever observed.

When an Indian has to pay a brief visit on a Ladino at his house or in his yard, he first asks permission to enter. No Indian I ever observed failed to do this. When a Ladino comes to pay a call on an Indian, he almost never asks permission to enter. Only one Ladino I knew was polite enough to ask permission.

When a Ladino confronts an Indian, the Indian usually takes off his hat when being spoken to. A Ladino never doffs his hat to an Indian. But not all Indians conform. This lack of conformity usually invokes curses and vociferous contumely by the Ladinos about the parents and training of the Indian.

In accidental "touch and go" encounters, Indian men are especially polite to Ladino women. Ladino men make no distinctions in their behavior with Indian women. Indian children show especial respect to their elders, whether Ladino or Indian. Ladino children are generally polite to Ladino elders, and are almost never polite to Indian elders.

Ladinos greet each other with "Hello, friend," or "Good day, sir," or, if there is intimacy between the two, the names of each are mentioned. Indians greet each other in similar respectful fashion. Ladinos do not greet an Indian unless they are greeted first, and their usual acknowledgment is simply a nod of the head to indicate that they have heard the salutation. Indians greet Ladinos with the respectful title of "Don." No Ladinos ever use "Don" to an Indian. The customary form of address, no matter what the age, is by the first or last name of the person, but such familiarity is not born of friendliness or intimacy with the Indians. Ladinos whistle, wave, or shout at an Indian to call him if he is distant and wanted. They frequently shout "Hey, boy!" No Indian was ever observed shouting, whistling, or waving at a Ladino to beckon him. No Indian was ever heard addressing a Ladino without using his or her "proper" title, such as Señor, Don, Señora, or Señorita. In all these situations, the Ladino is decidedly less aware of the presence of the Indian, and the presence itself produces less changes in the behavior of the Ladinos than is the case with the Indian. Indians who can escape direct encounters with the Ladinos on the street, in the plaza, and on the roads, do so. They move off the sidewalk long before it is necessary. They go into Ladino houses as little as possible. Ladinos behave as though the Indian were not present, except on occasion to acknowledge curtly and briefly any salutation they may receive.

It is clear that such different behavior indicates different attitudes of the people toward each other. But it is likewise clear that the definitions of the situations are sufficiently compatible to produce agreement as to what is to be done in the situations.

There remains, finally, the occasions of encounters in the pueblo plaza on marimba concert nights, when there is a rather large gathering of both Indians and Ladinos, and participation by them in the same events. The chief of these events is called "taking a turn" through and around the small park. Ladinos usually walk in mixed couples. Indian pairs usually consist only of young boys, chiefly because no Indian girl who lives in Indian style ever comes to the park on such nights. The observer of this event can note Ladino couples interspersed by pairs of Indian boys, and an occasional pair of Ladinoized Indian housemaids, usually orphaned or disowned. Ladinos and Indians sit around the kiosk side by side. They sit side by side on the outskirts of the park, on the park benches (Indians usually get up to give a Ladino man or woman a seat), and on the church steps. But in these situations of nearness to the Indian, the Ladino behaves as though the Indian did not exist. Indian behavior and conversation, however, is attuned to the Ladino neighbors. And, except for an occasional laughing slur by Ladino spectators cast at a pair of Indian boys who may be putting on airs, the

Indian is ignored by the Ladino. Contrariwise, the Indian who comes up to the plaza on these nights obviously emulates Ladino behavior in as many regards as possible, from the one-cent cigar in the mouth to the bell-bottomed white duck trousers and uncomfortable sandals with heels which Indians put on for such occasions, to be as near to Ladino shoe style as their purses and their customs allow them.

In all of this welter of events on these concert nights, there is only one where Indian and Ladino participate as equals. That is the playing of the marimba. It is not uncommon to find marimba crews composed partly of Indian and partly of Ladino men. Indian marimba players are considered generally better than their Ladino colleagues and there is greater demand for their services than for those of the Ladinos. These joint musical efforts result in the closest semblances to fraternity between Indian and Ladino to appear in all of San Luis life. The situation is perhaps closely analogous to that in which Negro and White musicians here in the United States sometimes team up for an occasional performance, and consideration of skill is the only criterion by which each judges the other during such performances.

It is interesting to note in summary that a basic rationality pervades the social system of San Luis, permitting the performance of those functions indispensable to the continuity of the status quo, no matter how nonrational the stratification of responsibility and reward may be. As in any continuing society, the larger number of people, if unorganized, and if limited in their conceptions of alternatives by ignorance and the security of the traditional, tend to evolve adequate rationalizations for their situation, no matter how unfortunate and deprived they may seem to the outsider.

One may perhaps speak here of the concept of the tolerance level of cultures. In our own expectations, the Indians of San Luis live in a way that we would tend to consider as deplorable in the extreme and calling for immediate revision. But a tolerance level has been culturally devised which permits these humans to "take" much more than we here customarily expect people will take without "kicking back." A set of values and beliefs has been fitted into the situation so that the Indians do not consider themselves particularly unfortunate. Indeed, in some regards, they tend to view their Ladino masters as more unfortunate than they because of the obvious dissatisfactions which the Ladinos manifest.

CHAPTER 14

WHERE THE PEOPLE STAY APART

IN CONTRAST with the situations of joint participation are those in which, by mutual consent, or by reason of the deliberate avoidance by one of the groups, the groups stay apart as much as possible. These are instances in which the groups are not compelled by any external force or custom; they do not mutually depend on each other for the success of the enterprises; the meetings are not unavoidable, and they would not involve mutual profit if jointly engaged in. Indeed, the likelihood is that joint participation would be found vexing and unpleasant by most concerned.

It may therefore be inferred that Indians and Ladinos avoid each other wherever possible to the degree possible, without implying thereby that this avoidance is mutually desired in the same degree by all members of both groups. The general round of situations to which this description applies includes: (1) housing location; (2) funerals; (3) street-corner gatherings; (4) recreation and leisure; (5) school functions; (6) local and national public celebrations; (7) social visiting and friendship units; (8) exchanges of meals, attendance at weddings, baptisms, and wakes; (9) private social affairs; (10) Indian religious affairs; (11) intermarriage.

Some principles appear to run through a number of these situations. Thus, for instance, it can be said that at least as far as some of them are concerned, joint participation in these circumstances by Ladino and Indian would express genuine sharing of mutually felt loyalties, respect, and cultural ties. At least some of them allow for the maximum of informal construction of relationships within only loosely formal definitions. Joining together in such occasions as weddings and wakes, and eating together and intermarrying tend clearly to imply intimate mutual commitments on the parts of those concerned. Generally, one finds such commitments willingly expressed only where there are a number of felt bonds of common tradition, loyalty, and mutual respect. It is well known that where these latter are absent, the social situations of mating, eating, friendship, and the like are filled with social uneasiness and anxiety.

Similarly, in situations which permit a maximum of latitude in informal construction, rather than being sharply defined beforehand, the assumption of equality or near equality of the participants is implied. It may be said, indeed, that such social situations are not ordinarily left open for informal construction when it is known beforehand that the participants are not mutually considered socially equal. In the San Luis case, for instance, when there are Ladino godparents present at the baptism of an Indian child, the principles of social priority which operate in the more well-defined areas of interaction are carried over into what would otherwise be a loosely constructed instance, so that when the time comes for serving food, Ladino men are served first, then Ladino women, then Indian men, and then Indian women. Indians and Ladinos do not eat at the same table or at the same time in this approach to an intimate situation.

It is important to note that situations which one can describe as subject to spontaneous construction, as far as the interaction of the parties is concerned, cannot at the time be situations where people know what "their place" is and feel they must keep it. However, this is an ideal distinction and not one which is ever totally actualized. For there are no culturally defined and sanctioned situations which are left totally open for spontaneous construction in any society, nor any which are totally closed and completely defined beforehand. At best, societies vary in their culture patterns from extremely loosely defined to very rigidly defined situations. In short, some chance element is always present in human interaction, no matter how many rules hedge it in, and, conversely, some rules are always present, no matter how loose the construction.

These remarks are relevant to the following qualifications concerning the situations in which Indians and Ladinos tend to stay apart: (1) In none of them is there one hundred per cent uniformity of behavior. Thus, it is not possible to say that Indians never eat with Ladinos or never intermarry with them. The generalizations concerning avoidance in these and other matters refer to the predominant tendencies. They are the cultural norms, to which, as in all societies, one finds exceptions. The exceptions do not contradict the rules of normative behavior. Rather are they instances which, when understood, help clarify the imperfection which is ever present in the normative structure of any society. (2) It is impossible from the available data to state precisely the number or percentage of occasions on which there are definite violations of the normative expectations. The evidence that one mode is the normative and the other the deviant has been gathered from as many sources as possible, including questionnaires, direct observation of overt behavior, informal conversations, participant observation, and various combinations of these techniques as are used by most investigating sociologists when studying the life of a community. It is here felt that the evidence is sufficiently conclusive to remove any reasonable doubt as to which is expectable and which deviant in this culture. (3) Since much of the material on avoidance pattern comes from questionnaires, and since the questionnaires were administered to approximately seventy people, it was clearly impossible to check at all times, with all interviewees, to see the extent to which their actual behavior did conform with their verbal assurances. At the same time, one feels secure regarding such questionnaire material when all other facets and facts of the culture fall in line with it, and when no good reason is thrown up by other materials to doubt it.

1. HOUSING LOCATION

A pervasive idea throughout many human groups is that one should live in the neighborhood of one's social equals, for communities tend to define one's social position by one's ecological location. San Luis is no exception to these rules of position. It was earlier noted, in this regard, that the frequency of Ladino houses decreases from the plaza outward to the edges of the pueblo, while just the reverse situation characterizes the Indians. It is reasonable therefore to envision the pueblo as consisting of a central core of Ladino dwellings surrounded by Indian dwellings.

It was also stated earlier that one finds the best houses in the center of town with their quality deteriorating as one moves to the outer edges. This conforms with the earlier material on the higher economic status of the Ladino. Housing location and quality thus become part of the prevailing definitions concerning rank and prestige. Since the pattern works out so that one can identify Indian sections from Ladino sections of the pueblo, questions of dubious parentage or group membership of an individual tend to be settled at least partly in terms of where the individual lives.

This pattern of ecological segregation tends to be self-perpetuating, since the Ladinos try to locate in the Ladino section when they construct new houses, and the Indians generally build near their families when the occasion arises. Moreover, since the segregation reduces the frequency of contact and the visibility of actions, and since these are mutually desired by both groups, there is no concerted effort whatsoever to alter this pattern in any way. Whatever stereotypes the Ladinos have regarding the "dirty shacks" of the Indians and their own "very pretty and commodious" dwellings are thus given credence by the actual facts one can observe as one walks about town. Thus, when the writer rented a subsidiary dwelling in the Indian section of town for purposes of interviewing Indians where they would feel more comfortable, he was asked by some of the Ladinos why he chose a place among the Indians instead of coming to live among "decent" people.

WHERE THE PEOPLE STAY APART

2. FUNERALS

Though the fact of death and the holding of wakes and memorial services sometimes bring the Indians and Ladinos together in one social situation, they appear to keep distant from each other in the funerals each holds for its dead. In the numerous funerals this writer witnessed during some nine months in the pueblo, there was never a Ladino in the funeral march for an Indian or an Indian in the funeral march for a Ladino. It seems noteworthy that this applies as well to Ladinos who professed to be friends of Indians who died, and to Indians who professed to be friends of Ladinos who died. Several extenuating factors must be noted: (a) There is general reluctance to attend any funeral, for fear of contracting "hijillo," an illness which is believed to emanate from the dead. (b) Not all the Ladinos one would have expected to be in attendance at certain Ladino funerals were present at those funerals. Nor were all the Indians present whom one would have expected to be in attendance at certain Indian funerals.

3. STREET-CORNER GATHERINGS

Gatherings about street corners occur most frequently in the evenings, during the daily noon hour, and on Sundays. The number and not only the percentage of Ladinos who come out in the evenings for idle banter is greater than the number of Indians who sally out. In all the street-corner gatherings witnessed, not one was ever a genuine mixture of Indians and Ladinos. Indians could be seen on the fringes of Ladino gatherings, hovering in the shadows, perhaps so as not to be conspicuous, but never joining in the circle.

In the afternoons, during the midday siesta hours, street-corner gatherings again are mainly Ladino, with few Indians about. Most Indians are at work, while most Ladinos are in the pueblo during these hours. The pattern of the structure of these gatherings is more apparent in the daytime. Again Ladinos form the nuclei of such gatherings, and even more definitely perhaps than in the evenings, Indians stay near enough to hear the chatter but far enough distant, apparently, so that it is clear they are not attempting to join the circle. If the gathering is in the cool interior of a store, Indians cling in the doorways, while the Ladinos cluster about the counter or on a bench. If the gathering is in the park, in the shade of a tree, Indians occupy places within earshot, and obviously follow the conversations of the Ladinos, but maintain a decided distance. If the gathering is at the city hall, Indians form an outer fringe about the Ladino nucleus, again following their conversation, but again not attempting to join in.

All that has been said above applies with even greater force to street-corner gatherings on Sundays, when there are many Indians circulating in public. Here the tendencies toward separatism are even more apparent, for here one notices Indians forming their own groups, as much as being fringes of Ladino groups.

This writer never witnessed any Indian gatherings formed around a Ladino or Ladinos. On the contrary, the passage of a Ladino tended in each instance noticed to bring about a silencing of the chatter that had been going on previously. Ladinos do not, however, stop chattering because of the presence of Indians.

Further, no prolonged gathering of Indians and Ladinos mixing in common was ever seen. Nor did the writer ever see any Indian attempt to join a Ladino circle, so that it is not possible to say whether an Indian would be rebuffed if he did.

It is at such street-corner gatherings that the most informal and amiable chatter is bantered about among the Ladinos. It is reasonable to infer, from the writer's own experience at these gatherings that bonds of intimacy and friendship are solidified at such gatherings, bonds to which the nonparticipant Indian is never a partner.

4. RECREATION AND LEISURE

Organized play and recreation are foreign to the culture

pattern of the Indians, but intrinsic to that of the Ladinos. Perhaps the principal reason is that Indians have no definite concept of leisure, their world being made up almost totally of work and rest periods, whereas Ladino culture strongly emphasizes the concept of leisure. Within these limits, however, there are enough situations in which Indians are available, eligible, willing, and able to play at the same time as and with the Ladinos, so that one may judge from their failure to do so that a clear pattern of avoidance exists.

These facts stand out: (a) All organized athletic deputations from the pueblo consist solely of Ladinos. (b) All organized games of soccer and basketball, the two principal group sports, are played only by Ladinos. (c) Organized parties, for swimming, fishing, picnics, horseback riding, and hunting, are made up either only of Ladinos or only of Indians. The incidence of the former is much greater. Indian indulgence in these things is usually solitary or, at best, consists of two people.

Some Indian boys know how to play soccer and some Indian girls know how to play basketball and, presumably if given the chance, could develop skills adequate to team playing, if in fact they do not already have them. A number of factors work against their getting this opportunity: (a) Ladino denial of the chance; (b) the culturally natural shyness of the Indian children; (c) the greater demand on the time of the Indian boys and girls for chores about their house; (d) the pressure by Indian parents to keep their children out of association with Ladino children.

This pattern is repeated on the adult level. The best example is seen in the pool parlor, where there is a tendency for Ladinos from various classes to mix with each other, but never to play with Indians. Of course, the cost of playing pool and the usual money stakes are prohibitive for many of the Indians. But some of the younger Indians do have ready cash, hang around the pool parlor, watch the games, toy with the cues and balls when no game is in motion, but never play at the tables. It is not possible to say, however, whether they would really like to play at the game, and, if they did, whether the Ladinos would refuse to play with them. The evidence suggests that refusal would be forthcoming, if and when any Indian was bold enough to make the suggestion.

All other things aside, one can see how this separatism in recreational and leisure-time pursuits helps integrate the total pattern of avoidance. Out of shared play and leisure, with the pleasure involved, a type of camaraderie tends to be developed which is unique to these activities. It is a kind of camaraderie, especially among young people, which is one of the principal ingredients of the social cement binding them together. Here, again, at a critical point in the socialization of the two groups, the pattern of avoidance and separation is strongly reinforced.

5. SCHOOL FUNCTIONS

Such functions are not frequently held in San Luis. They occur at the end of the school year and only a few times during the year. Theoretically the public is invited to all of them, with special invitations issued to the parents of schoolchildren. There were no Indians present in the audience at any of the functions attended by the writer. No Indian children participated in the school dramas or plays, whether they were ordinary school plays or special dramas worked up for national holiday celebrations. It is clear that there were not a few Indian children who could have taken some of the parts. It is not known whether any wanted to, or whether they were asked and refused. At commencement exercises, there were Indian children present to receive their reports, but there were no Indian parents. Most of the parents of the Ladino children were present.

6. LOCAL AND NATIONAL PUBLIC CELEBRATIONS

In these celebrations, the most spectacular of which is the national Day of Independence, some Indians and Ladinos jointly participate in some aspects of the affairs. On

WHERE THE PEOPLE STAY APART

Independence Day there is usually a march with a military band around the plaza. Most of the musicians are Indians. The Indian aldermen (regidores municipales) take part in the rededication of the pueblo to the principles of Guatemalan liberty and to the reaffirmation of the loyalty of the pueblo to the president, evinced by a document signed by all the paid officials and all the municipal aldermen. But aside from the Indian aldermen, there is little active interest shown by the rest of the Indians. The major constituency of the parade is Ladino, and the major portion of the audience at the actual ceremonies, whatever they are, is Ladino. There appears to be an identification of the Ladino people with the pueblo as a patriotic unit. There is nothing to keep an Indian from joining in the celebration, should he so desire. After such patriotic demonstrations, there is usually a dance in the public market place or in the school hall. The nuclei of participants at these affairs are all Ladinos. There is some tendency toward class lines being drawn at these events, because usually "presentable clothing" is expected. A good many Ladinos are no doubt excluded by this implicit rule. But lower-class Ladinos were observed joining in more closely than any Indians ever did. If the dance is in the market place, Indians usually hover around the railing and watch; or, if the dance is at night, Indians can be seen dancing, boy with boy, in the shadows nearby, on the steps of the church. If the celebration is in the school hall, Indians hover around the doorway or can be seen dancing with each other near the open windows.

7. SOCIAL VISITING AND FRIENDSHIP UNITS

Informal social visiting occurs often and regularly in San Luis. It is among the favorite recreational pursuits, and is open to rich and poor alike. Unlike formal social visiting, which is rare, there is no previous announcement of the intended visit, and there are no expectancies of food being served, unless the visit occurs at mealtimes. Formal visiting occurs only on special occasions, such as a family celebration or a simple, planned social reunion. On such occasions, the time and hour are set, and food and sometimes entertainment are provided.

The figures on the social visiting practices of the twenty-two Ladinos and forty-nine Indians interviewed are as follows:

TABLE 15

Pays visits	Ladinos	Indians
To family	18	43
To Indians	10	41
To Ladinos	19	19
To no one	2	2
Is paid visits		
By family	17	43
By Indians	12	39
By Ladinos	19	16
By no one	3	4

These figures are summaries of answers from the informants. But if by social visit there is meant a visit of some duration, of some intimacy, and of a nonutilitarian (i.e., not for business reasons) nature, there is considerable question as to the extent to which the figures accurately reflect the situation of intimate social visiting in San Luis. A distinction which was learned too late to be of value in interviewing was one between a business visit (*visita*) and a friendly social visit (*visita solamente para chansear*). The latter are the kind of visits which Indians make on Sunday to their friends and which Ladinos interchange with each other, but which apparently rarely occur between Indian and Ladino. The writer never saw or heard of any such social visits between Indians and Ladinos except between a few Indians and Ladinos living on the outskirts of the pueblo.

If it may be assumed that social visiting is confined to friends with whom one can exchange intimacies, then, from the figures on friendship groups, it would seem that the figures on visiting given above do not accurately reflect the limitations on that practice in the pueblo, at least so far as Ladino-Indian visits are concerned.

Those data on friendship may be summarized as follows: The Indians and Ladinos were asked to name their five best friends. If, in so doing, they named people only from their own group (i.e., either Ladino or Indian), they were then asked whether they had any friends in the other group. The writer knew beforehand that a distinction is made in San Luis between three types of friends, or "amigos": (a) *amigos de confianza,* or friends of confidence, who, most generally, are people to whom one can tell secrets, and of whom one can ask a favor; (b) *amigos de lejos,* or secondary friends, or people with whom one is generally friendly, greets when he meets them on the street, and with whom he has had generally amiable relations; (c) *amigos conocidos* or acquaintances. It is "friends of confidence" on whom personal calls of a social nature are generally paid in San Luis. The question about friends asked specifically for "friends of confidence" in each instance.

The Ladinos reported as follows:
1. None cited any Indians among his best friends. However, only 11 could cite 5 friends at all.
2. Three cited 4 friends, 1 cited 3, 2 cited 1, 3 said they had no friends. One said he had many friends *de confianza* and they were all Ladino. Data on one were not obtained.
3. On being asked if they had any Indian friends, 4 Ladinos cited 3 Indian friends each, and 1 cited 2; 4 of these 5 who had Indian friends also had cited 5 Ladino friends each, and the other had cited 4.

The Indians reported as follows:
1. 36 cited only Indians among their 5 best friends; 22 of these said they had no Ladino friends *de confianza.*
2. Of the other 14 of those 36: 7 cited 5 Ladino friends, 1 cited 4, 2 cited 3, 1 cited 2, and 3 cited 1.
3. 13 cited Ladinos among their best friends. Of these 3 cited all Ladinos; 2 cited 1 Ladino, 4 Indians; 1

TENSIONS AND EQUILIBRIA

cited 2 Ladinos and 3 Indians; 4 cited 3 Ladinos and 2 Indians; 2 cited 3 Ladinos and 1 Indian; and 1 cited 2 Ladinos and 1 Indian.

Several net impressions arise from these figures on friendship and visiting. The first is the persistence of separateness between Indian and Ladino in these matters. The second is that there is decided asymmetry in the way the Indians and Ladinos view each other. Indians count among their best friends certain Ladinos who never think of those Indians in such terms. Likewise, Indians cite many Ladinos as secondary friends (*amigos de lejos*), whereas but few Ladinos cite any Indians in these terms. There is much less of this asymmetry in the intra-group friends cited by both groups.

Comparing intra-group with inter-group visiting, the tendency toward separatism becomes more adequately documented. For we find that Ladinos tend to visit Ladinos and Indians tend to visit Indians far more than they tend to exchange visits with each other. Of course, some of the same objections raised to the validity of the inter-group visiting apply to the intra-group figures. But from the friendship figures it would appear that the distortion in the latter is far smaller than in the former.

Still another consideration is involved here. It is quite likely that Indians interpret as social visits certain brief visits from Ladinos whose chief objects are utilitarian but who pause, in the process, to exchange a friendly word or two, and that Ladinos do likewise with such brief visits from Indians. The writer has no doubt but that most of the inter-group visits cited by both groups were of this nature. And, in conformity with expectations, there was a greater percentage of these visits from Ladinos to Indians than from Indians to Ladinos. The "superior" social status of the Ladino, and his role as employer with work to be done, would lead to the expectation that he would feel free to drop in on the Indian more than the Indian in turn would feel free to drop in on him. The writer has witnessed many such visits. He was never witness to any social visit between Indians and Ladinos of anywhere near the same intimacy and duration as those which he witnessed between Ladino and Ladino and Indian and Indian. This is not to say, however, that such visits do not occur. But it is offered by way of some doubt that any regular inter-group social visiting does transpire. The fact that in no other realm of "social" activity is there manifested any inter-group intimacy or friendship of the same quality as that very much visible in intra-group relations would tend to document the impressions noted above.

8. EXCHANGES OF MEALS, ATTENDANCE AT WEDDINGS, BAPTISMS, AND WAKES

The tendencies toward separatism between Indians and Ladinos on occasions when joint participation involves intimacy and friendship can be seen rather clearly in the figures on exchanges of meals and attendance at weddings, baptisms, and wakes.

Before presenting those figures, certain qualifications must be introduced. (a) The writer has never seen an Indian eating at the same table with a Ladino, nor was he ever able to secure any adequate documentation of any such occurrence in San Luis. Where the figures show that an Indian or Ladino had been invited by or had invited a member of the other group to eat at his house, all other evidence points to the fact that these were not social occasions, and that the Indian did not eat at the same table with the Ladino, but rather these were occasions which called for food being offered, and food was offered, and accepted, but eaten apart from the member of the other group.

With respect to the figures on baptisms and weddings, it will be noted that there is a much greater percentage of Ladinos who have attended Indian affairs than Indians who have attended Ladino affairs. This is in conformity with the expectation, for it has already been noted that Indians ask Ladinos to serve as godparents for their children but Ladinos never ask Indians.

TENSIONS AND EQUILIBRIA

With respect to the figures on wakes, it will be noted that there is more exchange of visits on this count than on any other of the three. The qualifications noted in the earlier part of this chapter, to the effect that on occasions involving crises and deaths there is a tendency for the social barriers to be lifted, apply here.

TABLE 16

MEALS

Invites	Ladinos	Indians
Family	12	34
Indians	3	35
Ladinos	11	12
No one	10	13
Is invited by		
Family	17	36
Indians	8	35
Ladinos	16	8
No one	3	8

TABLE 17

BAPTISMS

Has been to	Ladinos	Indians
Family	14	15
Indians	10	19
Ladinos	15	1
None	4	28
Will, would, or has invited		
Family	11	35
Indians	4	35
Ladinos	12	19
No one	7	10

TABLE 18

WAKES

Has been to	Ladinos	Indians
Family	15	41
Indians	6	39
Ladinos	13	12
None	2	4

Will, would, or has invited

Family	9	35
Indians	4	30
Ladinos	9	6
No one	3	8

The figures on wakes must also be interpreted in light of the fact that usually invitations are neither expected nor given. Anyone may attend who wishes, and all who arrive are received. It is interesting in this light to note that tendencies toward separatism are still very marked. Ladinos attended many more Ladino than Indian wakes, and Indians, likewise, attended many more Indian than Ladino wakes. In view of the fact that wakes are "open affairs," special significance may be attributed to the figures. What they seem to point up is simply the fact that Ladinos mix with Ladinos far more than they mix with Indians, and Indians mix with Indians far more than they do with Ladinos, even when there are no formal barriers to free intercourse between the two groups.

The figures on baptisms reveal the same separatist tendencies. Ladinos attend more of their own group baptisms than those of the Indians, even though they are often called upon to serve as godparents for Indians or are invited by Ladino godparents to be their guests. The very large discrepancy between Indian attendance at Ladino baptisms and Ladino attendance at Indian baptisms should also be noted. Lastly, such separatist tendencies are clearly visible in comparing the figures on whom the Ladinos have, would, or will invite with the comparable figures for the Indians.

In the figures for attendance at weddings, the persistence of these tendencies is clearly to be noted. But again the qualification urged upon the figures for baptisms applies here: namely, that Ladinos attend Indian weddings as godparents for Indian couples or as guests of the Ladino godparents, whereas it is the rare Indian who attends a Ladino wedding in any capacity other than that of house help.

TENSIONS AND EQUILIBRIA
TABLE 19
WEDDINGS

Has been to	Ladino	Indian
Family	19	39
Indian	13	35
Ladino	19	1
None	3	7
Will, would or has invited		
Family	17	44
Indian	4	42
Ladino	17	15
No one	5	4

Note that (a) a far greater percentage of Ladinos attended Indian weddings than the comparable percentage for Indians; (b) far more Ladinos have attended Indian weddings than would invite Indians to theirs; (c) Ladinos would invite many more Ladinos than they would Indians; (d) the same applies, but with less force, to the Indian figures. It is not rare, however, that Indians are present at Ladino weddings. But they serve as house help, sometimes by special request of the Ladino family holding the wedding, with whom they have been generally friendly.

The chief wedding of the entire social year which this writer witnessed was that of the daughter of one of the five most prominent Ladinos in the pueblo to the son of a merchant from nearby Ipala. The father of the girl had the reputation with almost all of the Indians of being one of the very few Ladinos to whom one could go in an emergency and be sure of sympathetic attention. Some Indians cited this man as one among their best friends. Yet, at the wedding, not one Indian was present in any capacity other than house help. A good many Indians stayed at the doors to the house, peering in much of the day. Among them were some of the Indians who had cited this man as being one of their best friends. None of these Indians was asked to come in. Many Ladinos who had not been invited (some of whom were no better-dressed than some of the Indians who peered in at the doors) were invited in when they were noticed standing around at the entrances to the house. Some Ladinos voluntarily joined in the wedding procession to the office of the justice of the peace and back to the house without having been invited. No Indians did this.

This writer also witnessed two Indian wedding celebrations at which Ladinos tried to come in without being invited, and were effectively asked to leave. The comments of the Ladinos on these occasions indicated that they were not accustomed to being refused by such occasions, and, above all, not by Indians.

No weddings of Indians with Ladino marriage sponsors occurred during the time of this writer's stay in the pueblo. Hence, no reports from personal experience can be given.

In summary, it may be indicated that no data are available on how many Indians would attend Ladino affairs, if invited, nor whether any of the Indians had ever been invited and refused. Lastly, no data are available on how many Ladinos had received invitations to Indian affairs and refrained from going. Ladinos who had been asked to attend Indian weddings indicated they had been asked by Ladino sponsors of the wedding couple. None had been directly asked by the Indians concerned. Apparently none had refused because of any lack of desire to be present at an Indian wedding. Some had refused because they had other things to do. But they had sent gifts of food to the Ladino sponsors.

9. PRIVATE SOCIAL AFFAIRS

In the affairs which are strictly private, there is a similar separation of Ladino from Indian, whether the affair be Ladino or Indian. But noncommemorative social gatherings, parties, and private dances are held often by Ladinos and only rarely by Indians. Such social gatherings are mainly upper-class Ladino in constituency, but an occasional middle- or lower-class Ladino family itself holds or participates in one. No exact figures are obtainable. But judging from the affairs witnessed, it may be asserted that strict separation of Ladino from Indian is practiced. Likewise, at the few Indian gatherings witnessed, the same separation of Ladino from Indian held true.

10. INDIAN RELIGIOUS AFFAIRS

The tendency for Ladinos to remain uninterested and nonparticipating in Indian religious affairs has already been noted. It has likewise been noted that an occasional Ladino does come to a cofradia reunion, but usually only out of curiosity. It seems important to stress the absence of Ladinos from these reunions, because they represent for Indians the peak of expression of Indian communal life, attenuated though that indigenous communal feeling may be. The reunions usually last all night, with music from the *chirimia* being played at regular intervals. There is food served close to midnight. Religious leaders get up from their places at different times to offer a prayer to the saint being adored. There is a constant coming and going of Indian men of all ages. Indian women are forbidden to enter the cofradia house, though they remain at hand, cooking food or doing such women's work as is necessary to the maintenance of the reunion. Young Indian boys do any other errand work necessary. The prevailing tone appeared to the writer to be one of general ennui and fatigue. But every Indian asked declared that it was *muy alegre* ("very joyful") at the reunions. With very few exceptions, most Indian men go to such reunions at least several times during the year, and those who are members spend several days during each month performing necessary missions preparatory to the convocation of the reunion.

When Ladinos do enter, there is no reorganization of seating, nor any concrete manifestations that the presence of Ladinos has been noted. This is contrary to behavior in every other situation of relationship between Indian and Ladino which was witnessed by the writer. For at all such other times there is a marked change in behavior of the Indian from the time when alone or with other Indians to the time when he is in relationship or even in the company of a Ladino. Thus, of all the situations of relationship between Indian and Ladino, that which occurs at the cofradia reunions is perhaps the only one whose tone and content is set by the Indian, and to which the Ladino in part conforms.

11. INTERMARRIAGE

The extent of genuine concord between peoples in day-by-day contact may perhaps best be measured by the extent to which they intermarry and the way they assign status to and behave toward these couples and their children. In light of this, the figures on intermarriages between Indians and Ladinos and their attitudes toward such marriages are enlightening.

In the pueblo of San Luis, there are no cases at present, and in the memories of the present inhabitants there never has been a case, of formalized marriage between Ladino and Indian. Various people report they know mixed couples living together at the edges of the pueblo, but when they are asked to identify them it turns out that they "had heard from someone else that Fulano de Tal was living with Fulana de Tal," but that they themselves did not know of any case personally. When the secondary informants are checked, it turns out that they, likewise, do not personally know of any such cases.

All attempts to locate such mixed couples living together failed. No one could produce any convincing evidence that any such couple was then living together or had lived together.

Apparently, the most sustained connubial mixed relationship in the known history of the pueblo was the joining of a young Indian man with the most disreputable Ladino prostitute in town for a period of several years (1940-1942), during which time they frequently separated for periods of several months, but during which total period they also had two children, the birth of the older of which was the occasion for them starting to live together. That relationship ultimately resulted in open dispute between the two; a jail sentence for both as a result; a period of one month of living together without talking to each other after the period in jail, they having been ordered to live together by the jefe politico; and, finally, the desertion of the man by the woman, with the man dying some four months later. The woman moved to a different pueblo about a month prior to the death of the Indian man.

Their living together and their difficulties were the major topics of pueblo gossip for several months, with daily gossip bulletins issuing from people sympathetic to each of them. In none of that gossip to which this writer was witness was there any mention of any similar case. Direct questioning failed to reveal any other case where an Indian, known as an Indian, and living as an Indian, had cohabited with a person known as a Ladino, accepted by the Ladinos as a Ladino, and living as a Ladino.

CHAPTER 15

INTRA-GROUP STRATIFICATION

THROUGHOUT the foregoing materials we have described the behavior of Indians and Ladinos as though each of these groups had one uniform pattern of behavior. For the purposes of the report up to this point, such an assumption has been both necessary and justifiable. The materials presented were not significantly distorted, and it was possible, in assuming this homogeneity, to explore some of the most significant aspects of behavior one sees in the pueblo.

The question now arises as to whether additional refinement in description can be made by paying attention to such intra-group differences as may be found to exist. In concrete terms, do Ladinos and Indians distinguish among themselves the "better" from the "worse" members of the group? Are there observable hierarchies of prestige and power? What are the criteria employed for establishing such rankings? What are the consequences of occupying various positions on these social ladders?

Briefly put, both Ladinos and Indians make sharp distinctions among themselves of the more worthy from the less worthy people, but the criteria each group employs are markedly different. Moreover, each group focuses its rankings on its own members, sharply excluding members of the other group from consideration. No Ladino, for instance, no matter how humble or denigrated his position, is ever considered by the other Ladinos socially equal to or below any Indian. Put conversely, no Indian is ever considered by Ladinos the social equal or superior of any Ladino, no matter how many of the criteria of distinction he may possess.

Similarly, when Indians think and act in terms of more and less worthy ratings, they think almost exclusively of other Indians. The main difference is that the Indians exclude Ladinos because they feel them to be a very different kind of people, whereas Ladinos exclude Indians from their social ladders because they think them both different and inferior. In the next chapter, the details of these reciprocal group images will be presented. For the present, it is enough to indicate that the sharp caste line which operates in all other facets of the pueblo life also functions to maintain a dual hierarchy of ratings and two sets of relatively incompatible criteria on which these ratings are based.

It should be remembered, however, that this separation of hierarchies and criteria does not mean that no Indian possesses qualifications which the Ladinos value or that no Ladino possesses qualifications which the Indians consider worthy. The important thing is that in spite of the overlapping, each group does exclude the other from its own hierarchy. This testifies importantly to the basic significance of the caste demarcation, above all other distinctions which operate.

LADINO SOCIAL HIERARCHIES

Living for some time among the Ladinos, one notes considerable agreement as to who are the most important and powerful people in the pueblo. This holds true though there are bitter family feuds of long duration among some of those who are ranked highly. In spite of their dislike for each other, they tend to agree that their enemies are important people. As one watches the careers of these highly rated people, one notes that they are among the wealthiest people in town; that they give the biggest and most admired parties; that they own the most land; that they are the elite among whom political power circulates, each caucus or party taking its turn, depending only on the regime in power at the moment. One also notes that their children get the most formal education; their wives are the best-dressed; their houses the most sumptuous; their claims to reputable family lines the best-established; their intimations of important connections with social life in Guatemala City the most frequently heard and widely accepted;

and that each tends to control, singly or in collaboration with others of their friends, the respect, admiration, and political subservience of estimable blocs of Indians and lesser-ranked Ladinos.

The kinds of things just listed can be considered as both criteria of ranking and the consequences of being ranked highly. Certainly there is a mutual reciprocity of cause and effect in such matters. At any given moment, however, two criteria above all tend to predominate, in the sense that they are considered by others as the most important single items and that objectively they are matrix criteria from which the others tend to diffuse. These are (1) family name or reputation, and (2) economic position.

The various dimensions of family reputation have already been specified. It need only be remarked, by way of refresher, that these include its antiquity, ubiquity, and public-mindedness.

Economic position, as a criterion of social rank, is somewhat harder to clarify. But as a minimum, it includes occupation, or source of income, and the amount of income.

If it is occupation which is being ranked, one can abstract from the occupations of the most prestigeful people the following elements: cleanliness of work, skill, lucrativeness, professionalization, and freedom from specified routine. But it is not possible to rank these in any consistent order, since the people themselves do not single any out for special attention, nor do they consider them in terms of which are most important. Thus, it is not enough that a man is wealthy. He must acquire his wealth either from family income which is inherited, or from a skilled job of a semiprofessional or professional nature. Nor is it enough, either, that a man has a profession as his occupation. It must be somewhat lucrative and give him command over leisure time. Nor is it enough that a man has a job which is lucrative and professional in character. It must also have been achieved by an educational route which is prestigeful for what it implies concerning one's father's job and social standing.

Some examples from the ranks of the prestigeful people will help clarify this issue. The occupations of five of the ten most highly ranked people were (1) druggist and "empirical-doctor" (two years of medical school); (2) landowner; (3) doctor; (4) landowner and trader; (5) director of the mails and communications. Each of these five men owned plots of land which, relative to local conditions, were considered substantial. Each employed Indian and/or Ladino day laborers to work their lands for them on a tenant, sharecropping, or straight wage basis. Each engaged in trading crops from his land. Each was married to a woman whose family carried prestige. Each was relatively wealthy, by local standards, though the differences in property among some of them were as large as between them and others not rated nearly so highly. Each had served one or more terms in a variety of nonpaying public offices. And, in various degrees, each commanded a considerable body of Indian and Ladino partisans who thought they were the "best" people in town.

Each of these five would agree that the other four deserved to be rated highly, though perhaps not so highly as the individual himself would insist he merited. Yet, among them there were a number of distinct feuds, so that several of them would not speak to each other, or formally visit each other, or more than casually acknowledge the presence of each other in a room or public gathering.

None of them could claim he enjoyed a uniform rating from all people. In the ratings which various partisans assigned, the professional work of the doctor and the druggist would be singled out. Even here, however, since the druggist and the doctor were not on good terms, the partisans of the doctor would tend to sneer at the so-called medical work of the druggist, and the partisans of the druggist would deprecate the age and feebleness of the doctor and his old-fashioned methods of cure. The druggist in turn tended to deprecate the landowner, claiming that everything he owned he got from his wife's family, while the latter in turn claimed that the druggist had gotten his money and position dishonestly, through a long history of chicanery and swindling in combination with autocratic political pressures. At various times, several of these five would deprecate the office of the director of mails and communications, pointing out he was nothing much more than a postal clerk and telegraph operator. He in turn would emphasize the honesty of his work by comparison with the unproductive idleness of the so-called work of the landowners and traders.

These examples could be multiplied many times over, but the resulting picture remains the same: namely, that in spite of many local disagreements about the particular importance of particular aspects of a man's work and life, there are generalized criteria of rank which prevail, by token of which the highest prestige is assigned to individuals on the basis of some combination of occupation, wealth, and family reputation. These criteria are sufficiently objectively compelling so that even worst enemies agree about each other's generalized social positions.

Expectably, these criteria also operate throughout the rest of the Ladino social hierarchy, marking others off as more or less distinguished in their own places on the ladder. At a point on the ladder coinciding approximately with the ranking of the twentieth family, a generalized distinction is made separating the members of these first twenty families from all others in the Ladino population. This distinction is phrased locally in terms of *la sociedad* versus *el populacho*, or, roughly translated, between society people and the common people.

The sociedad includes the majority of the elite who constitute the roster from which are drawn names to invite to the best parties, church functions, school boards, women's religious auxiliary celebrations, leadership in public celebrations, entertainment of visiting dignitaries, and the like. These are the people who visit each other on socially equal terms, though by no means does each of them visit all others, since these ranks are themselves rift with social feuds of long standing. These are the people who, as a minimum, live near the center of town, have a decently paying job, own a black suit or evening-style dress and a decent pair of shoes; and, further, have some land or whose families own property from which income, without work, is derivable. They are the people to whom the titles of Don and Doña are given with the greatest emphasis upon the traditional significance of the words. They are also the people of whom the Indians are most aware as occupying positions of importance and to whom special deference must be paid. This classification includes 100 to 200 of the 1,100 Ladinos in town, depending on how far out into kinship extensions one goes.

Below these families are the populacho, or the common people. They are the ones who, on examination, tend more and more to approximate the Indian in appearance, occupation, speech, residence, and income, as one goes down the social ladder. Indeed, one may say that one of the best criteria by which to judge the rank of a Ladino is to estimate how significantly different he is from the Indians in those regards just mentioned. This is a functionally useful mode of judgment since the Indians, by pressure from the outside and by compulsive force of their own customs, minimize their display of wealth or consumers goods, live on the edges rather than the center of town, tend to do their own hard work, eat simple meals, stereotypically talk bad Spanish, are rarely if ever invited to any social affairs among the Ladinos, and fail to provide their children any extended formal education.

If it could be shown that Indians aspire after the same marks of distinction as the Ladinos, then it would be circular to state that one can measure a man's rank by the extent to which he is differentiated from the Indian. But the Indians do not generally aspire to the same things, and hence do not try to present the same public image as the Ladino. It therefore makes sense to estimate a Ladino's social worth by the extent of his differentiation from the Indians.

It is difficult to delineate many sharp lines of class dis-

INTRA-GROUP STRATIFICATION

tinction among the populacho themselves. One notes various degrees of poverty, landlessness, propertylessness in general, illiteracy, inadequate housing and poor housing location. Also present is a consistent tendency on their part to think in terms of socially superior and inferior people. But it is most difficult to locate any significant clusters of traits or of opinions regarding these matters at definite points on the social ladder. It is thus not possible to say that the lowest lowest class, or the most middle class, or some such other division acts or thinks in any uniform way about anything in particular.

A number of the populacho, for instance, are barely distinguishable from a number of the Indians. In some cases only skin color and certain cultural clues which no money can buy—such as attitude toward the Indians themselves—help distinguish the impoverished Ladino from the average Indian. In other cases, not even skin color is different, and only the person's own insistence that he is a Ladino makes the difference between him and some Indians, at least so far as higher ranking Ladinos are concerned.

One might almost say that for many intents and purposes many Ladinos and Indians share the same fate in the pueblo—with one significant exception. This is the fact that any Ladino, no matter how depressed, can theoretically count on some mobility in Ladino society, so long as he is considered a Ladino. That is, the lines of class mobility are theoretically as much open to him as to any other Ladino, whereas they are not open to anyone defined as an Indian. At least as far as the present attitudes in San Luis are concerned, no Indian can hope to be fully accepted in Ladino society, no matter how wealthy, well-dressed, literate, well-educated, or professionally employed he may be.

When one seeks a more precise measurement of income differentials among the Ladinos in San Luis, he is faced with the difficulty that people are very reluctant to give income figures. It is thus also difficult to estimate properly how much weight should be given the occupation of the individual, since, by local criteria, the prestigefulness of the occupation is heavily dependent upon the income derived from working at it. Accordingly, in trying to derive an index of class status from available interview materials, I was urged to the following procedure: (1) Use housing and clothing as indices of the income of the family. For whether or not there was real income to back up the apparent status connoted by types of houses and clothes, there was imputed income in the minds of others, and prestige is allocated in accordance with this definition. (2) Use landowning as an index of the real income and the freedom from manual labor of the family. (3) Include some measurement of family reputation, no matter how crude, and join this with the measurements above into a composite index. (4) Revise the estimate based on the three indices above only where the nature of the occupation is such that, despite economic impoverishment, the individual commands prestige for the kind of job he holds. Interestingly enough, no such revision was called for.

The use of housing and clothing as indices of apparent economic status is justified by the fact that a considerable amount of the conspicuous consumption of income is concentrated on these two items. There is no electricity in the area and one could not therefore judge by electrical gadgets and equipment. No one has an automobile, and this item is therefore out of the question. Various animals, especially mules and horses, do represent sources of investment and are taken as measures of wealth, but it is difficult to secure reliable data on these things. Both positively and residually, therefore, housing and clothing, about which information is easily and reliably obtained, emerge as significant and convenient indices.

The use of land as an index of status is strongly suggested by the great prestige emphasis placed on landownership in the area, and by the fact that it is the principal means of gaining income without work or of earning a

INTRA-GROUP STRATIFICATION

large income. There are no business enterprises of any significant scale in which persons with money can invest and receive income except the management and renting or working of farm land.

Family reputation, to be sure, is a loose and somewhat ambiguous category, since it tends to be so subjectively determined. On the other hand, it has been noted that no matter how poorly individuals or families think of the "character" of each other or of each other's families, they do agree on which families enjoy the greatest social reputation among others, even though they may think these are undeserved estimates. It is easy enough, if enough persons are interviewed, to locate the approximate ranking of a given family in the social hierarchy of San Luis.

1. HOUSING

On the basis of a house-to-house survey of the pueblo, including a description of all variations in housing type and a knowledge of the costs involved in constructing such varieties, it was possible to erect a continuum of prestige-types in dwellings, as follows:

a. *Upper rank*: professionally cut and finished wood supports for the roof, covered with a high-grade tile; brick floors, adobe walls; finished doors of wood; windows in each room, grilled or ungrilled; whitewash on the exterior and interior of the walls. It may not have a thatched roof, dirt floor, or unblocked mud walls. It must have more than one room.

b. *Middle rank*: tile roof on unfinished wood supports; walls of either adobe or unblocked baked mud, locally called bajareque, with the latter predominating; floors of brick or dirt, with the latter predominating. Some approximation at windows and doors, but not throughout the house. Must have more than one room.

c. *Lowest rank*: thatched roofs on raw wood supports; bajareque walls; dirt floors; one room; may or may not have windows and doors.

TENSIONS AND EQUILIBRIA

2. CLOTHING

Through interview materials and observation of the clothes worn by individuals whose approximate social ranking, as determined by other criteria, was already known, the following constituents of prestige in clothing were observed:

a. *Upper rank*: (male) at least one wool suit, with pants and jacket matching, and dark enough to be worn to evening affairs; a pair of shoes in good repair; incidental appurtenances such as shirts, underwear, etc.

b. *Middle rank*: (male) no wool suit, but at least three shirts and three pairs of pants, and one cotton jacket.

c. *Lowest rank*: (male) anything less than the above.

3. LAND

Individuals ranked on other counts were examined regarding landownership and the following rough divisions, correlating highly with the foregoing, were determined:

a. *Upper rank*: ownership of at least 100 cuerdas.
b. *Middle rank*: ownership of 1 to 100 cuerdas.
c. *Lowest rank*: no land at all.

4. FAMILY

Rankings, of upper, middle, and lowest were assigned on the basis of the pooled rankings of other Ladinos interviewed. The majority opinion was taken as the standard in each case.

COMPOSITE INDEX

Given the four indices of housing, clothing, land, and family, it was possible to assign numbers to each of the three rankings possible, 3 for upper class, 2 for middle class, and 1 for lower class. In this way a person could achieve a total of 12 points as his class score, if he got an upper-class rating on all four items, or he could get as low as 4 for his score if he was rated lower class on all four items. Such a range is evenly divisible at every fourth number so that it was possible to use the following measures:

INTRA-GROUP STRATIFICATION

a. Score from 12-10: upper class.
b. Score from 9-7: middle class.
c. Score from 6-4: lower class.

The table on page 220 indicates the individual rankings for all twenty-two Ladinos interviewed on each of the four items on which they were rated, and then sums up their ratings into a composite class index.

From this table it will be noted that 10, or 45.5 per cent, of the 22 Ladinos interviewed ranked as upper class by the standards set down above; 9, or 40.9 per cent, rated middle class; and 3, or 13.6 per cent, rated lower class.

It is clear that this distribution is not representative of the Ladino population as a whole. The sample was not randomly drawn nor was it in any sense representative of already known strata within the population. In the field situation encountered in San Luis, significant and perhaps distorting compromises had to be made with time, energy, availability of subjects, and a host of other circumstances which prevented even an approximation at an ideal sample.

It should be remembered that the terms upper, middle, and lower are arbitrarily assigned terms, and their real significance lies in the kinds of possessions and characteristics which give the people the rankings which were assigned to them. As we examine the things one has to possess to get into the upper class, it will be seen that it is a markedly different kind of upper class than we are accustomed to imagine from our stereotyped or real familiarity with similarly ranked individuals in modern American society.

The distinction between upper and middle class on the previous table corresponds with the distinction between la sociedad and el populacho. From repeated attendance at parties and dances of the sociedad it was estimated that about 20 families, comprising approximately between 100 to 200 people, constituted the bulk of the sociedad. This means that between 900 to 1,000 Ladinos fall below the ranking of "society." This provides a very rough estimate

TABLE 20. LADINO SOCIO-ECONOMIC STATUS INDICES. (N = 22)

Indices	Housing			Clothing			Land			Family			Composite index		
Rank	U	M	L	U	M	L	U	M	L	U	M	L	U	M	L
Case No. 1	X			X						X			X		
2	X			X						X			X		
3	X			X									X		
4	X					X	X								X
5		X			X		X				X			X	
6		X			X				X		X			X	
7		X			X				X		X			X	
8						X			X			X			X
9	X			X			X			X			X		
10	X			X				X						X	
11	X			X				X			X			X	
12	X					X			X		X		X		
13								X	X			X			X
14	X			X			X			X			X		
15	X			X				X		X			X		
16	X			X				X		X			X		
17	X			X					X		X		X		
18	X			X											
19		X			X			X		X				X	
20	X			X				X			X		X		
21		X			X			X			X			X	
22	X				X				X			X		X	
Number	16	6	0	11	8	3	4	7	11	8	9	5	10	9	3
Per cent	72.7	27.3	0	50	36.4	13.6	18.2	32.8	50	36.4	40.9	22.7	45.5	40.9	13.6

INTRA-GROUP STRATIFICATION

of the extent to which the sample is overweighted on the side of the wealthier and more prestigeful Ladinos.

It was noted before that by and large it is only the families of the sociedad who can and/or do send their children away from the pueblo to be educated; that they were the political and religious leaders of the pueblo; that they set the styles in language, recreation, and general behavior. The remainder of the Ladinos tend more closely to resemble the Indian in their economic situations, the amount of education given their children, the extent of their political power, and the amount of social distinction they enjoy. Though they are not barred, theoretically, from intimate social intercourse with the high-ranking Ladinos, they do not actualize this relationship in any noticeably different degree from the Indians. They tend to mix among themselves and to form a distinct segment of social life. They are, as a group, on a somewhat higher economic level than the Indians to begin with, and tend to pass on their skills and fortunes along family lines. But the economic difference is not sufficient to enable them to purchase admission into prestigeful Ladino society. Indeed, there is marked overlap in the distribution of their incomes and those found among the Indians. One may say of them, then, that in many regards they share a considerable amount of common fate with the Indians.

In spite of this shared fate, they distinguish themselves from Indians in their own attitudes and are similarly distinguished by other Ladinos and Indians. Cultural tendencies and culturally learned attitudes thus emerge, in these cases, as more important differentiators than income and occupation.

In searching out the truth of these contentions, it is important to see the extent to which the Indian sample overlaps the Ladino sample in its class ratings, using the same indices of ranking. However, family reputation is not an important criterion of ranking among the Indians. The judgment of their relative class positions was based on housing, clothing, and land alone. It is therefore necessary to reexamine the Ladino data and draw up a revised class estimate on the basis of these three criteria, family excluded. Referring back to the previous chart it will be seen that if we exclude family from consideration the class ratings remain absolutely the same: i.e., 10 in upper class, 9 in middle class, and 3 in lower class. (It is unquestionable that there was a tendency to assign upper-class family status to those interviewees who rated upper-class status on the other indices; but it is also unquestionable that people of old family reputations tend to be the ones, by and large, who have the necessary criteria for upper class rating.)

Translated into percentages, this means that 45 per cent of the Ladinos are upper class; 40.9 per cent middle class; and 13.6 per cent lower class. Table 21 indicates the rankings for the 49 Indians interviewed.

From these materials it can be seen that, using a composite index of housing, clothing, and land, there are no Indians in the upper class, 34.5 per cent in the middle class, and 65.5 per cent in the lower class. These figures reveal marked disparity in the economic situations of the two groups taken as a whole, but they should be taken in light of the known fact that the Ladino sample is heavily overweighted in the direction of wealthier Ladinos. It is difficult to estimate the extent to which the Indian sample is biased in any particular direction, since among them no distinction between sociedad and populacho prevails by which one may make an independent estimate, nor are there other social criteria which help one decide. From general observation of the average Indian way of life, I would not hesitate to assert that this is a fair picture of the Indian population as a whole.

It was asserted above that the comparison of Indian and Ladino class distributions reveals marked disparities in the statuses occupied by the two groups. This in no way violates our expectations in this regard. What is equally noteworthy, however, is the extent of the overlap in the class distributions. It will be noted that the percentages

TABLE 21

INDIAN ECONOMIC STATUS INDICES

(N=49)

Indices	Housing			Clothing			Land			Composite		
Rank	U	M	L	U	M	L	U	M	L	U	M	L
*No. of cases**												
15			X			X			X			X
9		X				X			X			X
8		X			X				X			X
8		X			X				X		X	
2		X			X			X			X	
2		X			X			X			X	
2		X				X		X			X	
1	X				X				X		X	
1	X				X		X				X	
1			X			X		X			X	
Number	3	22	24	0	22	27	1	7	41[1]	0	17	32
Per cent	6.1	45.0	48.9	0	44.9	55.1	2	14.3	83.7	0	34.5	65.5

* In order of decreasing frequency of occurrence. (Note that these are frequency of cases, rather than individual case numbers such as are shown on Table 19 for the Ladinos.)

of Indians and Ladinos in middle-class ratings are relatively similar. Measurement of the significance of the difference between the two proportions reveals that the difference between the two proportions is less than twice the standard error of the difference, indicating a statistically insignificant difference. This tends to bear out the contention that a considerable number of Ladinos and Indians share a relatively similar economic fate. The sharp disparity between the percentages in the upper and lower classes, in turn, indicates the expected and already described monopolization of land and other productive resources by the Ladinos and the economic impoverishment of significant numbers of the Indians.

If we look a little more closely at the meaning of these economic differences between lower and middle class, it will be seen that though it includes distinguishable items of property, the differences so included are not enough to say that these people have significantly different life chances or that their behavior is likely to become more similar when their incomes are made more similar. In short, no simple theory of economic determinism of cultural differences will suffice here. In both absolute and relative manners of speech, the entire economy of the pueblo, both Indian and Ladino, is depressed. And while that small portion of the population consisting of the Ladino elite or sociedad have a significantly better life in many material ways, the vast majority of both populations are relatively similar in their economic existence.

This gives added weight to our earlier contention that cultural mandates and dictates, exercising their customary force and compulsion, rather than simple economic differentials, must be taken significantly into account in attempting to understand the differences in the behavior patterns of the two groups, and their attitudes toward life in general.

The general picture of the pueblo which emerges at this point, so far as stratification is concerned, is one in which the entire pueblo is divided primarily by a caste line sepa-

INTRA-GROUP STRATIFICATION

rating Indians from Ladinos. Within the Ladino group itself, a line of demarcation separates the *sociedad* from the *populacho*, with significant consequences for political power, prestige, comfort, education, and the other concomitants of class position already indicated. Many of the populacho, in turn, tend to share a common *economic* fate with many of the Indians, but not the same kind of *social* fate. In terms of their aspirations and their values, the Ladinos would seem to be in a worse social position, since they are the subordinates and undervalued people in their own hierarchy, whereas the Indians are not considered by the Ladinos nor by themselves as being in this hierarchy.

What, then, of stratification inside the Indian community? The previous figures reveal economic stratification as measured by observable differences in clothing, housing, and land ownership and their concomitants. Are these distinctions of significance for the Indians themselves, so far as their organization of prestige, power, and general life perquisites are concerned?

The most general answer which can be given to these questions is that by and large the wealth of a man makes little or no difference in his rating in the traditional Indian community. As a matter of fact, as has already been noted, poverty rather than wealth is the norm in this traditional community.

From our materials it can also be inferred that the highest prestige in Indian circles is earned by the fullest exemplification of the traditional pattern of life. Since this importantly includes a high degree of religiosity and skill in religious lore, the highest prestige is reserved for those older Indians who are considered wise, religiously devoted, and skilled enough to conduct religious celebrations and rituals. These men are called *principales* and they are elected to that rank and title by the participating community. They are assigned various *cargos* or duties, such as tendering welcome to visiting religious processions from other towns, guarding of the crosses, initiating the planting and harvest festivals, and making prayers for rain. To them is also assigned the right and responsibility to act as intermediaries in marriage arrangements and to help in the religious ritualization of marriages. They are also vested with the power of justices of the peace by the Indian community, and disputes of all kinds are referred to them, though increasingly less so in recent years because of the increasing secularization of government. The Ladino community tends somewhat to recognize the strategic importance of this indigenous hierarchy by allocating responsibility for the good conduct of the Indian quarter to the principales.

The wives of the principales share with their husbands the prestige which accrues to that office. They are the leading dignitaries among the women, among whom otherwise no distinctions of rank prevail. They supervise the cooking of food at the communal celebrations. They walk with their husbands at the head of religious processions. Their houses are considered centers for reunion at festive occasions.

One further skill is covertly but widely recognized as estimable. This is the ability to produce magical cures for illnesses of various kinds. Since witchcraft of all kinds has been publicly outlawed, it is difficult to get accurate appraisals of the worth of various magical curers in town, or even to get uniform identification. My own inquiries lead me to believe that at least three and possibly four of the twelve most important principales also are presumably skilled in magical curing, though the observations of other students of San Luis suggest that at the most one of the principales is also a magic maker. Whatever the facts may be, it is clear that being able to induce cures gives considerable prestige to the individual, and, if this is combined with religious leadership as well, the person is likely to occupy the summit of available prestige-places in the hierarchy of Indian San Luis.

Perhaps the single most highly estimated person in the community at the time of my studies was an earlier mentioned young man, named Miguel Felipe,[1] who through a series of unique occurrences got a reputation in a relatively short time for being a marvelous curer and being especially endowed by God with the power of prayer-making that would produce results in all fields of effort. He was unquestionably the one genuinely charismatic figure in the Indian community, and his reputation was such that he enjoyed the confidence and the patronage of a goodly number of Ladinos as well.

It is unquestionable that he would have enjoyed a high position even if his skills had been limited to curing alone. For sickness and attendant anxiety are prevalent in San Luis, and are matched in their incidence only by the absence of secular-mindedness toward such matters and of secular cures for them. When this curing skill is combined in the same person with religious devotion and power, no matter whether it be real or assumed, the individual has two of the indispensable ingredients for a large following among the local populace. It is perhaps a trenchant commentary on the trend of affairs to note that had Felipe's skills been limited alone to religiosity, it is doubtful that he would have been as highly rated and esteemed.

Felipe violates, in the rating assigned to him, one of the most traditional expectations of Indian culture, namely, that wisdom, whether in matters of God or illness, is supposed to come only with advanced age. Uniformly, with the exception of Felipe, the principales are all in their fifties or older. Felipe, in his early thirties, shortcuts the traditional process of accession to prestige in a remarkable way. His ability to do so is perhaps itself indicative of the potential weakness of the traditional criterion of age as the mark of wisdom.

With this exception, however, generally throughout the culture the most significant line of division one can draw is that which separates the old from the young. This is not however a line of stratification in any simple sense of the

---

[1] See Bibliographical Note, Tumin, 1950 b, for citation of longer article on Miguel.

word. For it does not separate the socially superior from the inferior in the way we ordinarily think of these terms. That is to say, while older persons command prestige, power, deference, privilege, and other such accompaniments of high rank, they are not thereby considered as "better" than the younger people, nor the latter "worse" than they. The distinction is not one of social equality and inequality but rather of social quality or qualities, especially as these refer to those things considered most important, by the community, for its adequate survival and continuity.

The Indian code of evaluation, indeed, contains explicit reference to the social equality of all men and tends not to make a distinction between the humble and the elevated. Rather does it suggest that while all men are *socially* equal, some are endowed with greater wisdom and skills which are of value to the community and, as such, are entitled to greater prestige, deference, power, and authority to manage the affairs of the community.

When one tries to cut up the Indian community with other types of distinctions, more of the socially relevant and generally significant statuses fall out rather than in the categories. Wealth will not work as a significant cross-cut; nor will prestige given by the Ladinos; nor will sumptuousness of house or place of residence or amount of land owned. None of the traditional Ladino criteria, in short, will operate effectively to line up the Indian population as they themselves see the situation or as they actually behave. Instead, some combination of age, religiosity, wisdom, and skill in appeasing the supernatural constitutes the critical syndrome of prestige.

Since these characteristics sum up the peak of traditional achievement, it is both understandable and interesting that the greatest dissatisfaction with the traditional pattern is to be found among the young men who are beginning to operate within a cash economy; to forego religious devotions; to accept secular Ladino definitions of what is desirable; and to ignore the prestige and respect traditionally

INTRA-GROUP STRATIFICATION

commanded by old men of the group. It is mostly from these young men that one begins to hear invidious evaluations of the relative social worth of different types of Indians, phrased in Ladino-style values. In turn, as noted above, the older people attach a moral invidiousness to the activities of these younger men, not in Ladino terms, but in traditional Indian terms. Here we have a case, then, where a portion of the Indian community is being slowly fractured off so that it comes to share Ladino values and thus deprecate other portions of the Indian community.

The reaction of the Ladinos to this fractured-off segment of the Indians is instructive. The Ladinos do not accept these young men, at least not at this point. None of them can claim Ladino-style family reputation, nor can any of them lay claim to a prestigeful occupation. The leisure time they command by virtue of their cash income from working on banana plantations is not the right kind of leisure time in the eyes of the Ladinos. It is idleness. Nor are their conspicuously consumed fineries the right kind of finery or the right style of consumption. The Ladinos tend to exploit these youths by teasing them with pretended political favors, when, in fact, these favors tend to add up to obligations. As one watches these young men currying favor with the Ladino officials, the disparity between their definitions of the situation and those of the Ladinos who allow them to run high-type errands for them is all too apparent.

The most instructive example here is that of a young man named Secundino E. His father, until recently, was one of the most revered principales in the community. His very advanced age, however, has forced a gradual but sure retirement from active affairs, though he still tends to dominate, as a patriarch, the traditional hierarchy. Secundino, the son, is attempting to play both the Ladino and the Indian games. He maintains connections with the hierarchical religious structure of the Indian community through his father, and himself participates importantly in some quasi-sacred festivals. But he also acts as an errand boy of sorts for Ladino officials, with whom he curries favor rather openly, so that he himself feels important in both culture patterns. But the Ladinos consider him markedly unimportant, and the Indians deplore his dual or marginal position, at the same time that they show some deference to him because of his known connections with the official Ladino governmental structure.

Secundino is now, apparently, in such a position that it is no longer possible for him, in terms of his own attitudes, to fit again into the traditional Indian structure, and by no means possible, in terms of Ladino attitudes, to have any real mobility inside Ladino social organization. He is marginal to both cultural foci, and derives full satisfaction from neither.

This is a likely fate for any Indian who tries to bridge both cultures. The same kind of fate, though somewhat different in details, has befallen the barber in town, an Indian by public definition, who dresses like a Ladino, whose wife wears European or Ladino-style clothing, who operates inside a cash nexus, and who disavows any connections with Indian religio-political affairs. He likes to claim that he is accepted by the Ladinos, but they only scorn this claim when it is reported to them, and despite his ownership of the necessary style of clothing and housing for social acceptance, he is never invited to any Ladino affairs. It would be interesting to probe deeply into the psychic equilibrium of such marginal cases, to discover the extent to which the tensions which one hypothetically infers should be present are actually to be found.

From the foregoing materials it appears that one can talk of "class distributions" or "class behavior" in a number of different ways. If one is concerned with the way prestige is distributed, one gets one kind of picture of San Luis, including a separate exposure for Ladinos and one for Indians. The things that go into prestige and are associated with it have already been mentioned. But if one is interested in the way in which solidarity falls or is distributed one gets somewhat of a different picture. The

INTRA-GROUP STRATIFICATION

formulae would be somewhat as follows: Between any Ladino and any Indian, primary loyalty falls along caste lines, the Ladino being solidly with all other Ladinos by contrast with any Indian, and all Indians feeling primary loyalty to the Indian group over individual loyalty to any Ladino. The only possible exceptions here would be in those cases where godparental and compadre connections between Indians and Ladinos cut across the caste line.

Inside the Ladino group, loyalty is distributed along family lines and along lines of income-prestige rating. Since various members of Ladino families are distributed up and down the income ladder of Ladino society, this makes for some slight tension where there are competing interests. In general, however, issues promoting this type of conflict rarely arise. One must nevertheless keep in mind the fact that the ideal expectation is that loyalty falls first to one's family and only secondarily to any other interest groups.

Inside Indian society the same rule regarding loyalty applies. The Indian has his primary obligation to family. But since distribution of wealth is not a significant crosscut in Indian society, the competition of loyalties between family and class is virtually nil. The Indian loyalty pattern is thus virtually confined to family and to the Indian group as such. Since these are coterminal in many of their significant aspects, one can reasonably talk of a minimum of possible conflicts of loyalties inside the Indian group. When the traditional pattern is preserved, this makes for great stability and for a minimum of tension in social behavior. Conversely, however, when *any* departure from the traditional pattern is commenced, it means a departure from family as well as group standards and thus constitutes a genuinely significant break. Thus, while the Indian group is markedly solidary and tough in its traditional stability, this very traditionality makes it especially inflexible and incapable of meeting new situations. It is at least much more so than the Ladino group, which has marginal accommodations for various kinds of deviant behavior.

TENSIONS AND EQUILIBRIA

Since the Ladino concerns himself much more than does the Indian with questions of caste proprieties, and since he has competing loyalties within his own group, his society's status quo may be said to be that much more unstable, and the task of maintaining equilibrium in his social life is rendered that much more difficult. In turn this is compensated for somewhat by the satisfactions inhering in his superordinate position in the caste system.

The caste line emerges as the most significant overall cross-cut in San Luis. In a sense this is far more true of San Luis society than of American society, since in San Luis there is continuous mixture at all hours of the day and in many central places in the pueblo between Indians and Ladinos, so that the etiquette of caste relations is continuously under scrutiny. Were the Indians more isolated from the Ladinos, one could then say that the caste line is a very effective social divider but does not occupy too much of the attention of either group.

This is the case, for instance, in the relations between the pueblo Ladino and some of the aldea Indians, since these groups, or representatives of them, meet only infrequently. One notices in the more distant all-Indian aldeas a significant difference in the behavior of the Indians who, free from the necessity to observe caste etiquette, display far greater freedom and uninhibited behavior than do pueblo Indians.

In aldeas containing both Ladinos and Indians, the basic rules of caste etiquette are generally observed. But there are noticeable deviations in terms of inter-group visiting and friendliness which are not observable in the pueblo itself. The conditions of life in these aldeas are such as to make it virtually ludicrous to behave in any other way. Even the most caste-minded Ladino would feel silly and would be considered silly by other Ladinos if he tried rigidly to maintain some of the less significant rules of caste interaction which are observed in the pueblo. In the pueblo there is continuous reinforcement of the rules through their day-by-day ritualization and observance,

INTRA-GROUP STRATIFICATION

with the way being shown by prestigeful and highly caste-minded leaders of Ladino society.

In both the aldeas and the pueblo, regardless of the deviations from caste expectations in such matters as visiting and exchange of friendship, the fundamental taboos on miscegenation and commensalism are maintained literally without exception. That this is not simply a matter of economic class distinction is apparent from the fact that many Indians and Ladinos share relatively identical economic careers and patterns. The general principle is thus illustrated that the Indian is separated from the Ladino by barriers which money cannot destroy, at least not at present.

These barriers consist of group images held by the Ladinos of the Indians, resulting in consistently unfavorable and depreciatory attitudes toward anyone considered Indian for any reason whatsoever. It is therefore important to examine the image which the Ladino has of the Indian to see what it is about the Indian which makes him so invidiously viewed by the Ladino. But since the separation which is maintained among the people is also a function of Indian desires for separation, it is also important to consider how the Indians view the Ladinos.

CHAPTER 16

GROUP IMAGES

IN LIGHT of the situations of joint and separate participation which have been described, we will next consider the images each group has of the other. This involves what each believes and feels to be true about the other, and how each sets itself off from the other. An understanding of these group images should clarify the motivations underlying the behavior of each group toward the other.

To determine the group images, a series of questions was designed to find out what the Ladinos and Indians thought were the main differences between each other and whether they thought these differences were (1) plain differences or (2) differences which spoke poorly for the other group or (3) differences which spoke well for the other group.

After each informant was asked what he thought were the main differences, he was then asked to elaborate until it had become apparent what he felt such differences implied in terms of superiority-inferiority, or better-worse, so far as a comparison of the two groups was concerned. The results were tabulated according to the socio-economic class of the Ladino informants and the economic class of the Indians. In a few instances the specific answers to the questions did not decisively reveal what the informant felt such differences implied in terms of ranking one group as better than or superior to the other group. Where this was the case, the total interview was taken as a unit and the prevailing attitude throughout the interview was used. Because of the known bias of the writer in the direction of seeing conflict where others might not have seen conflict, any doubtful case was assigned to the group of "plain difference." For, there was never any doubt as between differences with appreciation and differences with depreciation. Whatever doubts there were always had reference to

GROUP IMAGES

whether the difference was being maintained as a plain difference or whether it was felt by the informant that such a difference spoke poorly of the other group.

Ladinos mentioned 38 items of difference which can be conveniently grouped under 7 major headings. Indians mentioned 30 items which can be conveniently grouped under eight general headings. The distinctions which were mentioned by both Ladinos and Indians were in: (1) language and speech; (2) family background; (3) work and travel; (4) physical characteristics; (5) material possessions; (6) character and personality. Only Ladinos indicated differences in "general social behavior." Only Indians mentioned differences in economic rank and amount of education.

The results in tabular form are given in Tables 22 and 23.

From these tables, it is seen that:

1. Ladinos see more differences, or are able to verbalize them (or both) better, than Indians. Ladinos cited an average of 5.1 and Indians 4.2 differences per person.

2. Ladinos see many more differences as depreciative of Indians than the latter see differences as depreciative of Ladinos. Ladino differences with depreciation were 50 per cent of all; the comparable Indian figure was 4.3 per cent.

3. Ladinos see no differences as appreciative of Indians, while Indians see 14.9 per cent as appreciative of Ladinos.

4. Twenty-eight instances of differences which Indians saw as *appreciative* of themselves were among the 54 instances Ladinos saw as *depreciative* of Indians. Indians saw 3 differences (in education and economics) as appreciative of Ladinos, while Ladinos did not mention these. Thus, there is about 50 per cent symmetry in their views here.

5. Ladinos see fewer plain differences, viewing only 50 per cent this way, while Indians so see 80.7 per cent of the differences.

6. Ladinos most stressed differences in language and speech, work, travel, and material possessions, these 3 com-

TABLE 22

INDIAN CONCEPTION OF GROUP DIFFERENCES

Differences**	Total		ECONOMIC STATUS*					
			Middle			Lower		
			Plain Difference	Difference with Depreciation	Difference with Appreciation	Plain Difference	Difference with Depreciation	Difference with Appreciation
	No.	%	No. %	No. %	No. %	No. %	No. %	No. %
	208	100	57 74	8 10.4	12 15.6	111 84.7	1 .7	19 14.6
Material possessions	85	40.8	24 31	2 2.6	6 7.8	39 30	1 .7	14 11.0
Language and speech	52	25	13 17	3 3.9	3 3.9	29 22.1		3 2.2
Physical characteristics	42	20.2	13 17	1 1.3		28 21.4		
Work and travel	17	8.2	2 2.6	2 2.6	1 1.3	11 8.4		1 .7
Family	6	2.9	3 3.9			3 2.2		
Education	3	1.4	1 1.3		2 2.6			
Economics	2	.9				1 .7		1 .7
Character and personality	1	.5	1 1.3					

*By the same criteria as those used to rank Ladinos into economic classes (housing, clothing and land, and excluding family which was used to make socio-economic rankings for the Ladinos) no Indian falls inside the upper-class grouping.
**The number of differences refer to the number of times the item was mentioned and not to the number of people mentioning them.

TABLE 23

LADINO CONCEPTION OF GROUP DIFFERENCES

Differences*	Total		Socio-economic status							
			Upper				Middle		Lower	
			Plain** difference		Difference with depreciation		Plain difference	Difference with depreciation	Plain difference	Difference with depreciation
	No.	%	No.	%	No.	%	No. %	No. %	No. %	No. %
	108	100	15	30	35	70	32 66.6	16 33.3	7 70	3 30
Language and speech	25	23.1	3	6	6	12	8 16.7	4 8.4	1 10	3 30
Work and travel	20	18.5	1	2	9	18	4 8.4	4 8.4	2 20	
Material possessions	20	16.5	1	2	7	14	6 12.6	5 10.4	1 10	
Social behavior	16	14.8	1	2	5	10	7 14.3	3 6.1		
Physical characteristics	14	15.1	4	8	3	6	5 10.4		2 20	
Family	8	7.4	5	10			2 4.2		1 10	
Character and personality	5	4.6			5	10				

* The number of differences refer to the number of times the item was mentioned and not to the number of people mentioning them.
** None of the differences mentioned by the Ladinos spoke in appreciation of the Indians. They were all either plain (non-derogatory; neutral), or depreciative of the Indian.

prising over 60 per cent of the differences cited. Indians most stressed language and speech, physical characteristics and material possessions, these 3 comprising over 86 per cent of all the differences. These figures indicate considerable symmetry in the way the peoples view differences between each other.

7. The largest asymmetrical item is "general social behavior" which took in 16 or 14.8 per cent of all the differences cited by Ladinos. Indians did not cite this item at all.

8. The upper-class Ladinos saw 30 per cent of the differences as plain differences and 70 per cent of the differences as depreciative of the Indian, while the figures for the middle and lower class are almost the exact reverse of these. So far as attitudes toward Indians are concerned, then, one may speak of a two-class division among the Ladinos.

9. There appear to be no significant differences in the opinions of the two classes of Indians, with the exception that lower-class Indians saw practically no differences as depreciative of the Ladinos while middle-class Indians saw 10.4 per cent of the differences speaking depreciatively of the Ladinos. So far as attitudes toward Ladinos are concerned, then, one may speak of a relative unity among the Indians.

It is further noteworthy that the Ladino depreciated the Indian most seriously in matters of language and speech habits, work and travel, social behavior and material possession. In actuality, with the exception of physical characteristics, Ladinos and Indians differ most widely in the extent of their material possessions, in their language and speech habits, in their occupations and modes of travel, and in their material possessions, including clothing and housing. This is especially significant since, with the exception of intermarriage, it is in social affairs, where social rhetoric, manners, and general appearance (clothes) are the vital criteria of eligibility for admission, that the groups are most often and most sharply separated. Inter-

GROUP IMAGES

estingly, it is also most particularly in these matters that acculturating Indians seek to emulate the Ladino.

It seems quite clear from all the foregoing that both Indians and Ladinos see each other as sharply differentiated, so sharply, indeed, that for all intents and purposes they form two separate types of human groups. It would further appear that the Ladino wants to have little or nothing to do with the Indian way of life. By contrast, there would appear to be at least some if not a considerable amount of verbally expressed desire by the Indian for the kind of life enjoyed by the Ladinos. For, the Ladino sees the Indian as a poverty-stricken, illiterate, unambitious, unclean, unintelligent, and untutored person. But the Indian sees the Ladino as a fairly wealthy person leading a life of relative leisure, living in fine houses and wearing fine clothes, engaging in diverting recreational pursuits, being himself literate and educated and insisting on the education of his children.

From these composite images it would be expected that Ladinos would tend to resist any attempts at amalgamation with the Indians, while Indians would be less vehement on this score. Expectably, therefore, it is found that Ladinos express considerable distaste for the idea of intermarriage between Indians and Ladinos, while, on the other hand, Indians feel more kindly toward the idea, at least when verbally questioned. The following figures summarize the expressed sentiments of the 49 Indian and 22 Ladino interviewees regarding intermarriage.

TABLE 24

	Ladino	Indian
Would let son marry girl of other group	10	20
Would let daughter marry into other group	9	20
Does not care	0	5
Says it depends on child	8	40
Says it depends on child, but prefers own group	7	25
Says children would not want to marry out	1	3

	Ladino	Indian
Would disinherit child who married out	9	0
Would accommodate self to intermarriage	3	2

Seven of the 8 Ladinos who said it depended on the wishes of the children themselves intended this permissiveness for both sons and daughters. The eighth was permissive regarding his son but not his daughter. Seven of these 8 also indicated that though they thought it depended on the children, they far preferred Ladinos to Indians as marriage partners for their children. The eighth indicated no preference. (This exception is not the same person who would not let his daughter marry an Indian.) Only 1 person indicated that it was not up to him, but up to his children, that he would let them do as they wished, but that he knew that they would not want to marry any Indian. Of the 12 Ladinos who said they would not let their children marry Indians, 9 said they would disown or disinherit the child if it did do so. Three said they would conform and give aid to their children and grandchildren if they were asked to. The man who would let his son but not his daughter marry an Indian was among the 9 who would disinherit or disown the child. One of those who said he would conform added that he would keep his parental love for his disobedient child, admit her to his house and recognize her as his child, but would let "her suffer until the day she died." Apparently, the suffering refers to her continuing to live in disgrace with the Indian.

In contrast to these figures and facts about the Ladinos, note that only 3 out of 49 Indians say they would not let their sons marry Ladinos and only 4 out of 49 would not let their daughters. Expressed in percentages, 6 per cent of the Indians say they would not let their sons marry Ladinos. For the Ladinos, 52.4 per cent would not let their sons marry Indians and 57.1 per cent would not let their daughters marry Indians. The one Indian who would not let his daughter marry a Ladino added that it depended on her. Of the 4 Indians who would not let either of their children marry Ladinos, 2 said they would conform if the children did, and the other 2 said they could not even consider the possibility.

It may be noted in further contrast that 5 Indians said they did not care, and added that it depended on the children, while no Ladinos said they did not care. It should also be noted that 8 Ladinos said it depended on the child and 7 of them added that they preferred Ladinos (the eighth indicating no preference) whereas 40 Indians said it depended on the child, with 25 of these adding a preference for Indians and 3 adding a preference for Ladinos. Of the 8 Ladinos who said that it depended on the wishes of the child, 7 had previously indicated they would allow their children of both sexes to marry Indians, while 1 had said he would not let his daughter but would let his son. Of the 40 Indians who said it depended on the wishes of the children, 17 had previously indicated that they would let their children of both sexes marry Ladinos, while 23 had not indicated either that they would give or refuse permission.

The net impressions from these figures are: (a) Ladino parents evidently feel they have a greater voice in the selection of the marriage partners of their children than do the Indians; (b) they have a greater concern about whom their children would marry; (c) their concern that their children should not marry Indians was greater than the concern of the Indians that their children should not marry Ladinos; (d) more dire consequences would be likely to befall a greater percentage of Ladino children than Indian children in the case of disobedience by the child of parental wishes; (e) all in all, the Ladinos feel far more strongly against the notion of intermarriage than do the Indians.

Further evidence for these contentions is to be found in the reasons given by Ladinos for preferring Ladino marriage partners for themselves and their children. (See Appendix.) An examination of those reasons reveals that (1) all of the reasons given by the Ladinos connote depreciation of the Indian; (2) 27 specific reasons in all are given by 27 Ladinos for preferring Ladinos or for not allowing their children to marry Indians, or both. Of these 27, 8 or almost 1/3 specifically mentioned blood differences; 1 mentioned the difference in "race"; 1 said the Indians were "worse people"; 1 said they were a different class of people with whom Ladinos should not mix; 2 mentioned the lesser intelligence of the Indians; 1 mentioned the lack of aspirations of the Indians; 6 of the differences concerned the lesser material possessions of the Indian; 4 differences noted concerned differences in customs; 2 cited Indian cruelty to wives; 1 cited the lesser education of the Indian.

Here it is found then that a preponderance of the Ladino reasons for abstention from desire for and permission for intermarriage refer to physical traits and material possessions. Counting intelligence as a "natural" difference, there are 16 or 59.3 per cent of the 27 differences cited which fall into these two major categories.

There is thus added to the fact of the differences earlier cited by Ladinos as separating Indians from themselves the further fact of a *belief that many of these differences—indeed, the most important ones, since they determine marriage eligibility—are based on biology and are ineradicable.* One can talk safely then of a caste relationship existing in San Luis in which, because of beliefs about differing genetic origins and a deprecatory evaluation of these differences, intermarriage is barred by the superordinate group. One of the principal avenues of social mobility for the subordinate group is thus effectively blocked.

From the Indian side of the question, the matter is viewed differently. It will be remembered that, aside from the 5 Indians who did not care either way about whom their children married, and the 3 Indians who preferred Ladinos as marriage partners for their children, there were 41 Indians who said that (a) it depended on the wishes of the child, but that they preferred Ladinos for their children, or (b) that they would not give permission to their

GROUP IMAGES

children to marry Ladinos, or (c) that their children would not want to marry Ladinos.

The reasons they gave were in substance as follows; 18 of these 41 said in effect: "Indians are poor people; they need to work and need spouses who can work along with them; Indian men and women know how to work and how to help each other; Ladinos do not"; 3 of the 41 said that Indians were not rich enough to marry Ladinos, since it entailed more money than they had to marry a Ladino; 4 of the differences referred to different customs as the blockage to intermarriage; 33 specific citations were made that it "was not customary for Indians to marry Ladinos"; 1 Indian cited differences in blood; 1 said that Indians should marry only Indians so as to keep the confidence and trust of the rest of the Indian people; 2 people said the Ladinos were less faithful to their spouses and would desert an Indian spouse after a period of marriage; 5 specific mentions were made of the fact that Indians should marry only Indians because the Ladinos were a different class of people; 1 person cited the different "character" of the Ladino people; 1 person cited religious, economic, and language differences as being obstacles; and, finally, 4 Indians said they preferred Indian marriage partners for their children just because that was their preference, and not because there were any differences between the peoples.

In reviewing these figures, the asymmetry with the comparable figures from the Ladinos stands out. Whereas almost 1/3 of the reasons Ladinos cited referred to blood differences, only 1 Indian mentioned differences of blood. Ladinos did not refer to differences in occupations or comparative laziness or industriousness of the Indians, while 18 or 43.4 per cent of all the Indian people mentioned the comparative orientations toward work. This 43.4 per cent is also the per cent of all the reasons given, as well as of the people giving reasons, for, not counting the 4 who expressed no reasons at all for preferring Indians, there were 41 specific reasons given in all.

The net impression which the writer here derives from

the foregoing facts is that Indians tend to see themselves as being in the nature of things tied down to the kind of life they now lead. Within that way of life, certain work skills are necessary, both for men and women. Marriage, to be successful within that way of life, must be a mating of two people with the requisite work skills. Indians have these work skills, Ladinos do not. Hence, it is better for Indians to marry Indians.

Only 3 Indians had the vision, if it be vision, to see that marriage to a Ladino would mean a change in one's way of life, and that considerable profit might accrue to an Indian who made such a change. One Indian, indeed, had an even more "advanced" view, to the effect that he thought it good for Indians to marry Ladinos all the time, so that at some time in the future there would be no one recognizable as an Indian and the Indian race would no longer exist, and then everyone could live like and be a Ladino.

It is further clear from the foregoing that the distance between Ladinos and Indians on the questions of intermarriage is in part mutually sustained. And it is likewise apparent that there are different reasons for whatever mutuality does exist. The reasons given by the Ladinos connote depreciation of the Indian, while the Indian's reasons do not depreciate the Ladino so much as do they consider his way of life so different from the Indian's that he simply is not to be considered as a possible candidate for marriage with an Indian.

It may here be urged, however, that if the Ladinos are so much more against the idea than are the Indians, and if the Ladino depreciates the Indian so much more than does the Indian depreciate the Ladino (again excepting the instance that Indians do not want to marry Ladinos), it is mainly the Ladinos who sustain the distance between them and the Indians on this score. And, it is even relatively insignificant, in this light, whether Indians do or do not wish to marry with Ladinos. The fact is that even if they should want to, the Ladino would not let them. The ultimate power in the matter lies in the hands of the Ladinos.

As to who initiates the distance, no clear answer can be given, unless, on the evidence presented, it may be taken that at least part of both peoples simultaneously initiate the distance in not approaching each other. What appears equally true is that if the Indian should begin to approximate the Ladino way of life, gradually taking over, along with other things, the work ethic of the Ladino, it is probable that at that time the Ladino, in view of his present depreciative beliefs about and feelings toward the Indian *in general*, will exert even greater efforts to keep distance, where he now only has to keep up one end of a quasi-mutually sustained situation of separatism. But it is equally probable that when and if the Indian comes to eliminate from his way of life such depreciated things as his poverty, his lesser material possessions, his occupation as a farmer, and his native dialect, he will then be a far more eligible candidate for marriage with Ladinos.

Now, although there is a total absence of intermarriage in the pueblo, there is a rather large number of children and adults who had Ladino fathers and Indian mothers. There were, so far as this writer could determine, no children by Indian fathers and Ladino mothers except for the children of the Ladino prostitute and the Indian man previously cited. Such unions for the most part occur between Ladino men and their Indian servant girls.

The manner in which both peoples regard children who are products of such unions throws significant light on how they tend to define each other. Relevant interview materials are available. They sum up as follows:

TABLE 25

LADINOS SAY

Child of	Ladino	Indian	Mixed
Ladino father: Indian mother: is	1	7	10
Indian father: Ladino mother: is	4	4	8
Ladino father: Indian mother: treated as	1	7	2
Indian father: Ladino mother: treated as	5	4	1

TENSIONS AND EQUILIBRIA

Orphan	Ladino	Indian	Mixed
Ladino raised in Indian house is	14		
Indian raised in Ladino house is	1	13	
Ladino raised in Indian house treated as	11	3	
Indian raised in Ladino house treated as	4	10	

INDIANS SAY

Child of	Ladino	Indian	Mixed
Ladino father: Indian mother: is	10	10	16
Indian father: Ladino mother: is	7	16	9
Ladino father: Indian mother: treated as	15	11	2
Indian father: Ladino mother: treated as	10	15	

Orphan	Ladino	Indian	
Ladino raised in Indian house is	19	7	
Indian raised in Ladino house is	9	21	
Ladino raised in Indian house treated as	16	10	
Indian raised in Ladino house treated as	10	10	

Several things are apparent from the above figures:

1. A person has more chance of being considered and treated as a Ladino by the Ladinos if he is of mixed blood and especially of a Ladino mother, than if he is born of two Indian parents, *even though he is then raised by Ladinos in Ladino fashion*. This would seem to indicate that for the Ladinos a person is to be identified as Ladino or Indian more by his parentage than by his training. And he is generally more acceptable as, and to be treated as, a Ladino if he has some Ladino blood, no matter what his customs, than if he has all Ladino customs but all Indian blood. This seems to indicate that the Ladino operates very much more with a biological definition of a person than with a cultural definition. The fact that only 1 out of 14, or only 7 per cent, of the Ladinos would consider an Indian orphan raised in a Ladino house as *being* a Ladino and only 4 out of 14, or only 28 per cent, would *treat* such a child as a Ladino speaks against any hypothesis that an Indian who takes on Ladino mannerisms and ways *is treated* as a Ladino. It speaks even more strongly against the hypothesis that such a person *is* a Ladino by local definition. Add to these figures the fact that there is no person of *definitely known* mixed parentage who is con-

sidered as and treated as a Ladino by the Ladinos and the Indians, even though not a few such mixed-blooded children have been raised completely in Ladino manners and ways, and even more doubt is cast on the hypotheses just noted.

2. Indians are more evenly divided in their opinions as to how to consider and how to treat children of mixed parentage and children of one-blood parentage whose customs are of the other group. No generalizations about Indian views are possible, then, except to note that Indians operate with both biological and cultural definitions. To the extent that they operate with biological definitions, there is confirmation for the hypothesis that biological considerations have important social consequences in San Luis. To the extent that they operate with cultural definitions there is similar confirmation for the hypothesis about the social consequences of cultural differences.

3. There is no way to compare actual behavior of the people with all the figures from the interviews, because, as has been indicated, there is no known case of a child of known mixed parentage who tries to be accepted as a Ladino. It was noted that there were not a few mixed-blood children (all had Indian mothers) who, though raised as Ladinos, are considered by both Indians and Ladinos as Indians and are treated as such, except for the fact that they are considered ineligible by many Indians as marriage partners. To the extent that some Ladinos and Indians both said that such children would be considered and would be treated as Ladinos, the interviews do not accurately reflect actual behavior. The discrepancy, however, indicates that the actual behavior is more antagonistic to closer amalgamation of the peoples and more promotive of distance than the prevalent verbalizations lead one to believe.

With reference to the opposite case of children of Ladino mothers and Indian fathers, there is only one case on which to judge, and that is such a special case that it is questionable whether it is a reliable index. It is the case of the children of the Ladino prostitute and the Indian man. Ladinos who were questioned about how the children would be considered and treated were in agreement that though the children were "mixed" and though they were being raised in Ladino fashion, they would be considered as Indians in San Luis, and would not be accepted as Ladinos. Indians were divided in their opinions, some rendering biological and others cultural definitions of the status of the children.

4. There is one case in the pueblo of a girl known to have had at least one if not two Indian parents, who grew up with Ladino training in the house of the two richest Ladino women in town. She dresses like a Ladino and does not speak the Indian dialect. But both Indians and Ladinos cited her, voluntarily, as an example of a person who tries to pass but who is known to be an Indian. She never attends Ladino or Indian affairs. Indians dislike her because of her pretences at a Ladino way of life. Ladinos ignore her.

5. Most of the "top-ranking" Ladinos in San Luis admit without hesitancy that somewhere in their families there is Indian blood, but add that it is very distantly removed in time, and that the overwhelming percentage of "blood" in the family is Ladino. This is an apparent but not a real contradiction of the earlier assertion that it is by a person's parentage that his Indian-ness or Ladino-ness is judged. For, in making such judgments, the people in the pueblo operate with recent and known parentage and not with distant and presumed parentage where the latter is "dubious." This connotes a biological definition by Ladinos of one's status as Indian or Ladino, but within that general biological definition there are tendencies to use *social* definition of one's status. For, according to the interviews, a child of mixed parentage has more chance of "becoming" either Ladino or Indian than does a child of Indian parentage, even though he is raised in one definite style. This applies for the Indian interviews as well, but not with so much force as for the Ladinos.

GROUP IMAGES

6. Perhaps the thing which most clearly emerges from the interviews with regard to these questions is that there is a very great diversity of opinion among the peoples. The fact that there are no real test cases which can be observed in operation in the pueblo makes it impossible to say to what extent the diversity of verbal opinion accurately reflects or would reflect a diversity in actual behavior. The only clearly observable behavior tendency in the pueblo is for a child of mixed parentage to be considered as Indian by both groups, regardless of the customs the child comes to learn.

CHAPTER 17

LEVELS OF ASPIRATION AND ASSIMILATION

IT HAS OFTEN been stated throughout the foregoing chapters that one of the principal sources of satisfaction the Indians derive from their way of life comes from keeping their aspirations within the range of achievements available in their culture. It has also been noted that in spite of the continuous exposure to the Ladinos and to their visibly easier mode of life, the Indians have for the most part held to those traditions which commend to them an acceptance of their own mode as the natural, the right, and the most fitting pattern for them to follow. The moment that, for any one of a variety of reasons, an Indian breaks off from the traditional pattern, the influences of the Ladino culture begin to show their impact, resulting in rather feeble attempts by the Indians to emulate some of the more superficial aspects of Ladino life. It is as though the Indian were guaranteed perfect safety and security inside his own cultural home, but the moment he pokes his head outdoors and begins to wonder what it is like outside, he begins to be culturally lost.

The apparent ease and leisure of the Ladino way of life can be a psychologically meaningful temptation to the Indian who, because he has somehow come to doubt his own value system, is susceptible to such temptation. How constant is that temptation and how aware the Indian can be of what it means to be a Ladino can be seen from the materials regarding changing of group membership which were presented in Chapter 5. There it was discovered that a rather large percentage (almost 80 per cent) of the Indians thought it possible for an Indian to become a Ladino, while somewhat less than 27 per cent of the Ladinos thought this transition possible. Similarly, a significantly larger proportion of the Indians, 54.5 per cent as against

13.4 per cent of the Ladinos, thought it possible for a Ladino to become an Indian.

It would seem quite clear from these figures—assuming the questions had the same meaning to all the interviewees—that Indians tend more than the Ladinos to view the differences between the two groups as primarily cultural and acquired rather than biological and inherited. This is borne out in the reasons both groups give for their respective beliefs regarding the possibility of the changeover. In those reasons we saw a significantly larger proportion of the Ladinos affirming the existence of native biologically determined differences between themselves and the Indians.

Perhaps more significant yet is the fact, which may also be inferred from the materials referred to, that the social attitudes of the Ladinos toward such a changeover are not friendly, and that this unfriendliness is itself a major factor in making any such change difficult if not impossible. Since the Ladinos are the superordinate group and thus control access to the membership in their own group, it would make little difference how possible the Indians thought the transition to be, or how effective they were in imitating the Ladino in his superficial phases. So long as the Ladino is determined to keep the Indian at a distance from himself—and it appears that he is so determined—it is unlikely that an Indian, no matter how Ladinoized in his behavior and appearance, will be accepted as a Ladino by the Ladinos.

Projected against these resistant facts, the percentage of Indians (66.6 per cent) who indicated some kind of desire to change over to Ladino status assumes a new significance. Assuming that they really meant what they said—that is, that they really desired to change to Ladino group membership—it would be reasonable to infer the existence of a great deal of tension in the society. For we would have a picture of a large number of Indians pressing for Ladino status and the majority of the Ladinos resisting this pressure. One would also expect at least some small percentage of the Indians to have contrived in one way or another to have gotten through the caste barrier and received acceptance.

But in actual fact these conditions do not exist. One does not find the degree of tension which should be there, and one finds no case of an Indian ever achieving Ladino status in the pueblo. Moreover, aside from the relatively recent phenomenon of a number of young Indians trying to emulate the Ladinos, one finds no persistent efforts among the majority of Indians to approximate those standards of behavior and appearance which are the indispensable prerequisites for consideration for caste mobility.

The apparent dilemma presented by these facts is in part resolved by examining the questions which were put to the Indians regarding the desirability of changing to Ladino status. For, asking an Indian whether he would like to become a Ladino was tantamount to asking a poor man whether he would like to become rich. That more Indians did not express this preference and this desire seems to me to testify that in spite of the apparently greater material satisfactions of the Ladinos, the Indians understand—perhaps only roughly and intuitively, but nevertheless understand—what is implied for them if they desert their traditional standards.

I feel further, from a knowledge of the Indian way of thought, that many of them never even think in these terms. That is to say, they never raise to the level of conscious question the desirability of their way of life by comparison with others. Few things in the Indian culture itself promote such comparison, while the majority of the major institutional pressures reduce the tendency to compare and instead emphasize the inherent naturalness of the Indian culture for Indians. In addition, every major pressure in the Ladino culture works toward keeping the Indians in their traditional status in spite of pious verbalizations that if only the Indians would become more like the Ladinos then the latter would accept them more readily.

Yet we must face the fact that Indians at least verbally state that the Ladino way of life is in some senses more desirable than their own, and the further fact that the Ladino does make at least verbal protestations about wanting to "bring up" the Indians to their level. That both of these facts have consequences is undeniable. We have seen the operations of these consequences in the cases of those younger Indians who have been deprived of the opportunity of participating fully in the traditional round of Indian life as a result of being deprived of adequate land holdings. The partial welcome which the Ladino extends to these Indians who desire acculturation tends to be grossly exaggerated by the Indians. In part this accounts for the apparent enthusiasm they come to develop for the Ladino patterns in spite of the equally apparent superficiality of the welcome they receive.

This interaction, though unevenly defined by the participants, functions as a drain-off of tensions generated by the discontent of the younger Indians. Objectively viewed, their social position is marginal and unstable. The fact that they obviously deviate from traditional Indian values makes them appear to other Indians as a continuous source of threat to those values. Since at bottom the Ladinos do not really want their company, their search for this company and for acceptance by the Ladinos would tend to produce feelings of uneasiness among the Ladinos themselves. Partial equilibration of these tensions is achieved by the provision of superficial statuses on the margins of Ladino culture. The Ladinos are thus able to define them into a safe niche. The younger Indians themselves find some sort of position they can define in their own terms and whose importance they can misdefine, without correction, so that they are for the moment subjectively satisfied. Finally, they serve as an example to the rest of the Indian community of what not to do, and thus in a measure help to reinforce the traditional standards of the Indians.

A fairly close analogy to this situation is provided by the case of the first reactions by Southern whites to the partial emancipation of Negroes in post Civil War days. Whereas in pre Civil War days there were no socially defined transitional statuses for Negroes, the emancipation brought forth that pattern of accommodation which is so amply illustrated in the case of Booker T. Washington. Without accepting him inside white culture, a status was provided midway between Negro and white patterns. In this fashion the Negro was still "kept in his place"; but at the same time he was granted a status sufficiently important to satisfy him regarding his own worth and to give him a vested interest in preserving that pattern of accommodation. In this way, any more aggressive demands the Negro might make were for the time being short-circuited, and partial and temporary equilibrium reached.

If we pursue this analogy further, however, we see that in the long run this type of accommodation pattern functions to slow up the achievement of full equality for the Negro. But there the analogy stops. For at the moment, there is no concerted pressure from within the Indian group for this type of social and economic equality. It is therefore reasonable to assume that the present type of equilibrium in San Luis is likely to prove more enduring than that of the South. This assertion holds, however, only under the condition that all other things remain equal. In terms of the dearth of presently expressed pressures by Indians for greater equality, all other things are likely to remain equal. In terms of the fact, however, that the alienation of Indians from the land is likely to increase, there is a promise of continuous pressure from the Indians for more such accommodative patterns to be developed.

These facts regarding Indian aspirations must be projected against the background of the aspirations of the Ladinos in San Luis. For, as we have seen, the realism of assimilation, the ability to achieve it, and the reinforcement of advance or withdrawal tendencies toward it by the Indian are in some significant degree a function of how the Ladinos define the situation.

In understanding Ladino aspiration levels, one must first and always take into account the geographical isolation and relative poverty of the pueblo and its environs. As has been noted, these factors tend toward cultural isolation and social poverty of the area, so that San Luis is almost literally left to itself so far as the outside world is concerned, and has therefore the dubiously valuable liberty to work out its own social arrangements.

Though trite, the phrase "big fish in little ponds" is the most apt description of the social positions enjoyed by the higher-ranked local Ladinos, and by all other Ladinos, to a lesser degree. The basic psychological components of persons occupying this status appear to be the same wherever they are found. Involved, first, is a general set of rationalizations to account for remaining within the local area. This almost always includes some reference to the ever-present possibility of one's going to the "big city" and moving freely in its social circles, if one really desires, but, "alas, for a number of reasons [only mysteriously hinted at and never made explicit] it is not possible now to do so; later, perhaps, when certain things clear up."

Secondly, there is a tendency toward everlasting depreciation of the social worth of others in the local community who claim prestigeful social standing. Of these others it is said, or at least hinted, that unlike the speaker, they could not move, even if they cared to, and that if they did attempt to effect an entry into other, more sophisticated, social circles, it would readily be seen that they were crude and ill-fitting. The functional value of this depreciation is rather evident: it serves as one additional prop to the dubious social prestige of the speaker and helps him rationalize his own local position as well as his own failure to move on into the larger social world.

One local figure, the druggist-doctor-dentist in San Luis, who was perhaps the single most powerful and prestigeful figure in the community, rarely lost an opportunity to assure the author of his intimate connections with affairs in Guatemala City; often described at great length his one real or purported trip to the United States, during which a visit to Coney Island was the high spot; recited frequently the details of an occasion when he had been principally responsible for bringing an internationally known opera singer to a nearby community for a performance; and never failed to denigrate the relative social worth of other of the outstanding Ladinos in town. Only rarely, when in a confessional mood, would he deplore his presence in San Luis, admit he had lost his real opportunities ever to move out of San Luis, speculate about what it might have been like had he gone to practice in Guatemala City, and display some real concern over the worth of being the big fish in the little pond.

Such Ladinos as he are, in a sense, in a marginal position, so far as their own definitions of their social worth are concerned. The realization appears to be gnawing at them that they are blowing up their own social worth beyond its real proportions. Since this is a decidedly uncomfortable state, all kinds of devices to reassure themselves of their social worth are employed. Certainly outstanding in this regard is the continuous humiliation of the Indian and the never-ending struggle to keep the Indian subordinate and subservient.

All of the devices employed serve the general function of making the social situation in San Luis analogous to the situation which prevails in more sophisticated and prestigeful areas. Wherever possible—and sometimes it is not as possible as the local gentry would like—the same kinds and details of social distinction are made as prevail in other areas. Indeed, sometimes, even more attention is paid to details of the criteria of social prestige than would ever be thought important in the more elevated circles. From being privy to the most intimate gossip routes, one soon discovers that every single conceivable criterion for social rating is at some time or another employed in elevating oneself or in running others down.

An interesting feature which one finds is different degrees of permissiveness concerning the roles played by Indians in the community. Under some circumstances— where the local gentry feel sure it will not be misinterpreted—it is considered fashionable to be extremely friendly and interested in the welfare of the Indians, and great plans are discussed, and then safely tucked away, for various kinds of welfare enterprises. Some of the middle-class strivers among the Ladinos are the most vehement in their denunciations of Indian laziness, dirtiness, and immorality, and some of the Ladino aristocracy are most apparently friendly. At the bottom of the Ladino ladder, among those few for whom striving is out of the question and most social hope long since gone, one finds an occasional individual expressing a considerable degree of genuine warmth of feeling for various Indian associates and friends. At the same time, so long as any realistic social hope is present, these same lowest-ranked Ladinos are likely to deplore the Indian and his presence in the community even more than the middle-class strivers. The apparent reasons are the economic competition which the Indians offer and the fact that the Ladinos recognize, in one way or another, that but for the grace of the social position of the Indians, they, the Ladinos, would be the lowest on the social ladder.

Since most members of the Ladino community are in one way or another involved in social striving for a higher standing, and since the accessibility of criteria of social rank is so limited, one finds a considerable sense of frustration at all levels of the pueblo society. The upper-class persons are blocked in their upward aspirations by their being fixed in the pueblo itself. The middle-class individuals are by and large frustrated by the presence of the upper class above them and their inability to climb, since their social origins are only too well known and since the economy is such that chances for economic mobility are minimal. The lower-class Ladinos feel keenly in many cases the presence of the Indians so proximate to them and the attendant depreciation of their own social worth by the two classes of Ladinos above them.

In a sense, then, the community is composed of individuals occupying only a limited number of status positions, each of which is fairly rigidly defined by local standards. Each person in some ways is a mirror of the other's possible or actual failure. Each person lower than oneself is a permanent reminder of the all-too-possible chance of social downfall. Each person higher than oneself is a bitter reminder of one's own lowered position. Everyone acts in one way or another as the potential or actual alter-ego of all others in the community.

The only group about whose relative social worth all Ladinos can agree is the Indian. It should be clear, then, how really important the subordination of the Indian is for the social status quo of the Ladino. Each of the divisions within Ladino society can use the Indian in a different way, all of which ways add up to inflation of Ladino prestige itself and to reduction of Ladino senses of insecurity and unworthiness. Moreover, with the material perquisites which accrue to the superior caste, life can be made a little easier and more tolerable.

The cultural and social pressures on Ladinos to treat the Indian in a relatively uniform way acts as a social cement of the Ladino community. The Indian community stands as a constant, though not necessarily pressing, threat to the Ladino community. The threat is minimized by keeping the Indian community subordinate and powerless. This is done by actual exploitation and discrimination, and by unrealistic high self-definition. In these techniques for keeping the Indian subordinate, the entire Ladino community joins to one degree or another.

In calculating the possibilities of social change in San Luis, therefore, one must always keep in mind the fact that no significant decrease in the resistance by the Ladinos to any plan for social equalization of the Indians can be hoped for unless one finds alternative devices which will help the Ladino feel socially worthy without keeping the Indians subordinate.

It would be wrong, however, to imply that the present relations between Indians and Ladinos are in any real sense rife with conflict. At the same time, the potentiality

ASPIRATION AND ASSIMILATION

of conflict inherent in the social structure and the division of labor and rewards must be recognized. For it is only against the background of the fears of the Ladino of being lowered socially by the social rise of the Indians that one can understand some of the features of the caste system which is maintained. As one group of students has pointed out regarding ethnocentrism and ethnocentric personalities:

"We can now consider the ethnocentric solution to problems of group conflict. The ingroup must be kept pure and strong. The only methods of doing this are to *liquidate* the outgroups altogether, to keep them entirely *subordinate*, or to *segregate* them in such a way as to minimize contact with the ingroups. . . . Ethnocentrism is based on a pervasive and rigid ingroup-outgroup distinction; it involves stereotyped negative imagery and hostile attitudes regarding outgroups, stereotyped positive imagery and submissive attitudes regarding ingroups, and a hierarchical, authoritarian view of group interaction in which ingroups are richly dominant, outgroups subordinate."[1]

San Luis represents one rather peculiar variation on this general theme, since at the same time that the Ladinos desire to keep social distance and maintain group purity, they also are mindful of the fact that the relative ease of their lives and their relative social standing is so very much dependent on the continuous presence of the Indians, to whom not all rewards can be denied. From the Ladino point of view, the social equilibrium between the two groups can perhaps best be seen, then, as the results of an attempt to maintain the Indian in a condition of relative subordinacy, at the same time that enough rewards are allocated to him to keep him satisfied within the confines of San Luis. It is no accident therefore that while Ladinos presumably urge the Indian on to various degrees of assimilation they tend to feel far more comfortable about traditional-minded and behaving Indians than about those

[1] T. W. Adorno, et al., *The Authoritarian Personality*, Harper & Bros., New York, 1950, p. 150.

who actually accept the invitation to come forward and change. For so long as the Indian remains traditional-minded, that long is he unlikely to challenge the existing status quo. As we have noted before, the devotion to the traditional way of life by the Indian is the Ladino's best guarantee of social stability of the status quo, at the same time that it is the Indian's best guarantee against dissatisfaction and discontent. It would appear, therefore, that any advance toward the civilization of a technological society would involve a significant social upheaval producing discontent both among Indians and Ladinos.

Yet, one cannot ignore the fact that in response to questions regarding desired occupations and level of education, a very large number of both the Indians and the Ladinos indicated some desire for more education and for a subsidiary type of occupation, not necessarily to replace their farm work, but in addition to it. May one infer from this that both Indians and Ladinos, though in different degrees, are really interested in some kind of change?

The answer to this depends on how much significance one wants to attribute to these verbal responses. Considerable caution must be exercised here since there is little by way of overt behavior to match these verbalizations. However, one cannot say that it is totally without meaning that Indians and Ladinos both express a set of desires regarding alternative ways of life. It indicates, at least, that they are not totally unaware of the diversities of the outside world, nor are they unmindful of the attractiveness of some of the promises it holds.

Yet, it would be dangerous to give more weight than this to the expressed preferences and desires for alternatives. And even this much is risky because of the possible implications of the term "awareness." It is not the kind of awareness which results in any change, without additional stimuli coming into action. In short, it is not itself a sufficient condition for change. At the most, it helps to sour the Ladino regarding his own way of life, without giving him the necessary impetus to do anything significant about it.

ASPIRATION AND ASSIMILATION

For the majority of Indians, it stands as a background against which they can project desires when they are asked, but it does not seem otherwise to enter into the calculus of felicity which they employ.

Missing these ingredients which would impel them to disrupt the local pattern, both groups thus tend to turn in upon themselves and the pueblo and to make of the pueblo life their real focus of interests and activities. Their participation and standing in the local society thus becomes for them as important as can be imagined. It is no accident, then, that the Ladino becomes so concerned with the stabilization of the order which places him on top of the heap, and resists, both unwittingly and deliberately, any efforts on the part of the Indian to disrupt that order.

What, then, happens to those Indians who do acquire skills and who do, by objective standards, possess the necessary qualities for acceptance in the Ladino society? That occasional Indians do achieve this status, or at least make efforts in that direction, is obvious. But the fact remains that no Indian, no matter how secularized and skilled, ever receives more than partial acceptance within Ladino social circles, and, in most cases, must leave the pueblo if he wishes to "pass."

Five such cases, more or less well-known to people in the pueblo, testify to the accuracy of these statements. They may be reviewed briefly.

CASE 1

Rigoberto M., a full-blooded Indian from San Luis, was sent at an early age to Jalapa to be raised. There he grew up as a servant in the office of the chief officer of the department, learned all the proper civilities, and acquired well above the average education. When he reached adult status, he had incurred enough favor from the political big-wigs so that he was given assignments in various places as pueblo secretary. Ultimately, he was given an assignment to San Luis. He lasted one year in San Luis, a feud with a local schoolteacher who had "connections" causing him to be shifted to a coastal area. While in San Luis, he was the best-dressed and most-educated Indian, and, according to reports, was far better-dressed, "cultured," and educated than most Ladinos. He was invited to Ladino affairs, but *questioning of Ladinos reveals that he would never have been invited had he not been secretary*. He danced with Ladino girls, ate in Ladino houses at the same table and time with Ladinos, and was generally socially accepted by some of the Ladinos. His best friend in San Luis was a young Ladino carpenter, an upper-class Ladino in virtue of his being nephew of the most dominant Ladino in the pueblo. This carpenter was one of the twenty-two informants to whom the questions were administered. He was likewise one of the constant and confidential informants of the writer during his stay in San Luis. His views on Rigoberto were solicited at length, and while he professed great admiration for Rigoberto, and considered him as a person and not "merely an Indian," he likewise asserted *that he would never let Rigoberto marry one of his children*. "*That touches one's self-pride,*" the carpenter asserted. "*Perhaps I would let such a thing happen in another place where Rigoberto was not known, but I could never let that happen here. I would be too ashamed of what people would say.*" All other Ladinos questioned about intermarriage of their children with Rigoberto answered in a similar vein.

It may be noted that this carpenter was one of the few Ladinos who thought it was possible for an Indian to convert into a Ladino, but it is clear from the foregoing to what extent he believed such a conversion possible and to what extent he would be willing to accept fully any such Indian.

Rigoberto M. is now living in a coastal area, employed as a secretary of a pueblo, married to a Ladino woman, but, according to letters to his carpenter friend, this is all possible only so long as the deception about his parentage

ASPIRATION AND ASSIMILATION

is maintained. His Ladino wife does not know that he is an Indian by birth.

CASE 2

The second case of an Indian now living as a Ladino is that of Marcario, the father of Rigoberto. This man lives in Santa Ana, in San Salvador, where he is married to a Ladino woman and runs a store. He is accepted by the Ladino community. People who visit Santa Ana report, some with amusement, that he is called "Don" in Santa Ana and treated fully as a Ladino, but that he pretends that he is not Indian, that his wife does not know he is Indian, that he denies to San Luis Indians who visit him that he knows the Indian dialect, and that he makes attempts when they come to visit him to hide any signs of previous acquaintance with San Luis. The Ladinos who commented on him to this writer indicated that he would never be called "Don" were he to reappear in San Luis and that he would never be treated as a Ladino.

CASE 3

There is a third person about whom there is generally less known than about Rigoberto and his father. This is Francisco M., formerly of San Luis, who went away as a fairly young boy to San Salvador, went to school, acquired a good education, and became a lawyer and a respected member of his community. His origins likewise are hidden, according to people from San Luis, and the Ladinos say that he, like the other two, would be treated, ultimately, as an Indian if he returned.

CASE 4

There is a fourth case about whom even less is known. This is the brother of Pedro M., who left the pueblo about 1932 to work at the coast for the United Fruit Company. He was supposed to return, but never did. He took on Ladino ways, saved money, started to wear shoes, and recently married a Ladino woman. His brother says that he too conceals his origins and says he is a Ladino. Pedro is himself contemplating doing the same thing as soon as he gets some money together. He insists that it is better to change because one gets treated better and leads a better life.

CASE 5

The fifth case, apparently known to very few people, is that of the nephew of Manuel P. Of his nephew, Manuel said, "I have a nephew who went away from here to Jalapa at a very early age. He grew up with Ladinos and is now in the town band there. He wears shoes and lives like a Ladino, and his children are totally Ladino and will marry Ladinos. They can't marry Indians now because now they are Ladinos. They are well-dressed and have shoes. My nephew's wife was an Indian from here, but now she dresses like a Ladino. They do not say they are Indians, and in Jalapa no one knows they are."

There are three other names of Indians who went to other places and assumed Ladino status, but they are not generally known at all, only one Indian informant and no Ladinos being able to cite them as examples of Indians who had changed over.

It is clear from these cases and Ladino comments upon them that the Ladino resists amalgamation of the Indian even when the Indian meets all the demands which could reasonably be made, short of changing his origins. Passage from Indian to Ladino status is thus by no means automatic, but does involve pretense and deception. Clearly the Ladino feels it important to hold to his belief in ineradicable biological differences, and thus to rationalize his maintenance of social distance from the Indian and his subordination of the Indian.

It is perhaps by this basic attitude of rejection more than by any other single thing that the tone of social relationships between Indian and Ladino may be characterized. From the earliest days of childhood when a disobedient or misbehaved Ladino child is reprimanded with,

ASPIRATION AND ASSIMILATION

"Don't be like an Indian" to the time when Indians who have been lifelong neighbors of Ladinos are buried and receive no more than "Oh, is that so?" recognition from the Ladinos when they are informed of the death of the Indian—throughout all this a sense of deep and pervading distance between the two characterizes their day-by-day and week-by-week contacts. They develop no important and meaningful friendships; they are separate from each other at the most happy and festive moments; they bear their sorrows apart from each other.

In their separateness, they can only confirm and not test those notions about differences which are passed on to them as readily as comments on the weather and a passing woman. Social distinctions, arising from notions of differences in biology and culture, no matter what their genesis, are self-substantiating. The Ladino, taught to think he is biologically different from and superior to the Indian, and seeing the Indian as a biologically and culturally different person, makes the easy joining of the two differences and reads culture into biology. Notions of superiority of the culture of his own group to that of the Indians thus become in turn notions of biologically determined superiority. These, in turn, have further social consequences. They become viewed as unbridgeable differences, and give rise to sets of feelings and attitudes by the Ladino with regard to the Indian which make him want to keep distance from the Indian, to exclude him wherever possible, to consider him undesirable, and, above all, to make sure that Indian blood does not get mixed into his family blood.

So, too, with the Indian child, but in a very much different way. From earliest childhood he is taught to stay away from trouble with Ladinos; not to fight with Ladino children; to get off the sidewalk when he sees a man with shoes coming. Until he is six or seven or even older he can understand only what people who look like his father and mother say to him. But the language spoken by the people with lighter skins and shoes on their feet is utterly incomprehensible. When he goes to the store with his older brother or sister, these same strange people are behind the counters, and people like his brother and sister and mother and father are buying things. In the fields, when he goes to bring his father his lunch, he sees people like his father and older brother. In the cofradias he attends with his grandfather, again only the familiar language is spoken by the familiar people and none of the other kind of people are there. He sees dances and parties going on, but none of the familiar and only the strange people are present.

In his first year of school, all these differences are sharpened. When he passes the soccer field or the basketball court, on his way home from work, only the strange kind of boys and girls are playing. All his own familiar friends he knows, are, even as he, coming home from work, loaded with firewood, weaving straw hats as they go. All the houses near his own contain only his own kind. In and around the plaza he sees the houses of the other kind of people, the big houses, out of which men come riding on animals or in which his father enters, hat in hand, "deferential, glad to be of use." Deference, fear, difference—all these and more are impressed on him at a very early age, and they are lessons in attitude and behavior he never forgets, almost always follows, and rarely rebels against.

There is, then, no mystery about why Ladinos and Indians keep apart from each other. The custom is there for each Ladino child to incorporate into his own private adaptation to the general culture patterns. The differences between the Indian and himself are highly visible. The revulsion for the dirt and ignorance of the Indian is taught the Ladino child very early in life, and, once sensitized, it is something he rarely ever fails to see and to comment upon. His earliest social experiences at home show him the different way in which his parents treat people known as Indians and those as Ladinos. Emulation of his parents' behavior brings him rewards, whereas failure to emulate that behavior brings him reprimand and punishment.

ASPIRATION AND ASSIMILATION

His first independent social experiences bring him into contact only with people of his own general color, his own general level of clothing, his own Spanish proficiency. He learns early to judge people's worth by the same criteria as those by which he knows he is being judged each time he appears in public. None of his elders or his friends associate in any intimacy with Indians; he does not either. By the time he is an adult ready to fit into adult social life in Ladino San Luis, he is a self-defined and self-distinguished person and the Indian is well stereotyped in his mind. There is no intimacy he has had with the Indian and no wish to test the truth of the stereotypes he has formed of the Indian. There are no negative community sanctions but plenty of community approbations for treating the Indian exactly as he has seen his elders and his friends treat him. There is no fear of retribution from the Indian for making fun of him and being rude to him. So the Ladino child continues to do so, and when he has children, teaches them to do so.

Because life is relatively so stable in San Luis, and because the differences are so very small in the way each child incorporates the patterns of his own culture, there is a predictable continuity of this social behavior from one generation to the next, and a predictable uniformity of that behavior.

There is, as has been shown, a relative uniformity in both Indian and Ladino behavior and attitudes. The differences in such attitudes and behavior are far more between the two groups than in either of them. Ladinos may be characterized as a *unit* in regard to the way they view and behave toward the Indian, and Indians, likewise, may so be characterized in the ways in which they view and behave toward the Ladino.

The first rule of behavior for each with regard to the other is to preserve distance wherever possible. The fact that each knows his place so well, and that there is essentially no overt conflict occasioned by anyone getting out of his place, makes life in San Luis relatively peaceful even though the basis for serious conflict is everlastingly present.

The apparent charm, the greater ease, the apparent gaiety of Ladino life causes an occasional Indian verbally to aspire after that way of life; to be ever-present on the peripheries; to aspire after manifest similarities with the people who enjoy it; to attempt to move over into it when the occasion arises.

The lack of charm, the heaviness and weariness, the lack of gaiety and reward in the Indian way of life cause the Ladino to reject that way of life, to want to have essentially nothing to do with people who live it, to keep as many sharp, manifest distinctions between themselves and those people who live that dull, hard, unrewarding type of life.

There appears to be every justification for transferring these general conceptions which each group has of the other, and the way they feel in general about each other, to each specific situation of joint and separate participation which has been discussed. If it is taken into account that it is primarily the Ladinos who set the tone for the relationships with the Indians, the reasons for the way the Indians behave in such situations become more clear. The Indian is raised to accept his role in San Luis society. He knows that the Ladino depreciates him, and he knows many of the reasons why the Ladino does so. He knows he is dependent in a very basic sense on the Ladino landlord, and takes his cue for deferential behavior partly from that dependence. The fact that Ladinos depend very heavily on Indians for producing the basic farm products is not something which is easily apprehended by the Indian. His concern is far more with getting a piece of land on which to raise his corn and beans so that he may be assured, at least, of existence and satisfaction of hunger, than it is with an overall analytical picture of the function of his work in the total economic system.

The sheer fact of greater wealth of the Ladino plays a very important role in determining the way in which the general social life of the pueblo is ordered. Ladinos have the money to make parties and dances and to indulge in leisure-time recreation. Indians do not. Indians could participate in these things only if the Ladinos were to invite them. But Ladinos have such a conception of the Indian as to make any invitations of the Indian out of the question, except under the most extraordinary circumstances. To transfer the custom of keeping distance from those affairs where the Ladinos initiate it to those situations where it needs to be mutually sustained is an easy step. Indians are rejected in the first and attune their own affairs to that rejection they experience. They do not invite Ladinos and do not expect Ladinos to attend, even if they should be invited. Indians get set off from the Ladinos by economically determined factors such as clothing, housing, and other appearance-criteria with which the Ladinos are so importantly concerned, and this initial set-off is almost the sufficient condition for their rejection when questions of choice and invitations come up. There has never been a tradition for close unity between Indians and Ladinos. There are not now any serious reasons why that custom of distance should be abrogated. The custom piles up every year, even as it apparently has over the past decades, of its own dead weight.

Other somewhat more ephemeral factors have an influence. The "small-town mind" is first among these. The need that Ladinos feel to distinguish themselves in some way from other peoples, to feel in some way superior to at least some other group, has its major outlet in the Indian group and in rejecting its members. The fact that there is class demarcation within the Ladino group itself lends testimony to this. It seems to say, in future terms as well, that when and if there is such an intermixture of peoples and a general leveling of all the peoples, so that differences are nowhere nearly as highly visible as they now are, class lines will form again around new criteria, even though the lines of division between the classes may be even more ephemeral than they are now, and even though there may not be any group clearly identifiable as Indian.

A second and very important set of factors tending to preserve the traditional ways of the pueblo is the service which the Ladino community provides as a cushion for the "shock of culture" to which the Indians might otherwise be more directly and disturbingly exposed. By this, reference is had to the fact that the Ladinos stand as the outward face of the community. For it is they who are most in contact with outside events and trends. And thus it is they who do the preliminary sorting and sifting of cultural stimuli which are then reinterpreted, in local fashion, for the Indian community. Given the fact that the Ladinos have a vested interest in keeping acculturative stimuli from being effective upon the Indians, there tends to be a reduction in the number of such stimuli as they are sifted by the receiving Ladinos. This process stands up and is important even in face of the fact that Indian men, by reason of their sales trips, are on the average out of the pueblo more often and for longer periods of time than Ladino men. We have seen earlier, however, that this contact with other communities and other ways of life is not an effective stimulus to change for the tradition-bound and insulated Indian.

The Ladinos serve as a culture cushion in still another sense, mentioned earlier, namely, that the changing Indian has a margin of social space between himself and the Ladino to traverse before he comes into direct contact with the outside world in any disturbing way. In the transitional area between his own traditional culture and that of the Ladino, there is plenty of social room and therefore time before the Indian can be expected to meet new impulses from the outside face-on. Of course, the existence of this cultural slack which remains to be taken up helps decrease the pressure which the Indian might otherwise exert upon the Ladino. Moreover, in its exemplary travails, it stands as a constant warning to the venturesome Indian and as a certain discouragement to the less venturesome. In so doing, it helps to reduce otherwise expectably serious tensions for the Indian. In turn, this makes it easier for the Ladino to preserve his own power position and thus to reduce the motivations, with which he might alternatively be affected, to seek new fields of social endeavor.

In somewhat the same fashion that Ladinos cushion the culture contact for the Indians, the Indian males serve as buffers between the Indian women and the faint stimuli in the pueblo itself. Cultural definitions calling for the greater isolation of the Indian women and for the absorption by the men of the contact with the Ladinos help to rigidify the traditionalism of the average Indian woman far beyond that of the average Indian man. Since the family system is such that the Indian woman plays an important part in decision-making in the household, and since above all she would be able to exert great pressure in decisions regarding initiating steps toward genuine culture change, any such inclinations tend to become minimized by the looking-inwardness of the Indian woman. Since the daughters receive their socialization in attitudes almost exclusively from the mother, there is a tendency for this process to be self-perpetuating. With the ban against intermarriage, and with the Indian male thus largely confined to marriage choices from among the inward-facing young females, a further support for this reciprocally reinforcing process is continuously being generated.

Against these and other factors tending to produce equilibrium are pitted the varied influences producing tension. These include, as we have noted, such things as the gradual impoverishment of the younger Indians and their being forced to seek outside employment; the consequent attrition in the kinship and religious principles and in their constraining and binding forces; the gradual democratization of the country as a whole, forecasting some radical revisions in the formal rights of Indians; the ineluctable impact of some aspects of the process of industrialization; the unceasing creation of idiosyncratic dissidents who venture forth along avenues of change and thereby challenge traditional equilibria; and, finally, the growing dissatisfaction of the Ladino with the traditional ways of the pueblo and with the highly localized kind of social prestige he enjoys.

The present balance of forces is perhaps best described as a slowly moving equilibrium. The term "stable equilibrium" would be preferred were it not for its connotation of the absence of any tension-producing forces. Such forces are present, but at the moment they are far less effective, so far as dramatic output is concerned, than are those tending to preserve the traditional way of life. At the same time, at least some of the forces tending toward change are likely in the long run to be irresistible, if our previous experience with so-called backward areas has any predictive value.